Going Home

Going

Home

Black
....
Representatives
....
and Their
....
Constituents

Richard F. Fenno

The University of Chicago Press

Chicago and London

RICHARD F. FENNO
is the William J. Kenan
Professor of Political
Science and Distinguished
University Professor at the
University of Rochester.
He is a past president of the
American Political Science
Association and the author
of a number of books,
including *Home Style*
(1978), *Learning to Govern*
(1997), and *Congress at the
Grassroots* (2000).

The University of Chicago Press, Chicago 60637
The University of Chicago Press, Ltd., London
© 2003 by The University of Chicago
All rights reserved. Published 2003
Printed in the United States of America
12 11 10 09 08 07 06 05 04 03   1 2 3 4 5

ISBN: 0-226-24130-0 (cloth)
ISBN: 0-226-24131-9 (paper)

Library of Congress Cataloging-in-Publication Data

Fenno, Richard F., 1926–
    Going home : Black representatives and their constituents /
    Richard F. Fenno.
        p.   cm.
        Includes bibliographical references and index.
        ISBN 0-226-24130-0 (cloth : alk. paper) —
        ISBN 0-226-24131-9 (pbk. : alk. paper)
        1. African Americans—Politics and government—Case
    studies. 2. African American legislators—Case studies.
    3. United States. Congress—Constituent communication—
    Case studies. 4. Jordan, Barbara, 1936– 5. Stokes, Louis, 1925–
    6. Fattah, Chaka, 1956– 7. Jones, Stephanie Tubbs, 1949–
    I. Title.

    E185.615 F396 2003
    328.73'092'396073—dc21

                                                    2002007704

⊗ The paper used in this publication meets the minimum
requirements of the American National Standard for Information
Sciences—Permanence of Paper for Printed Library Materials,
ANSI Z39.48-1992.

To Nancy

CONTENTS

ACKNOWLEDGMENTS

My debt to those who made this book possible begins with the four principals. All of them were candid and accommodating. They were altogether a pleasure to be with, to talk with, and to learn from. They wanted to help, and they did—a fortunate combination for me. Three of them read their segment of the manuscript, commented helpfully, and corrected factual mistakes. I thank them for their easy cooperation. The data, the interpretations, and the judgments in the book are, of course, entirely my responsibility.

In every case, my visits were arranged and made easier by the willing assistance of congressional staff members. In Lou Stokes's office, Sam Brooks, Art Nukes, John Leonard, and Owen Heggs were most helpful. In Houston, Cecile Harrison was an informed traveling companion. In Philadelphia, I benefited from the cordiality and knowledge of Rebecca Kirszner and from the logistical help of Raymond Jones and Thera Martin Connelly. Among Stephanie Tubbs Jones's staffers, the assistance of Nikia Graster, Betty Pinkney, and Beverly Charles was indispensable. I thank them all.

I gratefully acknowledge the very special assistance and support I received from several of my political science colleagues. Dick Murray provided an indispensable on-the-scene reading of the Jordan part of the manuscript. And had it not been for the timely intervention of Joe Cooper, I might never have reached Houston in the first place. Alec Lamis tutored me and kept me abreast of developments in Cleveland. Doug Arnold allowed me to utilize his unpublished work on Lou Stokes's press relations. Randy Strahan kept my intellectual spirits up throughout my more recent constituency travels.

For their interest and for a variety of advisory contributions to the book, I am also indebted to David Bositis, David Canon, Frederick Harris, Marion Orr, Lynda Powell, Valeria Sinclair-Chapman, and Carol Swain. I thank Zak Talarek for his talented and efficient research assistance. And I thank my cousin Bob Goddu for his unofficial clipping service.

To four friends—Lucius Barker, Matthew Holden, William "Nick" Nelson, and Michael Preston—who gave me the incentive and the confidence to tackle this project, I want to say a heartfelt thank-you. Without your early tutelage and continuing encouragements, there would have been no book of mine about black politics.

Rosemary Bergin has been my steady right arm throughout the entire project. I have relied daily on her expertise, her patience, and her good humor in endlessly shepherding the interviews and the manuscript to completion.

I have been most fortunate in being able to work with John Tryneski, an easy, supportive, and thoroughly professional editor. Above all, he secured the assistance of two anonymous reviewers, whose comments improved the manuscript measurably. I thank them for their time and their suggestions. I have profited measurably, too, from the expert and careful copyediting of Clair James.

I dedicate the book with my love and my gratitude to Nancy. For more years than I care to count, she has provided the support, the encouragement, and the good cheer necessary to make my research possible and enjoyable.

CHAPTER 1
AFRICAN AMERICAN HOUSE MEMBERS AND REPRESENTATION

CHANGE AND DIVERSITY

Thirty years ago, there were nine African American members of the U.S. House of Representatives. Today, there are four times that number. And therein lies a story of political accomplishment in America. Among students of the Congress, interest in that story has burgeoned as the numbers have increased. There exists, now, a varied and growing political science literature devoted to studying the ambitions, beliefs, interests, organizations, strategies, behavior, and influence of the black members of the House.

In that literature, two prominent themes are *change* for African Americans as a group and *diversity* among its elected members of Congress. The thirty years of change is treated as a recent chapter in a prolonged and continuing struggle by an excluded racial minority to win inclusion and influence in the nation's preeminent representative institution. In the current post–civil rights era, the ongoing group struggle has sometimes been written in terms of the diverse aspirations, activities, and accomplishments of individual black Representatives.[1] The first object of this book is to make a small contribution to these two stories—the macro-level story of change, and the micro-level story of diversity. The second object of the book is to suggest some conceptualizations that might be helpful to the larger study of congressional representation.

INCLUSION, INFLUENCE, AND LINKAGE

The "small contribution" mentioned above is designed to fit into a specific body of literature on African American representation in Congress. That literature has clustered around three broad subjects: inclusion, influence, and linkage.

Questions about *inclusion* revolve around getting, keeping, and evaluating representation for the nation's largest racial minority. In the congressional context, these questions center on entry and the barriers to entry. How do black politicians get into Congress? Who gets in? Under what circumstances? What explains the thirty-year increase in the number of black Representatives? Answers to these questions focus on the electoral aspects of racial representation—on legal barriers, on redistricting decisions, on citizen voting patterns, on the racial makeup of constituencies, on candidate emergence and on electoral strategies.

Early research centered on the social and legal changes that opened up participation to minorities—the civil rights revolution of the fifties and sixties and the Voting Rights Act of 1965, in particular. Recent research has given special prominence to redistricting decisions—as they affect both the adequacy and the fairness of minority representation.[2] Because it embraces these broad questions of legality and fairness, the large literature on inclusion has been normative as well as empirical.

Questions about *influence* have centered on the impact of the African American minority on the political life of the country. For the study of African Americans in Congress, the central question has been: How and under what conditions do black members of Congress exert influence inside, or through, the institution and with respect to what? The question assumes their election to Congress and calls attention to their legislative and oversight activities, to their committee assignments and committee work, to their roll call voting patterns, to their leaders, and to their alliances—inside and outside—the chamber.

Because of its longevity and its prominence, the Congressional Black Caucus (CBC) has attracted the bulk of this research on minority influence in Congress. Studies of the CBC's makeup, its representativeness, its internal cohesion, its legislative strategies, its bargaining leverage, its external relationships, and its overall accomplishments have dominated assessments of black member influence in the House—and assessments of their changing influence as well.[3]

Linkage questions have focused on the relationships of responsiveness and accountability between black elected officials and their separate constituencies. In a single member district system, that relationship is the essence of representation. The elected official makes an effort to respond to, and to influence, the sentiment of constituents within the district, and the constituents register a measure of approval. Within limits, House members can choose the constituents to whom they will respond, and the manner in which they will respond.

Member–constituency linkages may be forged out of policy preferences, personal contact, constituency service, symbolic activity, or group identities. Recent scholarly research has focused on policy linkages and the match between the policy preferences of constituents and the policy votes of their House members. These studies pay special attention to the relationship among the race of the member, the racial makeup of each district, and member voting patterns.[4]

Political science research within these three subject areas—inclusion, influence, and linkage—has given us three windows on African American members of Congress. Of course, the three windows are related to one another. In the real political world, we do not have a separate politics of inclusion, a politics of influence, and a politics of linkage. Research that deliberately cuts across all three rubrics reminds us how interrelated they are. Two successful studies of these interconnections are Carol Swain's *Black Faces, Black Interests* and David Canon's *Race, Redistricting, and Representation*.[5] The view adopted for this book utilizes all three vantage points. Deliberately, however, it gives primacy to the "linkage and representation" window.

REPRESENTATION AND THE HOME PERSPECTIVE

The linkage research to be reported here differs from most previous linkage research in two related respects. First, it does not center on questions of policy congruence. Second, it has been conducted almost entirely *in* the constituency. To date, the great bulk of political science research on congressional representation has focused on policy linkages, and it has been conducted at the Washington end of the linkage, where policy votes occur. The present study is built on the assumption that there is more to representation than policy relationships and that there is, therefore, value to be added from research conducted outside of Washington, at the constituency end of the linkage.

Indeed, a notion underlying the research is that representation is, at bottom, a home relationship, one that begins in the constituency and ends there. The research plan, therefore, is to watch, listen, and talk to some members of Congress as they go about their work in their districts and, thereby, to uncover the broadest repertoire of perceptions, attitudes, and activities that link that "at bottom" to their constituents. Home, not Washington, is the place where most House member–constituent contact occurs and the place where judgment is ultimately rendered.

In the literature on black politics, the linkage and representation window has often been treated in terms of two basic linkages—*descriptive* and *substantive.*[6] Voters gain and politicians provide "descriptive representation" when the two share some distinctive and defining characteristics. In the case of black voters and their elected black officials, the common characteristic is race. The idea is that black voters will feel represented when the person they elect is black. By contrast, voters gain and politicians provide "substantive representation" when the two share fundamental policy interests and policy preferences. The idea is that voters will feel represented when the elected official acts in ways that promote their shared policies. The distinction is sometimes stated in the language of someone "standing for" or "acting for" someone else.

Among students of black politics, a great deal of empirical and normative discussion centers on the two types of representation, their importance and their compatibility, in linking black citizens to their elected representatives. In discussions about the drawing of congressional district lines and about the overall representation of minority interests, questions involving descriptive and substantive representation are dominant. Their prominence requires that these two linkages be kept in mind. But in this book they will not dominate. They will be present, but in a different framework and in a different form.

In a study of four separate Representative–constituency relationships, conducted amid the hurly-burly of ground-level activities, the distinction between descriptive representation and substantive representation is not very helpful. It is both too general and too restrictive to use in organizing and analyzing observed behavior. Descriptive representation, to the degree that it is interpreted as "standing for," is too static a notion to be useful in thinking about the continuous member-to-constituent interaction that takes place in a real constituency. Even when descriptive representation does encompass some symbolic activity, its common statistical rendering constitutes an impediment to ground-level description.

As for substantive representation, it is equally restrictive in helping to identify the fullest range of a Representative's activities at home. As the term is commonly used, substantive representation encompasses one activity— policy representation as reflected in voting in Congress. That usage is perfectly adequate if policy voting is the main matter of scholarly interest—as typically it has been. But the day-to-day activity of a Representative in his or her home district involves a good deal more than that. If the full range of observable activity is to be treated, the policy-centered interpretation of substantive representation impairs its usefulness.

These difficulties emerge, of course, when research involves uncommon venues and questions. It was only when I went to observe the representational relationships of House members in their home constituencies that I found *descriptive representation* and *substantive representation* to be inadequate to the descriptive task. And, as a by-product, I also found that the oft-debated problem of their compatibility simply did not arise. To make sense out of what I was seeing, I had to transmute the two categories into a different conceptual language. From time to time, therefore, while the conventional categories will be mentioned, they have, for the most part, been set aside.

CONCEPTUALIZATION: PROCESS, CONNECTION, NEGOTIATION, AND STRATEGY

In the home district, member–constituency relationships reveal themselves through constant activity. Representation, therefore, can best be observed and conceptualized as a *process*. And the idea that best conveys process is the idea of *connections*. Representation is about connecting, and I assume that all constituency connections matter in the process—and the study—of representation.

The links between constituency policy preferences and the roll call records of House members have been the most heavily researched connections. But vote choices are only one out of many sorts of connection choices House members make. When the idea of descriptive and substantive representation is transmuted into the idea of connections, a wider variety of choices becomes visible. The static idea of descriptive representation becomes useful when interpreted as symbolic connecting activities. The idea of substantive representation is useful when limited to policy connections, and examined via roll call voting in the House and via policy dialogue at home. Then it becomes possible to examine separately several other active, observable connecting activities. In addition to symbolic connections and policy connections, three other connections—personal, electoral, and organizational—will be central in analyzing the representational relationships of House members at home.

Representation, as a relationship between an elected official and a constituency, is provisional and always subject to change. It is a relationship, therefore, that must be constantly worked on and worked out to the provisional satisfaction of both parties. Viewed at the district level and over the shoulder of the elected official, representation is a never-ending process whereby the politician works at building and maintaining supportive connections with some proportion of his or her constituents. We can, therefore, think of the representational relationship as a negotiated relationship, and we can think of the process of *negotiation* as central to the process of representation. In this book, I will use the idea of negotiation in a nontechnical, commonsense way. It is the basic idea of adjusting and matching, over time, the performance of one side to the expectations of the other.

As a negotiating process, representation is both incremental and experimental. Its incremental characteristics are reflected in the sheer number and variety of contacts between Representative and represented that occur—continuously—in the district. The experimental aspect of the process is reflected in the trial-and-error efforts of Representatives to bring their performance over time into some sort of equilibrium with the expectations and the monitoring routines of their constituents. Constituents want responsiveness, access, and two-way communication. House members want support—votes in the short run, trust and durable connections in the long run.

ELEMENTS OF STRATEGY: PERSONAL GOALS, CONSTITUENCY CONTEXTS, AND EXPERIENTIAL LEARNING

The research vantage point for this book is the home constituency. In the constituency context, each House member chooses certain connection patterns that he or she believes will result in constructive political activity and constituent approval. A member's pattern of connection choices can be thought of and analyzed as a *strategy* of representation. The basic elements of every House member's strategy are *personal goals, constituency contexts,* and *experiential learning.* They will be the guiding conceptualizations of the narrative. A brief elaboration of each follows.

All House members are *goal seekers.* They have ambitions; they want to accomplish things. They make choices and actively pursue such goals as getting reelected, making good public policy, accumulating influence in the House, building a political party locally, performing a civic duty, and helping individuals with their problems. Each member's representational strategy is driven by his or her goals.

Most members pursue a mix of goals. Election is, of course, the all-absorbing goal of every would-be House member. And reelection subsequently becomes the first-order goal of almost every incumbent House member. But election is not the only goal that drives the aspirant toward politics in the first place, and reelection is not the only goal that keeps the member in politics afterward. Nor, observably, is the electoral goal the crucial trace element in doping out each member's strategy of representation.

Thus, while it is always necessary to recognize that the first-order goal for most members is election or reelection, this single goal is rarely sufficient to explain their representational behavior.

Most members want to stay in Congress in order to pursue some broader, more satisfying goal—often the same one that attracted them to politics in the first place. In the observable mix of goals, it is this second-order goal that turns out to be the distinguishing feature of each member's district-level representational relationships. In discussing their district-level representational strategies, therefore, I shall treat the reelection goal as both common and instrumental. And the more sustaining goal will be treated as distinctive and dominant. I assume that a House member's dominant goal is the key to understanding the preponderance of that legislator's connections.

All House members are also *context interpreters*. They make choices and take action not in the abstract, but according to what they believe to be rational or appropriate in the circumstances or context in which they find themselves. And it is they who will interpret that context and act accordingly. The two main contexts in which their interpretation is called for are the constituency at home and the House of Representatives in Washington. Some important aspects of home context are fixed—proportions of blacks and whites, for example. Others are interpretable—constituent preferences and expectations, for example.

With respect to the constituency context, it will be helpful if I assume that each Representative perceives not a single home constituency, but a set of constituencies that nest, like a series of concentric circles, within one another. The largest circle, the district, contains all the residents of the legally prescribed geographical constituency; the next smaller, the reelection constituency, contains all voters who support or might support the member, and the smallest, the primary constituency, consists of their most active and most reliable supporters. African American members, as this book shows, perceive a fourth constituency to which they respond, one beyond the district—a national constituency of black citizens who live beyond the borders of any one member's district, but with whom all black members share a set of race-related concerns.

Finally, all House members are *experiential learners*. Over the course of their political careers, they negotiate their constituency relationships and develop recognizable connection patterns. Their negotiations do not take place all at once. They are sequential. They take time. My basic research strategy—of observing and tracing member activity over time—is predicated on that very condition. In thinking about member activity over time, the most useful perspective is a developmental one. The idea of careers is one such developmental idea. And the idea of learning is another. Members learn by their experience, and their experience guides them. Negotiating experiences are learning experiences. And their experiential learning can be traced in their negotiating sequences.

The negotiating experiences of House members are matters of mutual adjustment between them and their constituents. From the member's perspective, these adjustments proceed largely by trial and error. They must learn from their trial-and-error experiences how to size up situations and how to act in the service of their goals. When they have to make choices, they often begin with the question: "When I was faced with this situation or this kind of situation before, what did I do and what was the outcome?" If the outcome was satisfactory, there is a strong predisposition to do this time what they did last time. To do otherwise is likely to draw special attention from other players, and, since special attention can often be unfavorable, they tend not to risk it. They may, of course, update their situation—with new information, for example—and decide not to follow past practice. But there is a strong tendency to follow it.

Students who trace member vote choices in Congress have found a similar tendency to learn by experience and to follow it. That is, members make a large number of their vote choices by consulting their past votes and—if the outcome was satisfactory and the content roughly similar—they vote the same way they did before. Thus, as Herbert Asher and Herbert Weisberg describe it, members develop, over time, consistent and recognizable "vote histories." [7]

In his careful tracing of member career patterns inside the House, John Hibbing finds experiential learning to be reflected in member choices about voting and legislating. Vote choices tend to be fairly stable over time, constrained by past experience and past lessons. But choices about legislative involvement, on the other hand, reflect member openness to new experience and, as such, show a distinctive and positive learning curve. [8] These studies provide both rationale and support for some extra attention to the constituency-based negotiating sequences of individual House members.

THE STUDY

My first research adventure in the home districts of U.S. House members took place in the early 1970s, when I observed and wrote about the district-level activity of eighteen House members. [9] Among them were Louis

Stokes of Cleveland, who served in Congress from 1969 to 2000, and Barbara Jordan of Houston, who served from 1973 to 1978. In that study, details of person and context and experience—which might have provided a more nuanced picture of each individual member's political life—were squeezed out of the story in order to compare broad behavioral patterns. I used case studies for illustrative purposes, but kept the individuals unrecognizable. Stokes and Jordan grouped together anonymously with all the others, and race was not a relevant analytic category.

Because of the burgeoning interest in black politics, however, and because I had this small, two-person baseline from which to work, my curiosity led me to take a second, more focused and more contemporary look at a couple of other African American House members. They are Chaka Fattah of Philadelphia, whose current service began in 1995, and Stephanie Tubbs Jones of Cleveland, whose current service began in 1999. Because the present study examines only four individuals, it maximizes detail and, of necessity, removes anonymity. It necessarily sacrifices explanatory precision in order to gain descriptive richness. Readers will, of course, judge the merits of that trade. It is, however, important to note at the outset that—except for election results—this book presents *no* systematic evidence of constituency sentiment. It has been written almost entirely from the perspective of each individual Representative.

From beginning to end, the present research was curiosity and case-study driven. It had no overall "design." With Stokes and Tubbs Jones, I seized the opportunity to observe representational change from one Representative to another within the same district. With Jordan and Fattah, there were no continuities. The four individuals are treated here in the order in which I first met them—in an effort to match my own learning curve. I do want to make clear at the outset that I began and ended without any preconceived notion about a "best" strategy of representation or a "best" Representative. Each individual became, in my view, a successful U.S. Representative.

In no sense do these four people constitute a "sample" of African American House members. There are, however, important commonalities. I met all of them near the start of their congressional careers. All four lived their entire lives in the district they represent, and all four have represented dominantly urban constituencies. This latter characteristic is especially important because it eliminates from consideration the growing number of African American members from less urban and more heterogeneous constituencies—the very group of post-1990 Representatives that sparked and leveraged the important studies by Swain and Canon. This book does find and does describe both representational change and representational diversity, but it does so within a narrow range of the available possibilities.

Within districts, as well as across districts, sampling was impossible. With research of this type, the researcher does not make up the House member's home schedule or dictate the timing of a visit to the constituency. Much of what the researcher observes or converses about with the Representative and can report at firsthand is controlled by others. And the researcher cannot be certain what has been left out. Narrative accounts must be constructed from a series of intermittently gathered snapshots. The reliability of generalizations can be improved by repeated visits to the district, and author experience counts for something in drawing conclusions. But in the end, all generalizations, both across and within districts, are unusually tentative. Which condition, it is hoped, will serve to encourage—not discourage—more research of this nature.

My window on the constituency life of black members of Congress has been intermittent and tiny. More important, perhaps, my window has been opaque. I am a white researcher immersed, briefly, in the affairs of black communities. I am, of course, a stranger in any community beyond my own. But the strangeness of race is an extra hurdle in achieving rapport and in trying to figure out what is going on. I feel somewhat confident of my intellectual grasp of the rational aspects of the behavior I observe. But it is difficult for me to appreciate or evaluate the historical and emotional aspects of the larger inclusionary struggle.[10] The difficulty increases when, as in these cases, anonymity is foregone and relevant personal and circumstantial detail is sought.

Very early, I recognized that African American scholars are best equipped to do the job. But I also recognized that there is not yet a surplus of African American scholars doing it. And I believe I do have a story worth telling. My intent and my hope, therefore, are that these four narratives will be of some help to the larger, mainstream research community studying black politics in America. I hope, too, that it might provide an incentive for members of that community to proceed further. As another by-product, perhaps, the conceptualization, the argumentation, and the narrative content of this book can be of some help to students already researching the large subject of political representation.

CHAPTER 2
. . . .
LOUIS STOKES
1970 – 1976

THE PIONEER COHORT

From the mid-1960s to the mid-1970s, Louis Stokes and Barbara Jordan belonged to a recognizable cohort of African American House members. A half-dozen other black members were already there when Stokes arrived at the Capitol in late 1968. And those six early arrivals had surely been pioneers. But they could not be described as a cohort. They had come to Congress one by one, with their elections scattered in time from 1942 to 1964—over the course of eleven elections and twenty-two years. In a period less than half as long and in only four consecutive elections, the number of black House members had tripled. And the dozen new ones had come in clusters of four, four, three, and one. In terms of timing and context, they could reasonably be described as a cohort (see table 1).

All members of this cohort were products of the civil rights revolution of the 1960s. They were the first group of African Americans elected to Congress after the Voting Rights Act of 1965. All but one were "the first" to represent their districts. They were the group that initiated, and then dominated, the process by which the Congressional Black Caucus was created and institutionalized. The clustering of their elections, their common civil rights heritage, and their history of collective action inside Congress, encourage us to think of them as a recognizable and substantial "pioneer cohort" of African American House members.

The first part of this book looks at two members of that cohort—Louis Stokes and Barbara Jordan. I followed both of them in the 1970s. Studying them separately says something about the diversity of representational strategies among African American House members. Studying them together provides a baseline against which to measure change among African American House members who arrived in the 1990s.

There is no reason to expect African American House members to be

TABLE 1

AFRICAN AMERICAN MEMBERS OF CONGRESS: 1969–1975

Name	Year Entered	Year Left
Early Individuals		
William Dawson (D/Ill.)	1943	1970
Adam Clayton Powell (D/N.Y.)	1945	1971
Charles Diggs (D/Mich.)	1955	–
Robert Nix (D/Pa.)	1958*	–
Augustus Hawkins (D/Calif.)	1962*	–
John Conyers (D/Mich.)	1965	–
Pioneer Cohort		
Louis Stokes (D/Ohio)	1969	–
Shirley Chisholm (D/N.Y.)	1969	–
William Clay (D/Mo.)	1969	–
George Collins (D/Ill.)	1969	1972
Ronald Dellums (D/Calif.)	1971	–
Ralph Metcalf (D/Fla.)	1971	–
Parren Mitchell (D/Md.)	1971	–
Charles Rangel (D/N.Y.)	1971	–
[Walter Fauntroy (D/D.C.)]†	1971	–
Barbara Jordan (D/Tex.)	1973	–
Yvonne Burke (D/Calif.)	1973	–
Andrew Young (D/Ga.)	1973	–
Cardiss Collins (D/Ill.)‡	1973	–
Harold Ford (D/Tenn.)	1975	–

* Off-year election because of a House member's retirement or death.
† Nonvoting member.
‡ Replaced George Collins.

interchangeable in their representational activities. To the contrary, there is every reason to expect differences. And that, indeed, is a major legacy of previous research on patterns of representation among African American House members.

James Wilson pioneered the comparative analysis of black House members and their political styles at home in his study of Representatives William Dawson of Chicago and Adam Clayton Powell of New York City.[1] The two House members were leaders of constituency organizations, and Wilson emphasized the sharp contrast in the way each individual approached the common problem of organizational maintenance—Dawson by providing tangible incentives, such as jobs, to organization members, Powell by providing intangible incentives, such as ideology, to organization members. Differences in organizational context and in local political context explained differences in member behavior at home and in Washington. Without making representation his central idea, Wilson vividly captured important differences in the constituency relationships of two African American House members.

Carol Swain's research in the 1980s reinforced Wilson's conclusion about the variety of constituency relationships among African American members.[2] In so doing, she deepened and broadened his analysis. She made representation her focus, and she personally visited several districts to help her describe varieties of representational relationships. She explained variation using a four-part typology of districts—different types of districts, she argued, accounted for different representational patterns.

In his study of African American House members in the 1990s, David Canon further enlarged the analysis of race and representation.[3] He broadened the setting with philosophical and legal analysis, and he included all black members in a series of careful statistical analyses of their representational behavior in the House and in their constituencies. For him, too, variation in representational behavior is the central theme, and two varieties emerge. One is grounded in the pursuit of racial differences; the other is grounded in the pursuit of racial commonalities. He explains this variation using a typology of campaign contexts and strategic responses.

The micro-level emphasis on representational diversity in *Going Home* follows the work of these scholars. Its explanations, however, begin neither with types of districts nor with campaign strategies, but with individuals.

Louis Stokes reflected many of the characteristics of his twelve-member pioneer cohort. All but three of the twelve represented majority-black districts, all but one represented major U.S. cities, and all but three came from outside the South. Stokes was modal in each of these categories. He came from the largest of Carol Swain's district types: "historically black districts." And he came from the most populous of David Canon's representational categories: "difference representatives." In all these respects, Stokes is an anchoring template for an exploration of African American House members in their constituencies. "When I began this journey," he once said, "I realized that I was the first black American ever to hold this position in this state. *I had to write the book.* There was no book."[4]

PERSONAL GOALS AND REPRESENTATIONAL STRATEGY

When I first met Louis Stokes, in Cleveland in the fall of 1970, he was forty-five years old, serving in his first political office, and engaged in his first reelection campaign. His career milestones were these: educated in the Cleveland public schools; U.S. Army 1943–1946; Cleveland College of Western Reserve University, 1946–1949; Cleveland-Marshall Law School, 1949–1953; private practice of law, 1955–1968; Chairman, Legal Redress Committee, Cleveland Chapter of NAACP; elected to Congress, 1968. He had spent his entire civilian life in Cleveland.

I visited him there in October 1970, May 1971, and September 1976. I talked with him in Washington in December 1970, February 1972, and May 1974.

Lou Stokes was born into a poor, working-class family. His father worked in a laundry, and he died when Louis was three. His mother worked for forty years as a domestic. She did everything in her power to instill into her two boys the value of an education—to "get something in your head so you will never have to work with your hands the way I have." His early years were spent in a dilapidated two-family house and, from the age of thirteen, in the first of Cleveland's public housing "projects." He grew up in poverty; he had to work after school; he served in a segregated Army; and, thanks to the GI Bill, he went, at night, to college and law school. His earliest life experiences mirrored those of a large majority of his fellow black citizens in Cleveland. His educational achievements and qualifications, however, gave him the potential to be of extraordinary help to them in his later life.

As a congressional candidate, Lou Stokes was *not* a prototypically ambitious, self-promoting, entrepreneurial politician. He was a self-starting, community-minded lawyer. And as such, he says, "I had no political ambitions whatsoever."[5] He was very different from his younger brother Carl who, as a two-term state representative and two-term mayor of Cleveland, said of himself, "I took to politics as a duck does to water."[6] Said Louis in 1970, "For a long time, I had very little interest in politics. I was a lawyer and I loved my practice. Carl was the politician in the family and I left politics to him." Indeed, when they were partners, early on, in the "Stokes and Stokes" law firm, they had "bitter arguments" when Louis objected to Carl mixing politics and law by conducting his political activity in their office.[7] "My dream," he said, "was that Carl and I would establish the top black law firm in America. Carl had no such idea. He was going to utilize the law for his political career."[8]

When asked to identify his politically relevant experience, he emphasized, instead, his prior participation in the life of the community.

> I have to go way back. I worked in the community for eighteen years.
> People knew who I was and knew I was involved in the community—the
> NAACP, YMCA, Boy Scouts, you name it. That way people know you.
> You aren't an isolated name. They know you for the personal relationship
> they had with you. If you were their lawyer, they know you are an able
> lawyer and that you didn't pull any deals on them. I don't always tell
> people what they want to hear. I try not to promise things I can't deliver.
> So I'll say to people, "I don't want to mislead you." I try to be sincere and
> dedicated. . . . And you have the unique situation of Carl and myself.
> People in the community feel a kinship to our family. They know where
> we came from. They know what our circumstances were. We're like part
> of the family.

He was not a total political neophyte. "I had done a little work for a friend
of mine who ran for Congress. . . . And I worked in a couple of judges races
and in Carl's [mayoral] races." But he harbored no political ambition.

His legal work on behalf of the community—his civil rights involvement
and especially his legal work for the NAACP—was highly visible. When the
Ohio legislature responded to the Supreme Court's one-man, one-vote decision by redistricting Cleveland in a way that kept its black population divided, the Legal Redress Committee of Cleveland's NAACP challenged the
decision in the courts. After losing in the U.S. District Court, the committee,
led by Stokes, filed a brief directly with the Supreme Court, and the court, in
1967 and without oral argument, decided in favor of the brief. Cleveland's
new, black-majority Twenty-first District resulted. "I led the team that con-
tested the Appellate Court decision in the Supreme Court, and we won the
case," he recalled. "After that, people in the community came and said they
felt that since I had played such a large part in getting the new district created, that I should run for it. Actually, the seat was drawn for Carl. He's the
one who wanted to go to Congress. That had always been his ambition. But
he was then mayor. So after a great deal of praying and thinking and lots of
family confabs, I decided to run." Already a soldier in the legal battle for inclusion, he had now enlisted in the political battle for inclusion.

His community service was a necessary condition for his political career.
But far outranking it was the nearly sufficient condition of his brother's
influence. It would be impossible to underestimate that influence. It was
Carl Stokes who, as a state representative, first agitated and worked for

Ohio's first black-majority congressional district. And he hoped to take it for himself. It was Carl who first cultivated the people of the new district. It was Carl who became, as the first black mayor of a major American city, a city-wide political leader. It was Carl who led the formation of the organization that would become his brother's political lifeline. It was Carl who—determined that none of his ambitious enemies should win in what he considered "my district"—talked Louis into running for it.

Louis himself was supporting another candidate, Dr. Kenneth Clement. But when a group of black leaders sought Carl's advice one Sunday, Carl took Dr. Clement into his kitchen alone for an hour and emerged saying, "Kenny is not going to be our candidate. Lou's going to run." To which he added, "Here's a guy who doesn't have an enemy in the world. Now he's going to find out what it's like to have enemies.[9] It was Carl's advice and Carl's allies that managed Louis's emergence as a candidate. "I ran my brother Louis," wrote Carl, "and put behind him all the machinery that just elected me mayor."[10] This sheltering relationship was a mixed blessing at times, but the brothers remained the closest of political confidants for the entirety of Louis's congressional career.

In May 1968, Lou Stokes captured 41 percent of the vote against thirteen opponents in the Democratic primary. In October, he captured 74 percent of the general election vote. He had come to politics and to Congress in the wake and in the shadow of his brother. "So here I am," he said to me in 1970. "I'm in it and I like it. But I would have been perfectly happy as a lawyer."

In an earlier study linking the goals of individual politicians to their strategy of representation, I highlighted two types of goals—person-related goals, and policy-related goals. Based on that distinction, I identified two representational strategies—distinct but not exclusive. The strategy dominated by the cultivation of personal connections with constituents, I called a person-intensive strategy of representation. The other, dominated by the cultivation of policy connections with constituents, I called a policy-intensive strategy.[11]

In Lou Stokes's case, however, these categories do not fit, not singly and not even in combination. He did have strong policy goals. But his dominant goal was broader than that. It was to promote and protect the interests of one particular group—the group he calls "the black community." And because of the dominance of that goal, it will be most helpful to think of his dominant representational strategy as a *group-intensive strategy*—in which the group being represented is "the black community."

In a composite 1978 study that featured Stokes anonymously as "Congressman F," I wrote:

He is sensitive to all the common experiences and common aspirations that bind black people one to the other. The term he uses is "the black community." And he works, every chance he gets, to deepen the sense of community among blacks. His own identification with the black community is obvious and total. Every expression he gives or gives off conveys the idea that "I am one of you." His view of "me-in-the-district" begins, then, with a feeling of total immersion in the black community. Congressman F sees himself as a microcosm of that community.[12]

Subsequent political science research has helped me to recognize how basic the idea of "the black community" is to the understanding of African American politics.

In his seminal study of the political attitudes and voting behavior of the nation's black citizens, Michael Dawson finds an extraordinary degree of group consciousness. And their group consciousness, in turn, underpins an extraordinary political unity. Their longtime exclusion as a group and their common struggle for inclusion as a group has left African American citizens with a well-developed and enduring sense of themselves as a group. That sense is so well developed that despite growing economic diversity within the group, they continue to think of themselves—and react to external stimuli—as a group, as a homogeneous racial community.

Each black citizen, Dawson theorizes, believes that his or her personal, individual interest is bound up with the interests of the group, and, therefore, each individual acts politically so as to fight for and protect their common interest as African Americans. Or, as Dawson puts it, black people believe that their "fate" as individuals has been "linked" to the fate of their racial group. He writes, African Americans "believe that their lives are, to a large degree, determined by what happens to the group as a whole . . . [and, therefore,] that African Americans' perception of racial group interests [are] an important component of the way individual blacks go about evaluating policies, parties and candidates."[13] The bonds of racial history and the bonds of group psychology would be evoked and tested when Lou Stokes presented himself to his constituents as a representative of "the black community."

As a congressman, Lou Stokes was both embedded in, and a representative of, the black community. When he spoke of the black community, he was evoking the remarkable degree of group consciousness that existed among his black constituents and the remarkable consensus on group interests that resulted. The language of group interests was his natural language.

For him, the community and his constituency were virtually coterminous. Certainly that was true of his reelection and his primary constituencies. When asked, "Who are your strongest supporters?" he replied, "The whole black community." That was the constituency surrounding him, and that was the constituency to which he responded. That was the constituency he had worked for and protected in his work with the NAACP. His dominant goal as a Representative was to promote and protect the interests of "the whole black community." He followed, I shall argue, a *group-intensive strategy of representation.*

The group interests of the black community, as I watched him in action, could be divided into matters of *policy, pride,* and *power.* And the new Representative was uniquely positioned to further all three of them. He developed constituency connections that would allow him to affect policy, invoke pride, and exercise power. And because he was *the first* elected African American representative to the national government from his city and his state, he could set the standard—"write the book"—in all three respects. Being "first" gave him special opportunities and a special reputation with which to exploit those opportunities. At the time of my initial visit, he had been in office less than two years. But it seemed clear that he was already in an unusually strong position to pursue each aspect of his representational strategy.

The precondition for adopting any representational strategy, of course, is the ability of the elected House member to get reelected. And reelection, I assume, is an instrumental goal of all members of Congress—unless they plan to retire or have term-limited themselves or have a death wish. A lot of what I shall call Stokes's representational strategy is, at the same time, his reelection strategy. A large part of the constituency that he worked to represent was the same constituency that voted its approval at election time. Which is to say that the study of a House member's reelection campaign can provide a useful—albeit a partial—view of his or her representational strategy.[14] Good representation involves more than reelection, but "good representation" ought to produce reelection. And both must be negotiated out, over time, between a particular House member and particular sets of constituents in a particular constituency context.

CONSTITUENCY CONTEXT

The district I first visited in 1970 was a newly-minted product of the civil rights revolution of the 1960s. It was both a success and a turning point in the drive for political inclusion by the black citizens of Cleveland. Its dimensions were demographic, geographic, socioeconomic, historical, partisan, organizational, and journalistic.

Demographically and geographically, the Twenty-first Congressional District was a highly urbanized district with a 65 percent black population, located on Cleveland's east side. Its makeup reflected familiar race-based residential patterns. There were eleven wards in the city with elected black council members, and eight of them were in the Twenty-first District. Ninety percent of the district's 355,000 residents, mostly black, lived in the city. The other 10 percent, mostly southern and eastern European whites, lived in two contiguous southeast suburbs. Most white ethnics lived on the west side of the city, which made the geographical distinction also a racial one. When I first arrived, Stokes's staffers drew a bright line. "There's no reason to go to the west side. It's where people move to when they want to escape black people. It's a rough area. As far as we're concerned, it doesn't exist." Demography, residency, and geography combined to give some spatial definition to the idea of the black community.

The district's boundaries were redrawn after the reapportionments of 1970, 1980, and 1990. As the 1972 redistricting approached, I asked the congressman what the worst-case scenario would be for him. He answered,

> If they packed my district with white ethnics from areas like Euclid [a large east side suburb]—as some people say they might—that would kill me. . . . People out there know I don't mince words. They know how I stand, and they don't like it. That would be the end. I need a black base. I have 65 percent now. I would need 55 percent at least. With only 40 percent black, I don't think I could win. I don't mind having whites in the district, so long as I have enough black support to start with. That's the way it has to be for me.

He needn't have worried. And he probably didn't.

When the redistricting process was over, he was pleased. Indeed, what he had earlier called his "best scenario," in other words, "lop off some of Garfield Heights and give me East Cleveland," had come true. "I didn't take any part in it," he explained.

> Things would appear in the papers, and the guys down here would come in and offer to make deals and swap parts of our districts back and forth. I took the position that wherever they put the Twenty-first District, that was where I was going to run. I said I didn't care what they took, that I'd

take whatever was left over and run in that district. But you know who was going to get all the blacks, don't you—me! Who else could they give them to? No one else wants them but me. So that's the way it worked out. . . . The new district is even better than the last one. It's about 70 percent black. I have every black ward in the city. I have East Cleveland, which is 50 percent black. I got Warrensville and Warrensville Heights— and Warrensville Heights is probably 40 percent black. I'm safe for ten years—as long as I do my job.

In subsequent redistricting, the district grew in size (to 571,000), and it spread out into the east-side suburbs. Those suburbs, once overwhelmingly white, became increasingly black. While the black proportion of the district slowly declined, it remained a majority-black district throughout Stokes's tenure.

In socioeconomic terms, the entire city of Cleveland was suffering during the time of my visits. Two Cleveland historians called the early 1970s "the most difficult period in the city's history. . . . tumultuous years for Cleveland, years when the city seemed to be in the midst of its own Great Depression."[15] A 1975 comparative study of social and economic conditions in fifty-eight big cities ranked Cleveland second worst.[16] Whatever Cleveland's socio-economic ills were, they struck hardest at its black citizens and at Louis Stokes's district. Among the four congressional districts that included parts of the city, Stokes's district was the lowest in median family income, the lowest in families with income over $15,000, the lowest in families above $3,000, and the lowest in median educational achievement.[17]

"By 1970," wrote the two historians, the "abandonment of entire neighborhoods [was] a phenomenon concentrated in all-black neighborhoods with high poverty and crime rates."[18] Other accounts of Cleveland in the period detail its two serious outbreaks of racial violence—the Hough riot in 1966, killing four people and wounding eleven, and the Glenville shoot-out in 1968, killing seven people and wounding fifteen.[19] Both events scarred Stokes's district. Out of this combination of urban problems arose the very basic policy needs of the black community. With respect to those policy needs of a dominantly black constituency, the Twenty-first District was markedly homogeneous.

Beneath this overall contextual homogeneity, there was, of course, some diversity. When I asked the congressman how he would describe his district, he differentiated among neighborhoods in socioeconomic terms.

I would talk about the black aspects—65 percent and so forth. I would say it ranges, in the black area, from very poor to middle class. In the white area, it's just barely middle class–lower-middle class. [Among the black areas] the Hough area has all the problems of an inner city. And the middle-class areas aren't anything fabulous, $18,000 to $20,000 [a year] in the Lee Harvard area. . . . Most of my welfare problems come from the inner city. The people in Mount Pleasant, they want more from the city than from the federal government—sidewalks. They are very home conscious there.

When they drove me around, his staffers would provide sharper descriptive commentary. Driving up Hough Avenue—the scene of the first race riot—one called it "the worst street in the city, a dying street." And added, "this is where the trouble was. It's just about as rough as any part of the city. . . . the worst place to travel after dark." "Mt. Pleasant," he pointed out, "is the closest thing to a middle-class black area there is in the city. But Mt. Pleasant is going to the dogs. And Hough is already there." Another staffer took me to see Lee Harvard, "the newest area"—a modest, suburban-feeling neighborhood of small one-and-a-half-story brick or wooden homes with residents watering grass and tending gardens. The picture there was one of a peaceful middle-class citizenry. Neighborhood differences emerged when low-income housing was proposed for middle-class areas.[20]

The historical context in which I studied Lou Stokes's representational pattern has been described by political scientist Robert C. Smith as a time of "transformation from protest to politics." A time of "black power" pronouncements and "ghetto riots," he wrote, had first stimulated and then given way to "the development of a black ethnic tradition and the development of emergent independent black organizational structures." The period from 1966 to 1972, he said, was marked by "a veritable explosion" of "a wide variety of black organizations active in the articulation of black interests."[21]

In the early 1970s, black elected politicians functioned—to varying degrees—within this transitional context. The racial disturbances in Hough and Glenville in the late 1960s signaled the presence of militant protest in Cleveland. When Stokes was elected, the black nationalism of these "ghetto riots" had waned. "The nationalists don't lay so thick around here," one staffer said in 1970. "I was at a meeting not too long ago when three Black Panthers came in, in full regalia," the congressman said in 1971. "One of them came over near me, and I made a point to talk with him. He just said,

'We're with you brother.' And he walked away. That's all I've seen of the Panthers. They don't write me for anything." Still, the transition from protest to politics remained incomplete.

"I was over at Cuyahoga Community College," Stokes said a year later,

and one of the radical kids asked me, "How come you're working within the system? You should be over here with us denouncing the system." And he went on like that. So I said to him, "All right, I'll get up and denounce the system. But before I do, answer me one question. What will your system be like?" That took him back a little and he said that the American and French revolutionaries never stopped to figure out what the new system would be like before they revolted and so forth. I said, "I know what this system is like, and I know what I can do in this system. But I don't know what I will be able to do under your system if you don't tell me. If I'm going to let you lead me, you've got to show me where I'm to be led." Then I asked him another question. "How are you going to win? They've got the Army, the police, the National Guard, the guns, the bullets, the tanks, the Navy, the airplanes. You can't win. So why should I follow you and get killed and get thousands of innocent black folks killed when you haven't a prayer?"

I'm going to keep on denouncing the inequities of this system, but I'm going to work within it. To go outside the system would be to deny myself—to deny my own existence. I've beaten the system. I've proved it can be done—so have a lot of others. But the problem is that a black man has to be extra special to win in this system. Why should you have to be super black to get someplace? That's what's wrong in the society. The ordinary black man doesn't have the same chance that the ordinary white man does.

Doubtless, some ideological diversity remained. And Lou Stokes's devotion to racial solidarity, to organizational politics, and to his constituency job can best be appreciated within a contextual combination of group transition and personal commitment.

For Stokes, the transition from protest to politics centered on creating an indigenous black political organization—one that grew out of the relationship of the black community to the Democratic Party. In an urban constituency, when the geographical boundaries of a House member's district are not coterminous with the reach of the dominant political party, a member of Congress must negotiate some kind of working relationship with the local party organization. For a first-generation House member who is *not* a prod-

uct of that organization, the choices involved—cooperation or conflict—
are crucial. Where—as in Stokes's case—no similarly situated black politician has ever faced the problem of getting along with his or her party, the
stakes for the newcomer are high. And prior negotiations provide no answers. The choice involves power for the black community and survival for
the House member.

For Lou Stokes, the partisan-organizational context made it virtually impossible to avoid a conflict. The interests of Cleveland's black community
did not coincide with the interests of the Cuyahoga County Democratic
Party. The Twenty-first District was an overwhelmingly Democratic district
in a strongly Democratic city in a Democratic-leaning county. At every level,
black voters were hard-core Democratic voters and essential to the party's local success. But black voters and their representatives had not been rewarded
with commensurate power in return for their support.

When African American ward leaders won election to city council, they
were granted only ward-level patronage and enough recognition to keep
them contentedly in office.[22] The party dealt with black politicians in this
one-by-one fashion, thus keeping them divided. No black politician was
given citywide or countywide power within the party. And no black politician had the incentive or the muscle to change the situation.

The coming of a black mayor and a black congressman, armed with broad
official jurisdiction and widespread personal recognition in the community,
changed the political context. These "new guys on the block" were in a position to carry the fight for fair representation directly to the white leadership of the Democratic Party. And it was in their own self-interest to do so.
The congressman's fight for political inclusion, therefore, became a major
time-consuming part of his representational activity in the district. His fight
centered on creating and maintaining an independent, community-based
political organization.

In terms of the media context, the city had two daily newspapers and
one weekly newspaper with political coverage. The morning *Cleveland Plain
Dealer,* with a circulation of approximately 400,000, and the afternoon
Cleveland Press, with a circulation of approximately 300,000, were the
largest. When Stokes was first elected, the *Plain Dealer* had recently caught
and passed the venerable *Press.* In 1984, the *Press* went out of business.[23] For
most of Lou Stokes's career, the *Plain Dealer* was the only major local paper.
The third paper was the *Call and Post,* an African American weekly newspaper, with a circulation of about 30,000.

Neither of the two large dailies supported Carl or Louis Stokes in their first, and crucial, electoral bids—Carl in his first, and losing, 1965 bid for Mayor, Louis in his 1968 Democratic primary. In Louis's race, the *Plain Dealer* supported a black city councilman whom Carl described as "desperately want[ing] white approval."[24] And the *Press* made no endorsement. The *Plain Dealer* did support both brothers in their subsequent election efforts.

As mayor, Carl drew constant press attention, and he depicted his day-to-day relationship with the press as "war." Gradually, he wrote, the papers "hardened into permanent adversaries," subjecting him to "daily attacks" and a "steady, slow assassination" by the people who covered him.[25] Whereas Carl was treated as an important local figure by the daily papers, Louis was not—and not, for that matter, by the historians and chroniclers of the city.[26] In the early years, at least, the congressman's relationship was characterized more by neglect than by confrontation.

The *Call and Post* and its publisher, William O. Walker, a Republican, was a different story. They were unfailingly supportive of both Stokes brothers. And they treated both men as important local figures. From 1957 to 1971, wrote Carl, "not a week went by that I didn't visit the *Call and Post* and counsel with Al Sweeney [city editor till 1967] or editor and publisher W. O. Walker."[27] The congressman, too, seemed in constant contact with Walker during each of my early visits.

During the 1970 campaign, the congressman's top staffer commented: "He's getting wonderful publicity from the Negro press. He's plastered all over the papers—they are very friendly to him. The *Call and Post* is worth a lot more than the *Plain Dealer* and the *Press* put together." Throughout my visits in the 1970s, the congressman expressed similar sentiments. "The Cleveland press doesn't cover black affairs," he said in 1976. Nor, he added, did it cover him in Washington. "On substantive stuff, nobody cares. I work on two bills, I get two lines. But let me get into trouble of some personal sort and it would get a whole page." Despite all of his locally based political activity, Lou Stokes—the most prominent figure in Cleveland's black community—did not command the attention of the daily metropolitan press. That, too, was part of the context in which I watched him work at home.

ELECTORAL CONNECTIONS

When we observe House members making connections at the grassroots, we are observing the bits and pieces of an ongoing process of negotiation. It is helpful, in thinking about these negotiations between members and constituencies, to think in terms of a *career*. Whenever an outside observer jumps into an ongoing negotiation between a member and his or her constituents, an immediate observation is that of a career in progress. A lot of member–constituent negotiation will have preceded that initial observational period, and a lot will follow afterward. To chart a Representative's career is, therefore, to chart a long-term negotiation. A useful way of framing a representational career is to divide it into two broad, overlapping stages. In the early stage of a career, a member's constituency relationship tends to be *expansionist,* involving the negotiation of stronger connections and more support within the district. In a later stage of a career, the relationship becomes mostly *protectionist,* with the member's district negotiations designed to consolidate existing connections and support levels.[28]

When I jumped into the 1970 Stokes campaign, the first negotiation of his brief political career—his baptismal 1968 Democratic primary victory— was over. It had been, and would remain, his most crucial expansionist effort. It had made him a political leader, and it had eliminated his near-term competition from within the community. When the new Twenty-first Congressional District came up for grabs in 1968, it had attracted a lot of attention from elected black officials. Three locally prominent black city councilmen—and two white city councilmen—entered the race. "Each one," said Stokes, "thought he had a base to start from. Each one thought, 'I have three thousand votes and Stokes has none.'" But no one came close. Against thirteen opponents, he took 41 percent of the vote, defeating his nearest rival by 20 percentage points. He carried fourteen of seventeen city wards, and he defeated every one of his black opponents in the opponent's home ward.

His campaign manager described Stokes's winning campaign.

We were one happy family of novices. We had a good, well-known candidate who had been active in the community from the NAACP and the Urban League on down. We contacted all the groups, church groups especially. Our greatest fear was that each of the politicians running in his own ward would pull strength from Lou. So we deliberately set up an organization in the home ward of every man in the race and we talked up Lou and talked down the local leader. "What has he ever done for you?" Our theme was that Lou was "the unity candidate," and it appealed to people.

He went around and made speeches—not so much at first. But later on, he spoke everywhere. His opponents made him angry saying that he was running on his brother's name. That made him work harder. We were surprised by the size of the margin. We beat every one of his opponents in his own home ward. We just out-worked, out-organized, and out-strategized them. It was the most fun I ever had.

Stokes, too, emphasized the importance of these initial ward-level connections. "We went into every ward and precinct and we organized it," thus tying him into his future constituents. "I didn't even campaign in the white area," he said, "except for one tea held by a fellow I used to work with years ago." His primary campaign created strongly supportive "ties that bind"—connections that would undergird his future prowess at the polls.

His postelection comparisons with his leading opponents suggest the breadth of Stokes's community connections. He took on and defeated both the most white-oriented black politician and the most black-oriented black politician. Within the black community, that is, he emerged as a political centrist and a political unifier.

Speaking of his strongest opponent—and the only one he debated in public[29]—Stokes commented,

He was a black man who was very popular with the white community. And the reason was that he was always criticizing the black community. He would tell them just what they wanted to hear—that the black people were hoodlums and bums and all that sort of thing. They thought he was a wonderful person. He ran with the endorsements of the Democratic Party, the AFL-CIO, the Cleveland press and one black church group. I had the endorsements of every other black church group, and all the organizations there were in the black community. I beat him two-to-one— even in his home ward and precinct.

The vivid contrast in their respective electoral constituencies expresses clearly Stokes's perception of his own support base. It was, indeed, "the whole black community."

Available accounts support this assessment of his strongest opponent. The *Plain Dealer* editorial endorsing that candidate did not mention the Stokes name. Calling their favorite "a standout," they praised him for keeping "the welfare of the entire city in mind" and for recognizing "the limitations of city government in providing jobs and housing for inner-city residents.[30] Ward-level analysis of the primary vote indicates that *Plain Dealer* support did give their candidate a boost—in white areas. In the three city wards carried by Stokes's chief *white* opponent—and *only* in these "white" wards—the *Plain Dealer* candidate ran ahead of Stokes.[31] In their postelection summary, the newspaper called it "a surprisingly strong victory" and attributed it to "the magic of his brother's image." [32]

His strength against another highly touted and more radical councilman opponent revealed the breadth of Stokes's support. "He ran as the candidate of the black nationalists," said Stokes. "But I had strength with the nationalist groups, too. I had been head of the Legal Redress Committee of the Cleveland NAACP. I had defended a great many Black Nationalists and others in civil rights cases. And I had defended Harllel Jones, leader of the Black Nationalists. So I had strength there." As one staff member put it, "The militants know the congressman defended them when they were in trouble. He took a lot of cases, and he did it for nothing. So they know they owe him 'a lot of bucks.'"

Stokes had attached himself, at many levels, to the civil rights movement, and that experience left him with connections to the diversity of ideological elements within the black community. His centrism within the community made his representational tasks at home much easier than otherwise. Subsequently, too, his centrism at home made it relatively easy for him to adjust to institutional politics inside Congress.

Lou Stokes's 1968 general election contest was no problem. But the tenor of it certainly helped him with old-line black Republicans and, doubtless, broadened his support throughout the community. His Republican opponent was the same African American who had initiated the redistricting case Stokes had argued in the Supreme Court. So Stokes was pitted against his own former client! Of whom he spoke warmly:

> He was a very fine, respected gentlemen in the community, with a wonderful record of service. He was the Executive Secretary of the NAACP and did the finest job ever done by anyone in that position. His position and mine on civil rights and things of importance to the black community were the same. We had very similar credentials. But I had a good organization. I was a Democrat in a Democratic area. And I had the name "Stokes." All those things helped. . . . Not one cross word ever passed between us. I hold him in the highest respect.

Stokes's relations with prominent Republicans would turn out to be of considerable importance to him in an upcoming bipartisan political negotiation within the district. At which time, his very positive relationship with his Republican opponent would be beneficial.

The scope of his 1968 Democratic primary victory—his overwhelming plurality in a fourteen-person race, his winning plurality in every "black" ward and his two-to-one margin over his strongest competitor—gave him plenty of reason to think of his supportive reelection constituency as "the whole black community."

From the comments of the candidate and his campaign manager, we can discern the makeup of his very strongest connections—his primary constituency. They are, by one calculation, all those who voted for him in the primary. But a more fine-grained picture will locate the heart and soul of his support where both accounts highlight it—in the black churches of the district. Not long after we met, he expounded on the necessity of their bedrock support. "My brother and I have been very fortunate in always having the support of the churches," he began.

> The other day, we had a meeting of eighty ministers. In the black community, ministers are very influential. Their members will do what the minister tells them to. If the minister stands up on Sunday and says, "You've got to support Lou Stokes," they say, "Yes, sir, yes, reverend,"— and then go out and do it. And if the minister speaks for you, why that's better than being there yourself. Some of these ministers have congregations of three thousand people. Eighty ministers . . . are a powerful force in the community. And we have always had support from them.

From the beginning of my visits to the end, the hard core of his support came from the leaders and the parishioners of the black churches in the district. And, as I shall show, he nurtured and negotiated for that support throughout his career.

For most House members, their first reelection campaign is the most pivotal in their careers. One victory can be regarded as an accident; two victories signify solidified support. Here again, the normal time-lines did not apply to Stokes. None of his primary opponents of 1968 ever tried again. "We took all the starch out of them," he said, "when we beat them so badly in the first primary." During his first term, he had been able to add increments of policy representation to his symbolic connections. In 1970 he had no primary opposition.

In broadest outline, the House member–constituent negotiating process is about bringing the responsiveness of the House member and the support of the constituency into some kind of "fit" or equilibrium. One sign of success in this negotiation is establishing constituent *trust*—that is, establishing a willingness among constituents to give the House member's decisions and actions the benefit of the doubt, accompanied by a willingness to listen carefully to his or her explanation should doubt arise. Building trust takes a lot of time, a lot of trial and error, and a lot of effort.

In the best of scenarios, the member will gradually develop, for example, a reputation, and the constituents will gradually develop reliable monitoring routines. For both sides, these moves cut the time and information costs of their negotiations. As constituent trust gets established, it will help underwrite success on election day at the polls. And, more than that, it will also give the member support and behavioral *leeway* during the two years between election days—a freedom to pursue personal goals other than reelection. If we want clues to the existing state of a House member–constituency negotiation, therefore, we might look for signs of trust and signs of inter-election leeway.

Building trust takes time. And the length of time will, of course, vary among individual members. In Lou Stokes's case, the length of time was minimal. "I realized I had to live with being Carl Stokes' brother until I could establish my own independent image," he said. "I knew it would take some time."[33] But it did not take long. Constituent trust seemed to me to have been given to him as early in his political career as it had been to any of the other seventeen House members whose careers I examined in the 1970s.

Given its historic significance, Cleveland's active black citizens could hardly wait to elect their first member of Congress. And once elected, he became, instantly, a topmost political leader of the black community and a symbol of newfound black power. His constituents tendered him their trust, it seemed, almost before he did anything. For most House members, constituent trust is theirs to gain and is the object of much effort. For Lou Stokes, trust was quickly given, and it quickly became his to lose. And I saw no inkling of that possibility. By the time I arrived for my first visit, he was already in the protectionist stage of a political career that was not yet two years old. Only once [to be discussed later] did he ever face noteworthy opposition in the Democratic primary.

In cultivating constituent trust, there are three threshold requirements. The person seeking trust must work to convey to his or her constituents some sense of being qualified for the job, some sense of identification with the constituents, and some sense of empathy for the situation of the constituents.[34] For Stokes, identification and empathy came without argument. Only "qualification"—a combination of competence, honesty, and experience— was not self-evident. And, because they were sending out their first representative to compete in the Washington world, the newly empowered black electorate might be expected to place the heaviest emphasis on qualification.

During my initial visit, I watched an early test of his "qualifications" and of constituent trust. At a "candidates night," Stokes and his African American Republican opponent spoke and answered questions from a diverse panel of community leaders before a sizable audience. The opponent launched an attack on Stokes as unqualified. Among other charges, he said, "you have done nothing in Washington," and "you are stealing." Stokes answered the first charge by asking how many in the audience had received a letter or other communication from him. Half the audience raised their hands. "Truth, like the earth ground to dust, will rise again," he declared. And he handled the second charge with what I recorded as "a withering stare" and a comment that he never engaged in personal attacks.

In the question period, people in the audience came to his defense. One woman got up and spoke directly to the challenger: "You don't have any qualifications for office. I could do a better job as congressman than you could. My three-year-old daughter is better qualified and could do a better job than you. How much did they pay you to run?" [Applause.] A second woman agreed, saying, "Why should I waste my time?" And she walked out. So did her husband, a panelist and former head of the district's major public housing organization. The meeting, my notes read, "dissolved in derision" until "the moderator finally stopped the massacre out of pity and respect for the office."

Afterward, the congressman's staffers commented that "there is a big emphasis on qualified candidates this year." I concluded that the new congressman's first term had doubtless strengthened the community judgment that he was, indeed, qualified for the job, and that they had already tendered him a good deal of trust. Commenting on the event the next day, the congressman said simply, "They know me and they trust me." A week later, he was reelected with 78 percent of the vote.

No elected official ever feels free from uncertainty. Even if an incumbent looks unbeatable, he or she will worry and prepare for the worst. Nonetheless, by 1970 the expansionist phase of Louis Stokes's career was over, and his protectionist phase had already begun. His basic electoral goal had been met, and he could turn his fullest attention to the pursuit of his dominant group-interest goals.

POLICY CONNECTIONS

First among these goals was making good public policy—the content of which was widely agreed upon within the black community. In representational terms, political scientists would categorize Louis Stokes's policy goals, his policy votes, and his policy decisions as "substantive representation." His community had serious, glaring public policy needs. They were the "givens" of his constituency context—the need to redress existing socioeconomic inequalities and to open up equal opportunity for the future. The goal of any African American representative chosen from the community would be, first and foremost, to lend every effort to meet those needs. They were needs—involving jobs, poverty, drugs, education, housing, and health—that could not be met without large infusions of government assistance.

As their Representative, Lou Stokes pressed, in Congress, for an activist agenda. He ranked consistently high on "liberal" vote ratings. For his first four terms, his average ADA (Americans for Democratic Action, i.e., liberalism) score was 95 percent. From 1970 to 1994, his average COPE (Committee on Political Education of the AFL-CIO; i.e., prolabor) score was 95 percent positive.[35]

When compared with that of his House colleagues, his liberalism is even more impressive. The widely used Poole-Rosenthal DW-Nominate scores—based on roll call votes for each two-year congress—allows us to place and compare each member's voting record on a liberalism–conservatism scale in relation to that of his or her colleagues. Those rankings of all House members place Lou Stokes, throughout his tenure, at the far liberal end of the House member spectrum.

In his first term, for example, Stokes's DW-Nominate voting score was the eleventh most liberal in the House. That is, only ten colleagues were—according to this measure—more liberal than he. Conversely, 424 members were more conservative than he. In his second term, he again ranked as the eleventh most liberal House member. In his thirteen remaining congresses, the small number of members with more liberal scores than Stokes's fluctuated from fifteen to twenty-nine.[36] By all available indicators, the congruence between the policy needs of the black community in Cleveland and the policy preferences of their congressman had to rank near the top of any linkage chart. And their approval of his policy-related activities undoubtedly followed at nearly the same level.

From my earliest visit, I found, alongside the signs of constituent trust, some related signs of representational leeway on policy matters. In his pursuit of the policy interests of his constituents, it seemed, he would be given the benefit of the doubt and not held to any strictly itemized accounting of his behavior in Washington. In policy terms, for example, leeway meant that when he voted in Congress, his constituents would give him wide latitude in making his decisions. And that is exactly the way he perceived his constituency relationship. "The fact is," he said in 1970,

> that I have freedom to do almost anything I want to do in Congress and it won't affect me a bit at home. . . . Some of my colleagues talk about their public opinion polls. My people didn't send me to Washington to check back every time there is a vote to see what public opinion in my district says. They sent me down there to use my judgment and to provide some leadership. . . . I don't have any trouble voting. When I vote my conscience as a black man, I vote right for my district.

If, he continued, a vote seemed to require an explanation, he would explain it to his constituents—especially, the churchgoers.

> When I come home every week, I go to the church groups and tell them what's been going on in Washington, and I explain to them why I voted as I did. For instance, I explained to them why I voted against the Voting Rights Bill because it was a fraud. Nixon wanted to remove the fifty-seven registrars that are working in the southern states, because they have been more effective than anything else. After they heard me on voting rights, they went home mad.

And he concluded, "I don't need public opinion polls."

In similar terms, he described his decision process.

> On most pieces of legislation, I have a certain attitude toward it as soon as I know what it's about, and I vote that way. On some controversial matters, I may ask the staff what correspondence we've had. But even if the mail is in favor of the D.C. Crime Bill, I'm not going to sacrifice my fundamental beliefs about "no-knock" and "preventive detention" and vote for the bill. And I know my people will agree with me on that. When I vote as a black man, I necessarily represent the black community. I don't have any trouble knowing what the black community thinks or wants.

And, finally,

> I don't know whether my district is peculiar or strange or what, but I don't get letters asking me to vote such and such a way on such and such a bill. I'll bet if you went into my area and took a poll and asked people how I voted on the voting rights extension or the SST, people wouldn't know. They don't vote for me for that reason. The have a blind faith in me. They

say to themselves that everything they know about Lou Stokes tells them "he's up there doing a good job for us." It's a blind faith type of thing.

Try as I might to get him to identify "tough," "problematic," or "killer" votes, I never succeeded—despite his obvious efforts to oblige. "I hardly ever have a problem on a vote. And that's the truth," he exclaimed after one of my efforts.

Louis Stokes had a clear perception of an inclusive "us" in "the black community"; he did not doubt that he represented "us" when he voted, and he did not doubt that they would approve of what he did. His words are powerful expressions—in the representational context—of Michael Dawson's idea of black group consciousness and its formidable pervasiveness in black politics. In Stokes's view, "I don't think any black congressman has difficulty voting in the interest of his district."

While roll call voting on matters of public policy is the most visible of a legislator's negotiating efforts, the sum total of a House member's effort at policy representation involves much more. It obviously means working for the legislator's policy goals wherever the policy-making process requires it inside the legislative institution. But less obviously, it also means advocating, discussing, and explaining policy matters in the home constituency. This latter activity—building and maintaining policy-based connections with constituents—is a mainstay of every House member's negotiating processes.[37]

In my three visits, I heard Lou Stokes give six formal presentations to audiences of sixty to three hundred people. In the order I heard them, they were delivered to: a candidates' night crowd, the Glenville Neighborhood Council, the National Sorority of Phi Delta Kappa, the Mount Pleasant Monthly Forum, Community Guidance and Human Services, Inc., and the Liberty Hill Baptist Church. In every case, he spoke of "the great problems facing the community and this nation" and the need to "reorder national priorities" to meet them.

He talked about the need for a politics that would "replace the broken down and dilapidated houses in Hough" with livable ones; correct the disparity "when a mother on welfare gets five dollars per child, per year for school clothing, and we spend $78 billion on armaments"; do something about the problem of "putting a $2,400 ceiling on welfare when the government itself sets the poverty level at $3,900 for a family of four"; change national health insurance from "a medical care system in which the poor get sicker and the sick get poorer . . . while we go to the moon for rocks and to Mars for dust."

He strongly opposed the Vietnam War, where "we take an eighteen-year-old and put a diploma in one hand and in the other hand we place a rifle and tell him to go to Vietnam and kill." A larger theme was his assertion that "young people are turning off in the society" and that "if the society they are going to inherit is like the society we have—with Vietnam, racism, and poverty—then they don't want it." Those are the policy messages he carried throughout my visits.

SYMBOLIC CONNECTIONS

A second set of representational activities is commonly categorized by political scientists as descriptive representation, by which is meant representation of some group by an individual who shares that group's defining characteristic—in this case, race. Members of the group will be, or will feel, underrepresented unless someone with the same descriptive, group-level characteristic represents them. When an identifiable group has been excluded, as blacks have been, inclusion via descriptive representation constitutes an early, recognizable step along the way toward fulfilling group aspirations. Representation by a member of the group means first-class status for the group—full participation, a recognizable stake in the system, and a "politics of presence" in which the first inclusion of the new group affects the political status quo.[38]

When Lou Stokes became the first black member of Congress from Cleveland (and Ohio), he automatically gave descriptive representation to the black citizens of Cleveland (and Ohio). His goal was to put it to work for them. But descriptive representation is a static concept. It says nothing about behavior. In Congress, it gets expressed as a given group's percentage of House membership as compared to the group's percentage of the nation's population. The measure is most often applied to minorities and to women. And disparities in percentages are used to measure the underrepresentation of each group. The numbers, however, say nothing about the activity of the elected members with respect to members of their group. It will be more helpful to think of *symbolic representation*—as the behavioral aspect of descriptive representation. In his or her behavior, the elected representative knows that he or she is standing for the group, exemplifying the group, setting standards for the group, blazing trails for the group—and, in that symbolic sense, representing the group.

With his election, Lou Stokes became an instant leader, prominent as well as powerful. He knew that he had become a symbol of the black community, and he knew that his behavior would be judged in that light. He was particularly cognizant of being "the first." He was "writing the book," and he wanted to be a positive symbol. He wanted to act in such a way that members of the black community would be proud of him and—because he was descriptively like them—proud of themselves as well. "Black pride" was a widely expressed group interest during the period.

Over and over, Lou Stokes commented on the success of his symbolic activity. In the beginning, the accomplishment was tied to his brother. "People take pride in our accomplishments. They like what we've stood for and they know the abuse we've taken when we've stood up for the black community." Soon, it was about himself alone: "People in the black community read avidly about what I'm doing. And almost every week, there is something in the paper [*Call and Post*]. They read it and they feel proud. Almost anything I do makes them feel proud. They know I'm a black man standing up for the black man. Even when I stand up for the Black Panthers, the sophisticated people in the community understand why I'm doing it, and they feel proud." As their representative, he was a symbol. By "standing up" and "standing tall," he encouraged them to do likewise. His policy goals were certainly relevant to this purpose. But the nurturing of "black pride" was a distinctive, personal goal and a basic element of his representational strategy.

His symbolic connections were actively pursued and could be observed when he was at home in the district. The very first event I observed in Cleveland was the dedication of the African American Cultural Center at Cleveland State University. It began with the Negro National Anthem, "Lift Every Voice and Sing," after which the congressman said, "This center symbolizes the hopes and ambitions of young black people who are struggling to bring unity and pride with the educational experience. . . . we can see their newly found pride in blackness and the sense of unity that binds them through their blackness. . . . It is here that you will reflect on the history of black people and their role in today's society." "Black pride," he once explained, "means pride in blackness, pride in accomplishments of blacks, pride in studying the history of blacks."[39] In his presence and his talk, he was forging a symbolic connection with his constituents.

As we drove around the city in a staff-driven Cadillac or Lincoln, people often waved. At stoplights, they would roll down the window and call to him. "It happens every night when I drive through the district," he said on one such occasion. "They took a poll at Case Western University and found my name recognition was 99 percent," he added. "People recognize the car, and they want to pull alongside and say hello. It makes them feel proud. You can see the smile break over their faces. They feel important, too, just to see and talk to the congressman." He was saying that they felt represented—and included. His inclusion could be taken as a symbolic warrant of their inclusion. And conveying that sense to his constituents was a nonpolicy element in Lou Stokes's strategy of representation.

A 1971 speech to one thousand members of the national, black women's sorority, Phi Delta Kappa—a college-educated, middle-class group—produced a similar reaction. He was introduced as "our leader," as "a man who has known poverty and overcame it, a man who knows what it is to be part of an oppressed people—our people," a man with "many, many awards and accomplishments and many, many qualifications." In my notes, I wrote: "He got a standing ovation when he was presented and a standing ovation when he finished. No other congressman I've seen gets that. There is a distance, I think, between Lou Stokes and his constituents, and yet he is one of them. But he is clearly more than 'one of the boys.' He is a qualified leader, respected, admired, and trusted without hesitation. His black constituents are not cynical about him or suspicious. After the talk, he was mobbed by these mature, adult, college-educated, professional women—for his *autograph* [italics in original]. I never saw that before."

When it was over, he described the experience as an exchange of energies—they to him, him to them. "A large group like that does something to me. It makes me want to prepare more and do a better job. But I'm relieved when it's over. They are a good cross section of concerned people—school teachers and administrators mostly. Some of them are campaign workers—more now than there used to be—with more black awareness. These people were the types who used to want to stay out of things and keep to themselves." The speech he delivered was loaded with policy content. But the connections he made and his location on a pedestal were loaded with the stuff of symbolic representation.

In these several ways, Congressman Stokes was providing something less than substantive representation and something more than descriptive representation. He was providing active symbolic representation. It was a representational activity that no white member of Congress could duplicate among his or her black constituents—however satisfactory that white member's policy connections might be. Lou Stokes's symbolic activity was a critical, indispensable element in negotiating for supportive connections among his African American constituents. And the same would probably be true for every other African American House member of his pioneer cohort.

ORGANIZATIONAL CONNECTIONS
AND EXPERIENTIAL LEARNING

A final goal, one necessary to the overall promotion of black group interests, was strengthening the black community's political power within the city. When I arrived in Cleveland, Congressman Stokes was leading the black minority in a classic battle for political inclusion. In their time of transition "from protest to politics," they were seeking a larger share of political power within the white-led Democratic Party. In a sequence of negotiations common to minority politics, a previously excluded group was changing from a longtime accommodationist approach to a new confrontational approach to the entrenched majority power holders.[40] It was a battle for empowerment.

The pathbreaking election of African Americans to the mayoralty and to the U.S. Congress—under the Democratic Party label—had demonstrated the political muscle of Cleveland's black community and had brought about a wholesale change in their political aspirations and expectations. The minority was demanding increased intraparty influence—more leadership positions, more candidacies, more appointments, more jobs, more contracts—in proportion to their demonstrable importance.

Moreover, they had recently created an organizational vehicle through which to press their claims. Eight months before I arrived, the Twenty-first Congressional District Caucus was born—the brainchild of four leaders of the black community: the mayor, the congressman, the Republican publisher of the *Call and Post*, and a veteran councilman. Lou Stokes became its chairman. Its executive board was composed of local African American leaders—elected, civic, and religious. When the Board first presented itself before a general community meeting, recalled Carl Stokes, "the crowd stood and cheered in a great display of unity and pride."[41] The Caucus had quickly become the political embodiment of "the whole black community."

Lou Stokes's leadership in the empowerment struggle of his constituency followed naturally upon his leadership in their legal struggle. And recognition of his leadership in the political battle crowned and cemented, almost indestructibly, all his other representational ties. Again, only an African American could qualify—no matter how congenial the policy positions of a non–African American representative might be. As Lou Stokes put it, "My constituents don't know how I vote on any issue, but they know me and they trust me. The more active I am working for them in the Caucus, the more popular I become, the more they trust me and are proud of me."

Caucus-related problems, therefore, became a major preoccupation of its leader. And his Caucus-related negotiations dominated my first visit. His subsequent negotiations figured prominently in our conversations to the end. Caucus origins preceded my arrival, and Caucus activities continued well after I left. But while I was there, the organization underwent a slow transformation. In the beginning, Stokes's Caucus-related negotiations were expansionist in outlook. Six years later, however, his Caucus-related negotiations had become distinctly protectionist. In the interim, he had learned a lot about political survival. His story is the premier example of experiential learning during the time I spent with him.

When the Caucus originally pressed its claim that a black man be given some regular position in the countywide Democratic Party hierarchy, they were rebuffed. Whereupon they decided to take the Caucus out of the Democratic Party and go to war with the party at the polls. "We're building a machine," said one Stokes staffer, "like Tammany Hall or like Daley did in Chicago." The idea was to demonstrate their independent power by endorsing, supporting, and electing some *Republicans*—both black and white—as well as Democrats. Topmost priority was given to the election of a white Republican, Seth Taft, as a Cuyahoga County Commissioner—a position long dominated by the party's white ethnic Democrats.

When I arrived, the Twenty-first Congressional District Caucus was in electoral high gear. In its basement headquarters, I watched the largest volunteer, grassroots effort of any I have ever observed. "People who ten years ago had dropped out of the political process are now politicized," said one staffer. "That's encouraging and exhilarating." I counted fifty people, old and young, stuffing envelopes and making phone calls. Others flowed in and out, picking up signs and literature. Some of the material explained the stakes—"help end bossism"—in terms of their group interests. Others were in the form of sample ballots for election day.

The campaign director was a political pro. He had previously done organizing work in the California campaigns of veteran black congressman Gus Hawkins and presidential candidate Robert Kennedy. He described their computer-assisted analysis of key precincts and discussed his plan that called for one thousand volunteers "working on election day" and for "hundreds of ministers walking key precincts with their collars on." Republicans as well as Democrats within the black community had thrown themselves into the effort.

Students of black politics have found that in cities where blacks have been empowered by winning the mayor's office, they adopt a "more trusting and

efficacious orientation to politics," "greatly increase their attentiveness to political efforts," and "become more active in politics than their white counter-
parts." [42] I certainly witnessed one case in point. "The Caucus idea," it
seemed to me, "was more audacious than the mere election of a congressman, because it involved teaching the most sophisticated kind of cross-party,
split-ticket voting patterns to an entire electorate, many of whom were new
to political activity." [43] In that effort, Chairman Stokes was the chief educator.

At four different events—the candidates' night, a neighborhood improvement association dinner, a dinner-dance, and a fund-raiser—he explained and preached the idea of the Caucus. At the candidates' night, for
example, he said this:

> The Democratic Party has had the black vote in its pocket for years. And
> what have they given us in return? Nothing. Why should they? They had
> our vote. Of course, they handed out a few menial jobs. You used to pride
> yourself on voting the straight Democratic ticket. And it got you nothing
> but a few menial jobs. This year, the Democratic County Committee said
> to us, "We've got a chairman, a vice chairman, a secretary, and a trea-
> surer, but not one of them can be black. And we've got the election board
> over here and none of them can be black." We presented the name of
> George Forbes, and they said he's not acceptable to us white folks. We
> have 25 percent of the vote in Cuyahoga County, and the Democratic
> County Commissioner wouldn't put one black man among the regular
> slate of officers.
>
> Well, we told them they can take their party and put it someplace else.
> They can still make their decisions in the back rooms, but we want no
> more of it. In the paper this morning, President Nixon said we should
> abandon party labels. There isn't much we can agree with Nixon on,
> but this is one thing. Party labels are taboo. That's what the Twenty-first
> District Caucus is all about. We screened all the candidates, black and
> white, Democrat and Republican, and endorsed those candidates we felt
> would be most responsive to the needs of this community. And we picked
> some black people and some white people, some Democrats and some
> Republicans.
>
> When a Republican councilman can sit down with a Democratic
> councilman and decide, regardless of party, what's best for this commu-
> nity, that's *beauty* [italics in original]. We're asking you to vote that way—
> some here, some there—cross the street. If you cross the street, that will
> teach the Democratic Party respect. As Congressman William Clay, who

spoke at my fund-raising dinner, said, "No one every gives up power. You have to seize power." ["Right on, right on."]

That's why we ask you to support the Caucus and what we're trying to do. We've got to stand tall. With the Caucus, you can stand tall, not, as Flip Wilson says, crawl small. This is not Lou Stokes's Caucus or the Mayor's Caucus or anyone's caucus. It's bigger than any one of us, because it's all of us. The Caucus is you. It's the unity of the whole black community.

On election day, the Caucus-supported Republican, Seth Taft, unseated a Democrat as County Commissioner.

Chairman Stokes declared victory. "We made our case with Taft," he said. "That's all we really needed and all we really wanted. We proved that black people would vote Republican—Republican! We would have liked to do more, but we didn't expect to. With Taft, we made our point—enough so that we can claim success." On behalf of the community, the *Call and Post* echoed his claim.[44] In the following year, in the 1971 Democratic primary for local offices, the Caucus was even more successful. Said the *Plain Dealer,* the Caucus "won a momentous victory and humbled the Democratic Party—by defeating the party's choice for Mayor in the biggest surprise in Cleveland's political history" and by "winning every council contest they got into."[45] These two successive sets of victories carried the Twenty-first Congressional District Caucus to the height of its citywide strength.

Success, it is said, has many fathers. The success of the Caucus stimulated the private ambitions of numerous community politicians. And their ambitions loomed ever-larger in Lou Stokes's constituency life. They did not challenge him at the polls, but they did challenge him for more influence in conducting the business of the Caucus—in negotiations with the party, and in setting the terms for the black community's eventual return to the Democratic Party fold.[46]

Some were anxious to start cutting deals beneficial to themselves; others were more cautious. Stokes was both cautious and protective. He saw the activities of others as a threat to his Caucus leadership, and he resisted, increasingly, any diminution of his authority as chairman to speak for the Caucus. If someone was to speak for the Caucus, or if there was to be a position in the party representing the Caucus, he wanted to be the one to do it.

A couple of years of byzantine, high-level, intra-Caucus and intraparty maneuverings disrupted and slowly weakened the Caucus idea. One by one, restive political leaders declared their renewed allegiance to the Democratic

Party and fell out of step with the Caucus and with Chairman Stokes. In 1972 some Democrats who had left the Caucus began to challenge at the polls some of the Republicans who had remained in the Caucus. The bipartisan unity Stokes had so proudly invoked in 1970 was gone.

Speaking of "the deserters" who had left the Caucus, he said,

> They wanted to make the Caucus an extension of the Democratic Party, a ward club of the Democratic Party. In order to be effective, the Caucus has to be bipartisan. It has to be able to switch back and forth in its endorsements. It is a community organization that is politically oriented. That's where you get your leverage, in your independence. You don't need a caucus if you are going to be a ward club. . . . What the guys have done now is to weaken the political strength of the black community. The Democratic Party owns them now. They have to do what the party wants and what the party tells them to do.

He gradually retreated to a more modest concept of the Caucus—as his own political base. Its organizational scope would remain community-wide, but its main purpose would be to protect Lou Stokes from whatever uncertainties a fractionated local leadership might bring. From his days as lead lawyer for the NAACP, he had been protecting black interests. Now, his political career had developed to the point where he had to think about protecting his own interests.

For the 1972 elections, therefore, "I devised a new strategy. . . . The question was: Was I going to place my own esteem behind other races? If I do, will they keep a scorecard on me? So I decided not to make any endorsements and to concentrate on my own race. The Democratic Party did not endorse me. If I hadn't had the Caucus, I'd have been in bad shape in terms of support for me. Now, I've beaten the party again. . . . As [*Call and Post* publisher] W. O. Walker says, 'Lou Stokes won big, and anyone who thinks his prestige has been damaged [by the defections] had better think twice.' "

Stokes continued, "I did it by having my own organization. They will be keyed primarily to me. The people in the Caucus will be loyal to Lou Stokes; they will rally around Lou Stokes. Nobody can take that away—whether I call it the Caucus or the Lou Stokes organization of the Twenty-first District. [But] the strength and beauty of it has been strangled by men who are tired, as they say, of sacrificing and want to start to get the spoils. The black community is the loser. The beauty of having twenty-five elected officials sit around the table and make decisions on the basis of what's best for the black community—that beauty is gone." And he added, "I've got to keep my organization, and people want to organize around me. I have to do it for my own protection every two years."

Still, he worried and wavered. "The community still believes in the Caucus concept," he said. "So the question for me is how much time I have to devote to that organization. Do I keep fighting and fighting alone or do I say I've done my part and shift my gears?"

His indecision lasted until 1976, when he was unexpectedly faced with an unusual primary opponent—the man who had once been the topmost member of Stokes's own district staff and who had been his 1972 campaign manager. The congressman took it personally, as a betrayal by an "old friend." "The whites downtown wanted to buy themselves a boy—in every sense of the word—that they could control." Stokes sought the support of the elected officials who had left the Twenty-first Congressional District Caucus. They gave it to him—on condition that the campaign be conducted by a "Stokes for Congress" committee and *not* by the Twenty-first Congressional District Caucus. It was an unwelcome stipulation, but he agreed that the Caucus be "subsumed within the campaign committee." The alliance effectively shut off his opponent's support within the black community.

The congressman campaigned on his incumbency. "You have an investment in me. It's like putting money in the bank. If you leave it there, it gathers interest and it grows. If you take it out, you have to start in all over again. Our people have just gotten started, and we're too far behind to start over so soon. I've been in Congress for 8 years, but we waited 180 years before we even got started." He won a lopsided primary victory.

The contours of his victory forcefully underscored the congressman's overwhelming support within "the whole black community." As he described it,

I set my strategy. He figured if he got the whole 35 percent of the white vote, he would need only 16 percent of the black vote to win. So I was determined to hold my strength in the black community. I knew I would get about half the vote in the white community no matter what, so I worked for solid support in the black community. The first thing I did was get the ministers. I called a breakfast meeting, and 125 ministers came. That's all of them! Then there is a group of ministers who have to work at other jobs, because their parishioners are too poor to pay them—some of the storefronts for instance. Fifty of them came. Once I had the ministers cemented in, I called a similar meeting of all the black elected officials.

Twenty-three of the twenty-four showed up for that. Then I had it all. *When you have the ministers and the black elected officials, you have the black community.* . . . In every black ward, I won by at least twelve-to-one, and I got nearly half of the white vote. Overall, I beat him four-to-one.[47]

His discussion nicely delineates his primary constituency.

He had learned a lot about politics since 1970. Part of it, about friends and foe, he had just learned the hard way. And while the winning alliance helped Stokes to confirm his community-wide support, he also learned that the circumstances had changed the status of the Caucus. From now on, he would treat the Caucus as his own personal organizational lifeline.

"After the primary, when I showed such great strength," he reflected,

> I toyed with the idea of giving up my leadership of the Caucus and my reliance on it. The Caucus people were upset when they had to be submissive to the campaign committee. They want their own identity. They are very loyal to me personally and take pride in working for me. They want to work within the Caucus. My workers tell me they can get more cooperation in the black community for Caucus events than for party events. We had three thousand at the Caucus picnic last week. . . . I decided that if I disbanded the Caucus, a lot of people would think I had weakened myself and might decide to run against me. If I had no district organization, I'd look just like everybody else in the black community. I've got to keep the leadership of the Caucus. It is my political strength.

Where once the Twenty-first Congressional District Caucus had been an expansionist political weapon for the whole black community, six years of negotiating had transformed it into a protectionist political weapon for the incumbent congressman. More clearly than ever, the Caucus was a crucial part of his primary constituency.

His postprimary comments reveal a familiar king-of-the-hill mentality— that he was clearly *the* top political person in the district and, as such, that he needed to guard against potential challengers. When a politician becomes king-of-the-hill in the district, it is only a foothold, not an entitlement. The Caucus gave Stokes a solid foothold. He still had to protect his interests inside the Democratic Party. In 1976, for example, when the Party chairman moved to reduce the influence of the highest ranking black official in the Party, Stokes stopped it cold with a threat: "I will not participate in his diminishment. If you do that, I will tear up the Party."

On another front, that same year, he acted to preempt potential challengers from within the Democratic Party organization by running a slate of committed Stokes delegates to the Democratic National Convention.[48] "I did it to get the black community to pull together," he explained.

> I'm the leader, and when you are the leader, people expect you to lead. As the highest elected official in the district, I can't let anyone lower in the hierarchy get the idea that I'm not the leader. That's why I always run for state committee membership. I don't want anyone to demonstrate more political clout than I do in any districtwide contest. If someone does better than I do in any congressional district election, they'll want to run against me. I can't let it happen. The ministers agreed with me that we should keep the unity of the black community by running delegates pledged to me for president.
>
> My name was on the primary ballot eleven times—beside the name of six delegates and three alternates, for state committeeman, and for Congress. It was such a confusing ballot, we had a job of educating to do. So we told them, whenever you see the name Stokes, pull the lever! That's what we taught them. . . . Later, when I introduced myself to [Jimmy] Carter for the first time, he said, "I know you, you beat me bad in your district." I said to him, "It was just a skirmish; you won the war."

Again, his primary constituents were crucial. "The ministers," he said, "were able to shut Carter out of the churches where his strength had been. Many were not anti-Carter . . . but they recognized they had to meet Carter's challenge to the community and demonstrate our political clout." At the end of our talk, he said, "Now I've got to . . . get something going in the community for Carter and [Senate candidate Howard] Metzenbaum. It's pretty late already; but if I don't do it, nothing will get done. *No one can move till I move.*" Coming from the king of the hill, it was not a complaint. And he doubtless hoped it was a secure prediction.

PERSONAL CONNECTIONS

When Representatives are at work in their home districts, much of what they do involves person-to-person contact with individual constituents. In groups large and small, in meetings formal and informal, in public appearances required or optional, in campaigns or noncampaign settings, in office consultations about personal or organizational problems, the Representative meets face-to-face, one-on-one with some of the real live individuals whom he or she formally represents. Such representational activity cannot be avoided. It is an essential part of the job. But there is a large difference between the constituency activity of House members who enjoy, thrive on, encourage, and emphasize person-to-person relationships and the activity of those who are less enthusiastic.

As House members go, Lou Stokes was among the "less enthusiastic." He was a much respected and much admired political general, but he did not spend a lot of time mixing and mingling with the troops. Unlike some House members, he did not have to cultivate all sorts of personal relationships in order to convince his constituents that he is "one of us." In his situation, that close identification was a given. Still, he kept a personal and psychological distance. In the closest of quarters, with his personal staff, they always referred to him, in or out of his presence, as "the congressman"—*never* Louis or Lou. When he had the choice, he kept his face-to-face, person-to-person contact to a minimum. He came home regularly; but he kept a light schedule. And he favored formal, large-group connections like speeches instead of informal, interactive connections such as town meetings and office hours. Connections "up close and personal" did not play a large or important part in his representational strategy.

Lou Stokes was not personally arrogant. With me, he was gentlemanly, forthright, and good humored—sometimes sharing his broad smile and his infectious laughter. To his staff, he was "the brainy reasoner," in contrast to his brother, "the flashy communicator." To the press, he was thoughtful and strong-willed. In thinking about the distancing that characterized his personal connections, therefore, we might consider the degree to which his path to politics was smoothed and sheltered by his brother, Carl. That custodial recruitment relationship relieved the newcomer of the grassroots ground-breaking activities—pursued in innumerable retail contexts—that most political neophytes must engage in. Because his brother brought him in at the top of the ladder, he was never put under pressure to cultivate the one-on-one routines so necessary—and so likely to become second nature—for someone who had to fight his or her way up from the bottom.

I made three trips of three days each to the district, for a total of nine "event days," in other words, days in which he had at least one scheduled event. During those nine days, he participated in a total of twelve events—an average of slightly more than one event a day. On six days out of the nine, he scheduled only a single event. On five of the six, his entire schedule consisted of a single speech. (On one of those days, we drove to Columbus for his speech to the Democratic State Convention.) All-in-all, it was a remarkably light schedule.

Formal, stand-up speeches, delivered to sizable audiences, seemed to be his preference. "I try to speak everywhere I'm asked in the district—unless I'm not home or too jammed up. I tell people I'll go anywhere I'm asked." In those settings, his preeminent leadership status in the community was on display, and it was solidified as he invariably drew a supportive reaction from constituency audiences. His staff said he worked hard on his speeches and said they "took a lot out of him," which may have meant that he considered one speech a good day's work. In each of his five one-speech days, he went home afterward. And I never heard him single out any individual constituent, or group of constituents, as a negotiating target for his personal ministrations. As I saw it, his preference for wholesale over retail connections with his constituents was strong and dominant.

Many members of Congress, when you ride with them around the district, fill the time by regaling a visitor with their detailed knowledge about their district and its various parts. Lou Stokes was not one who did. Again, I believe that his sheltered path to politics kept him from the ground-level experiences that bred an intimate familiarity with his territory. He did not display a working, hands-on knowledge of, or enthusiasm for, the finer details and nuances of constituency makeup and development. He was not a neighborhood-level politician. Unlike many of his colleagues, he had no ready-made repertoire of illustrative tales about life in the constituency.

Alone among my House member acquaintances in the 1970s, he deputized a staff member to give me a guided tour of the district. "John knows the district, and he knows ward politics," he said. The clear implication—and the evidence—was that the congressman did not. Again, he never had to learn such things. He was, I concluded, motivated and challenged by large-picture, community-level affairs and problems and not by small-picture, personal-level affairs and problems.

"I come home more often than a lot of the guys," he said in 1970, "not like the Philadelphia people who come home every night; but on the average once every week. I meet with church groups and other groups. And I let people see me to let them know I haven't lost touch with them." An examination of his yearlong 1973 schedule gives a more complex view of his home activities than my visits can convey.

According to his office records for 1973, he took thirty-four "event trips" home from Washington—for an average of (excluding the August recess) about three times a month. Six more trips were "nonevent" trips. During the thirty-four event trips, he scheduled fifty-nine event days—not quite two event days per trip home. In the fifty-nine days, he scheduled seventy-eight events—less than two per day. Those averages conform closely to what I experienced. And they seem to confirm my qualitative assessment of a relatively small agenda of constituency activities—smaller, at least, than most of the other House members I was following at the time.

In terms of the variety of events, however, his full 1973 schedule did reveal a greater variety than I had seen, especially an increase in the number of his ceremonial appearances—at dedications, celebrations, openings, receptions, anniversaries, and community fundraisers. These events might have involved "appropriate remarks" of some kind by the congressman, but not a "speech."

A convenient breakdown of the seventy-eight events showed the following distribution of activities: thirty-eight general community, fifteen church, ten Caucus, ten media (eight radio, two television), three Democratic Party, and two personal business. Ten of the thirty-eight community events and four of the ten church events were formal speeches. I did attend three non–speech making, mix-and-mingle, community events, but I witnessed none of the other sorts of activities. Still, I am not inclined to change my estimate of a fairly light, fairly formal pattern of home activities.

One set of personal-level activities left out of the previous listing were his one-on-one appointments with constituents in his city district office. It is hard to know what to make of them, because his schedule lists nine such appointments from January to March and none after that. However, the congressman himself made clear his lack of relish for such requests by individuals.

> Sam and the staff try to do all they can for them and put them off. But if they insist and Sam has gone all the way with them, then I will see them. It's their right. If they are getting action from the staff on their problems and things are moving along, then they won't care if they see their congressman. Congressman [Robert] Nix of Philadelphia goes home every Saturday and sits in his office talking to his clients. I don't do that, and I don't want to.

There were, however, exceptions, when requests came from people of some local importance.

There were, however, different levels of "importance." At one level, he met with individuals who, he said, "are not influential in the community, but they are influential within their own sphere. They don't really want help with their problems. They just want to go back to their friends and say, 'I saw the congressman and he said . . .' Then they'll make up their own story of what I said. They want to talk to me, and if I don't see them, they'll cause me ten years of disadvantage." He told the story of "a lady in church who insists that 'I must see the congressman,'" but who, when she gets into his office, says "'I know you are too busy to deal with my little old problem, but I just wanted to see you. You're looking well.'" He laughed. "She'll go back to her little domain and say, 'I saw the congressman today and he's looking well.' It gives her status."

At the highest level of importance was the publisher of the *Call and Post,* W. O. Walker, a Republican. After the 1968 kitchen meeting had settled his candidacy, the first thing Lou Stokes did was to go to Walker's house "to get his blessing."[49] Once elected, he continued to be especially attentive. "What he wants from me," said Stokes in 1971,

> is attention. He is very powerful and very rich, and there is nothing I can do for him. He doesn't want anything from me but recognition. Human beings want to be recognized no matter how powerful they are. So I have to nurse him and keep his goodwill. Sometimes, it's an imposition, but he's too powerful and I can't afford to lose his goodwill. All he wants is to be able to say, 'Oh, the congressman was here Tuesday afternoon,' or 'When I was talking to the congressman Thursday evening . . .' And so I talk to him every time I come home; he supports me, and we stay on the same team. If I didn't, I might lose his support, and I can't afford that.

Four years later, he again noted this one personal contact of penultimate importance to him. "I didn't know him [Walker] till I ran for office, because I had not been in politics. It was Carl who had the close relationship. But since I've been in office, we've had a very close relationship. We've been together on every issue—every issue."

In between the woman from church and the publisher are the local politicians. He did not go out of his way to develop personal relations with them unless the affairs of the Caucus demanded it. Of the party politicians, his attitude was, "The ward clubs are controlled by the councilmen. . . . During the campaign, the councilmen invited me to speak to their clubs. But other than at campaign time, I don't bother them and they don't bother me." When he had to, he did deal with local politicians on matters related to the Caucus. But he did not like it. "With Carl out of town," he exclaimed, "I'll have to sit with all the local politicians and hold their hands. The way they have me doing this is ridiculous. . . . Carl babies them. I can't."

It was a constant balancing act. "I can't stay involved in all the local problems. I haven't the time. I'm constantly on the telephone tending to all these little crises that come up while I'm in Washington. . . . I'm trying to strengthen my Washington office to take care of these problems. But all these guys [local politicians] that sit back home have a big advantage. They know everything that's going on and can take advantage of me. I've got to protect my back. It's my biggest dilemma." So he went home "to protect his back"—more by keeping a presence than by schmoozing individual politicians.

In 1976 the congressman's one-time aide and primary challenger made a major campaign issue out of the congressman's personal connections. As the *Plain Dealer* reported it, he "launched an all-out attack on his former boss by attempting to portray Stokes as out of touch with his constituents."[50] As a former top district staffer and his former campaign manager, his challenger was better informed than anyone else about Stokes's representational priorities. And he obviously considered "out of touch" to be Stokes's major vulnerability. While the argument did not work, the challenger's choice of issues provides at least some prima facie evidence that "keeping in touch" routines had a relatively low priority for the incumbent.

Stokes defended himself against his opponent's charge by emphasizing the choices he had made about where to put his time and energy.

> In the campaign, my opponent said that I'd lost touch with the community, that I wasn't coming home all the time like I should to stay in touch. I told my folks that I couldn't reply to that kind of argument—though it was a lie—but that they had to do it for me. I told them: I have a five-day-a-week job in Washington. I get up and go to work every morning, five days a week, just like you do. I work all day, just like you do. Then you get weekends off, but I get on the plane after five days in Washington and come home for two more. Five days and two on top of it. And I ask them, what do you want me to do, stand on the corner of 55th and Central, jive talking and slapping hands and giving the African handshake bullshit all week long? Or do you want me to spend my time working for you in Washington? If I stay here all week the way my opponent wants, I'd blow it for you in Washington.

It was a defense that elevated to top priority his policy connections to his constituency and relegated to a lower priority his personal connections in the constituency. And, while the two types of connections commonly intertwine, that juxtaposition accurately reflected his representational priorities.

MINORITY CONNECTIONS

The white minority in his 1970 district was concentrated in two city wards, fourteen and fifteen, and in suburban Garfield Heights. They constituted 35 percent of the population and the bulk of the anti-Stokes votes— 20–30 percent—at election time. In the redistricting of 1972, he lost Garfield Heights and added white constituents from three nearby suburbs. But the total percentage stayed the same, and the congressman's representational relationships with them remained respectful and modest. The district's white community was not consequential for him politically, personally, or policy-wise. He tried to give them the best possible quality of constituency service in handling their individual problems and requests. But it was the large-scale problems of the black community that absorbed his time, energy, and interest.

He and his staff were quick to affirm that when it came to help with their individual problems, his white constituents would be served as diligently as his black constituents. "When I was elected," said Stokes in 1970,

> The reaction in the white community was that they would be completely left out. They felt that a black congressman would have no interest in their problems. We have tried to overcome that, and we are making headway. Once they came to us for help, they found they were getting the same service as anyone else. They started saying, "Not only did he answer my letter, but he answered it quickly." That has helped. Maybe they don't feel like they did with Charlie Vanik [their previous Representative], but we're making progress. Ed Matt, my military specialist is from the white area. He said that at first when they came to him with Vietnam cases, they began, "I know Mr. Stokes isn't interested in us, but . . ." He would take ten minutes to explain to them that the staff had been instructed to treat everyone alike—and after that, they accepted our help and appreciated it. I visited with the mayor of Garfield Heights the other day and he said, "All I hear about you is good."

His top district staffer echoed the sentiment—with a slightly different conclusion.

> The congressman is very sensitive to the idea that he is the congressman of all the people. And he's made it clear in no uncertain terms that just because a man's name is Polish, doesn't mean he gets a different kind of service. . . . A few appointments to the service academies and a few Social Security checks unraveled can have a very beneficial effect. Of course, not

everything can be done and they may have to wait. That's what black people have been doing for one hundred years, so it doesn't bother me.

They were certainly conscious of the potential problem of reverse discrimination, and they tried to give personal "service to all." In 1994, after several more partly white suburbs were added to the district, he opened an additional three-person district office in the suburbs. With the passage of time, some benefit—if not pride and trust—might accrue.[51]

Three of the twelve events I attended in my visits involved major white participation—one during each visit. Two of them took place outside the district. The first was a cocktail party fundraiser in an adjacent suburb. The second was a school visit in the Fifteenth Ward. The third was a keynote speech at the Democratic State Convention in Columbus.

There was one group of whites to whom Lou Stokes did pay marked attention. They were the Jewish citizens—like-minded and liberal—in nearby suburbia. When I would ask him to tell me about his tough votes in Congress, he typically replied, "I hardly ever have a problem on a vote. And that's the truth." But on a couple of occasions, he mentioned the issue of Israel and his Jewish neighbors as possible "tough vote" examples.

"I had a little problem with a military bill last year," he explained in 1970. "I made a promise that I would vote against every single military spending bill that came before the House until I saw some reordering of priorities. But the bill had in it arms for Israel, which I favored. I don't have any Jewish constituents, but I do have a lot of Jewish friends outside the district—people I know and who have helped me. I visited Israel last year and I favor helping them. So I seized on the fact that money for the development of two ABM sites had been taken out of the bill, that this was a concession to our side, that we have won something, and, therefore, I could vote for the bill in spite of my promise."

Most of his Jewish friends lived in Shaker Heights—a wealthy suburb, heavily Jewish and slowly being integrated by well-to-do black professionals. The fundraiser was an integrated affair of twenty-four people in the home of a black architect. The congressman spoke briefly about the Caucus, but without any of his fiery "we've got to seize power" rhetoric he had used at the candidates' night the previous evening. To this group, he presented the Caucus as a rational, liberal reform effort inside an ossified political party. And he compared it to Eugene McCarthy's Democratic insurgency of a few years earlier—no doubt an apt analogy for this group. In this setting, the Caucus became cerebral "new politics." The speaker seemed to be soliciting the understanding of friends—not the commitment of warriors.

My second event took place in a 92 percent white junior high school serving the two white, ethnic wards—"unfriendly territory" the staffer-driver said, where the "white hoodlums" had beat up some black students. It was unknown territory, too, and despite written directions, he got lost. I asked the congressman whether he spoke often in this part of his district. "When I first ran, I did some," he said. "But I don't anymore. And they don't ask. . . . I didn't make any gains in this area in 1970. So in the progressive sense, my work went for nothing." Later, he added, "We don't do much with schools." It was never clear, however, why this particular group invited him and had been accepted. One staffer opined only that "they were probably very surprised when we agreed."

His performance generated the same warm reception and enthusiastic participation as the many other such school events I had attended elsewhere. He began with a ten-minute talk about his job, about the House of Representatives as a great place for "disagreement with dignity," about the Constitution as the greatest document ever, and about America as the most wonderful country ever, but as a rich country with poverty. In the question period, the easy answers brought cheers. "Is Cleveland dying?" "Cleveland is not dying because you aren't dying." [Cheers.] "Capital punishment?" "I'm against it." [Cheers.] "Cleaning up the river?" "I have money in the Rivers and Harbors Bill for a pilot clean-up project." [Cheers.] "Lieutenant Calley?" "A man should not be punished when he has been taught to kill." [Cheers.]

There were no adverse reactions—not even on gun control. The congressman, I noted, spoke "easily and confidently—without flamboyance. He is not a colorful personality, but he is immensely likeable." He was pleased. "When I see what happened today, I see hope for the future. If there weren't the children coming along, I'd say the hell with it. But these children have no prejudice, no hostility. They'll come along through high school and college and maybe things will improve. What a difference between the reception they gave me and the one their parents would give me. . . . Their parents are too far gone. I can't talk to them."

"Why didn't you talk about the Caucus?" his staffer asked. "The school has been trying to get the students away from the ethnic view of things," he replied. "If I pushed the black view of the Caucus and why we had to do what we did, then I would be talking just the way the school is teaching them not to talk, wouldn't I? So I thought about it and decided not to go into it, unless it came from them." It didn't.

The third presentation to a white audience took place in Columbus, at the

1976 Democratic State Convention. His acceptance of the invitation to keynote the convention was an exception to his rule of "no speeches outside the district without an honorarium." He did it, he said, for symbolic reasons. It was an "honor," he said. "The party has never had a black official as their keynote, so it is another 'first.'" Also, he had been pushing the party to run a black person for a statewide office and he thought his invitation might be a harbinger of just such a step and that he should keep up the momentum. I did not hear the speech, preferring to talk outside with his driver.

Afterward, the congressman ranked it as the least important and the least comfortable of his three weekend events. "I know some of the people there appreciate what I have to say. But I know many of them do not appreciate what I have to say. I know it. I can feel it. I can feel the prejudice, and I don't enjoy it." A couple of years earlier, he and his brother had been barred from that same convention. So it was a political plus for him in a symbolic sense. The statewide party was not, however, about to become completely hospitable. His representational connections and his leadership performances would be played out within the black community in the Twenty-first Congressional District.

LIBERTY HILL BAPTIST CHURCH

At the following day's engagement—the last event of my third and last visit to the district in the 1970s—Lou Stokes was at the top of his game. The occasion was an afternoon "Gospel Chorus Program" at Liberty Hill Baptist Church, at which he was the guest speaker. About sixty parishioners, between the ages of forty and ninety, were in attendance at this prayer and singing event. It was not a religious ceremony per se, but it took place in a religious setting. And it drew, in Frederick Harris's terms, upon the "inspiration" that the combination of individual religious beliefs and the institutional black church imparts to political activism.[52] The congressman's talk was political and nonpolitical, warm and personal, passionate and worldly. And in all these respects, he spoke as someone totally immersed in and devoted to the black community—both inside and outside of the Twenty-first District.

Early in the program, when the visitors were introduced, my name was called with the added comment that I was writing a book about their congressman. The pastor asked me to stand up. When I did, he pointed his finger at me and put me on notice. "Now you write good things about our congressman," he said. And to the group, he added, "As you can see, I'm trying to persuade him." Everyone laughed. The mood was informal and the political merged seamlessly with the religious.

Various speakers praised him lavishly. One recited his "many accomplishments" and thanked him for honoring them in spite of his "busy schedule." Another praised him as a fine family man and an exemplary figure and spoke of how "proud" they were of him. Another said, "with all the things we hear about Congress these days, it's an honor to have with us as unselfish and dedicated a congressman as Honorable Louis Stokes, who is doing so much for people in the Twenty-first District and for people all over the country."

He began by identifying himself totally with the group. "Liberty Hill is like home for me," he said. "I know so many people here. My roots go back so far. I look out and see Ruth and Rose Collins [the leaders of the gospel chorus] with whom I went to Central High School and whose mother was mother to me, too. And Reverend Wilson married me. He has been an inspiration in my life. And I'm pleased to see so many members of the Twenty-first Congressional District Caucus here. We had three thousand people at the picnic two weeks ago. These are the people who make it worthwhile for me to go through what I go through day after day. If it were not for you people who are behind me, I wouldn't do it. I am blessed that you are back here."

He led himself into his talk by associating himself, in good-humored fashion, with the church. "When my office talked with your program chairman, Sister Bertha Banks—who has been such a help to me in the Twenty-first District Caucus—they asked her what you wanted me to talk about. And Bertha Banks said, 'He's been raised in the church. He'll know what to say!' I consider that statement a great honor. I assume you don't want a political speech. [Laughter.] Well, that's one way of insuring that I won't talk too long." [Laughter.]

In a serious vein, he continued to identify himself with his listeners. "Whatever I have achieved, it's because of my church background. You know, sometimes people forget from whence they came. They reach the heights, and they think they did it all by themselves. Men like Reverend Wilson have been my inspiration. Many black folks have felt they should be in the white church, in the integrated church. When I rassled with that question, I decided that my roots are in the black church. I decided that I had to stay there, where I had been given my start."

Then he linked Liberty Baptist Church and its parishioners to the wider black community. Church people, he said, should be concerned about problems in the world. As a delegate to the recent World Council of Churches conference in Nairobi, Kenya—"perhaps the greatest experience of my life"—he had been reminded of the difficulties of black people worldwide. Referring to the burden of apartheid in South Africa, he told his listeners, "Three hundred people have been killed, shot—women and children—in Soweto. And you know, those people look just like you do, just like you." And he concluded, "Our roots are in that part of the world. We as church people have an obligation to be concerned about our brothers and sisters in that part of the world." It was a reminder that this broad black constituency, with "linked fates" beyond his own district, was also a representational concern of his in Washington.

His talk turned to problems of the district. Among the twenty-three congressional districts in Ohio, he said his district—their district—"has a concentration of the greatest social problems. In many areas, we rank twenty-third in Ohio—in education, health care, housing." Whereas the Cleveland suburbs had one doctor per eight hundred people, his district, he said, had one doctor per three thousand people. And it is, he said, "the right of every human being to have free medical care from the time they are brought squealing into the world until the time they are laid to rest in a casket."

District education levels, he continued, were the lowest in Ohio. As for housing, two district homes had burned in recent months. On abortion, he spoke of the need to be concerned about the living as well as the unborn. And he closed with a story about a woman who left her house and while she was gone her dog chewed her baby—the story which, he said, brought home "better than anything, the plight of people in poverty." He repeated that "we as church people, have to be concerned for our brothers and sisters."

Reverend Wilson gave a rambling benediction about the importance of the church as a guide in "a collapsed society." He ended with "Well, may God bless you and may Congressman Stokes keep getting elected to Congress. May you continue your unselfish work. I'm proud of you and I'm pullin' for you." The political endorsement was totally natural and unexceptional—evidence, again, of what I took to be an easy blend of spiritual fellowship and political support in the crucible of the black church.

When the speaker and the pastor greeted people in the vestibule afterward, I stood well off to the side. Several people went out of their way to greet me and wish me well with "your book." It had been, I thought, an exemplary reinforcement of his earlier negotiations with a group of his primary constituents.

As we drove downtown afterward, the congressman closed the circle of political and personal connections. Asked to rank the events of the three-day weekend in terms of "personal enjoyment" and "political importance," he ranked Liberty Hill as both the most important and the most enjoyable event. "I get the greatest enjoyment out of something like this," he concluded. "I like the church. I enjoy the ministers. They have been so important to the whole black experience. And they are my strength. I enjoy being around them and with them. And the people there are people of warmth, sincerity, and appreciation." After our previous day's engagement at the Democratic State Convention—which he ranked at the bottom—the difference was especially large and palpable.

When we parted, his final comment of our time together struck a familiar note. "I've decided not to go to that reception tonight," he said. "If I go, I'll be stuck there till ten o'clock. I'm going over to W. O. Walker's for dinner, and then I'm going home to bed." Never one to squeeze the last drop of juice out of every constituency contact, he remained as secure in his pattern of representational connections as any member of Congress I had yet met.

INSTITUTIONAL CAREER AND REPRESENTATION

THE HOME CONSTITUENCY

Inside the House of Representatives, Lou Stokes pursued his group-intensive representational strategy in ways that were superintended by the partisan and organizational structures of the institution. While he had not, in the beginning, been ambitious to undertake a political career, once he became a member of Congress, ambition propelled him toward positions of influence—first within the formal committee structure and second within the informal system of specialized member caucuses. In these settings, he sought the same group-interest goals that motivated his activity in his Cleveland constituency. And he applied them to a larger national constituency as well.

As a freshman, he was assigned to the Committee on Education and Labor. It was a good committee in which to pursue his representational goals. According to one account, he called it "the most important committee in Congress" because of its jurisdiction over "the mass of urban problems which have led to unrest in the major cities of America."[53] On the committee, he could pursue the same kind of policy representation he had advocated at home. "The background I bring to the [Education and Labor] committee," he said, "having lived with the problems of the ghetto, along with my legal experience and community involvement, will stand me in good stead in pleading the causes of the poor, the uneducated, the jobless, the ill-housed, and the other forgotten people."[54] He described the committee as "a very liberal committee and a very friendly committee." He praised its white chairman as "liberal," "nice," and helpful to himself and to fellow African American newcomer Bill Clay of St. Louis—soon to become his best and most lasting friend in the House.

His relations with organized labor, in other words, the AFL-CIO, were, however, not strong.

> I did not have their support in the [1968] primary. They supported my strongest opponent, and I beat them. They supported me in the general election and ever since. But they aren't of any importance. I'll tell you what group was very important to me financially in the primary—the Teamsters. And do you know, they have never come back to me since for anything—not once. The AFL-CIO, they fly in your face every time you turn around. They endorse me but don't contribute one dime to my campaign. And they're always after me for something.

As a representative of working people, his affinity with the unions was naturally strong. And his COPE score from 1972 to 1996 averaged 90 percent. But he did not spend time with them or do their bidding. "When a vote came up on the Philadelphia plan," he said, "and the AFL-CIO is opposed to it, they send me the same letter they send everyone else. But they know I'm going to vote for it because it helps black people get construction jobs. And they don't do anything about it."

While the needs of his constituency made him a good fit for the committee, he soon learned that it was not "the most important committee in Congress." He wanted to move up the hierarchy of committees. And because an Ohio member of Appropriations had recently died, that committee vacancy held the most promise.

Stokes explained his preference. "There are only two committees in the House, Appropriations and Ways and Means. Those are the ones that have all the power. It looks like I'm going to be able to get longevity in the House. So I thought I'd rather endure the seniority system on a committee where the power is. It would also be another first—first black man to sit on the Appropriations Committee since Reconstruction." It was one more venue in which to carry on the racial struggle for inclusion. "In the history of Congress, no black [had] ever even sat as a member of these committees," he said. "We were not in the system. Essentially, we had no power in Congress."[55]

In the summertime, the Ohio member of the decision-making Democratic Committee on Committees, fellow Clevelander Charles Vanik, had agreed to nominate and support Stokes for the open "Ohio" slot. A month later, however, when I stopped by Stokes's Washington office, his application was in limbo. I found an "all politics is local" scenario. Stokes had been victimized by the ongoing local political feud between the county Democratic Party and the Twenty-first Congressional District Caucus. Congressman Vanik had withdrawn his offer to nominate Stokes and was preparing to nominate a freshman Ohioan instead. His reason: "Louis supported Republican candidates for office" in the recent election—and had failed to endorse Vanik himself.

Stokes fired off a reply that read, in part,

> I regret that Congressman Vanik has chosen to deny black people the first opportunity afforded them to have a black congressman sit on the most powerful committee in Congress. I regret further that he has chosen to deny the people of Cleveland this additional honor, along with the benefits which could have been derived from my membership on this committee.
>
> I do resent the fact that Congressman Vanik has now chosen to break his commitment to nominate me for this position. This commitment was made early in August. Obviously, he has taken it upon himself to reprimand me and the people in my Congressional District for the existence of the 21st Congressional District Caucus. This action is clearly consistent with his behavior this past May when he and the other Democratic Party leaders organized the party without consultation with the black community. His action today is clear and convincing evidence of the continued attitude of Cuyahoga County Democratic Party leaders in his refusal to recognize qualified black leadership.[56]

Stokes's eight African American House colleagues wrote a letter to Vanik that concluded, "We fervently hope that you will reconsider and nominate Louis Stokes based upon his merit."[57] Their intervention was crucial. And the experience of this proto-caucus taught them what a formally organized caucus might accomplish.

"Charlie is wrong," said Stokes.

> Some of the most experienced political experts in the House, Phil Burton and others, agree with me that if the [Committee on Committees] allows local political situations to enter into the picture in assigning committee

memberships in Washington, they will inject a new and dangerous element into the equation with consequences no one can foresee. If I had failed to support my party's candidate for president, that would be another thing. . . .

The members of the black caucus sent Charlie a letter making three points. One was that local politics ought not to interfere with committee assignments. The second is that he made a commitment to Lou Stokes and around here a person's word is supposed to be his bond. The third was racial. The fact of the matter is that Lou Stokes is black. That shouldn't enter into the picture at all, and a lot of people will be watching in this contest to see what happens.

I know what Charlie wants. He wants me to give up my leadership of the Caucus back home and he wants the Caucus to disband. He has no right to demand that of me. It's my political lifeline. He can't ask me to do that. He's thinking that if the Caucus goes, it will hurt Carl and then he'll be number one. . . . But Charlie is worrying a little bit now because other members of the House feel that the time is ripe, that a black man should have the position, and that Lou Stokes is the man who should have it. We'll see what happens.

Shortly thereafter, Majority Leader Carl Albert got involved, and "in the interest of unity and harmony within the Democratic Party in the House," persuaded Vanik to reconsider his decision."[58]

Back in the district, the Stokes's inclusionary struggle drew detailed coverage and intense support from the *Call and Post*. It was interpreted in the paper and in the black community as "the first of a series of squeeze plays planned by the Cuyahoga County Democratic organization to bring the troublesome Stokes brothers into conformity with the dictatorial operation of the County Democratic machine."[59] More specifically, it was interpreted by members of the Twenty-first Congressional District Caucus as an effort to blackmail them into disbanding in order to save the Stokes appointment.

Thus framed, the organized reaction of the black community was swift and strong. The Caucus executive committee passed a resolution stating: "The 21st Congressional District Caucus is not for sale. This Caucus stands behind its beloved chairman, Louis Stokes, in his qualified application for the important committee. We will not, however, be blackmailed into deserting our principles, our organization, and our unity. . . . We will not be intimidated by Congressman Vanik."[60] Editorially, the *Call and Post* echoed that "capitulation to the demands of county Democratic bosses for blind loyalty will mean an extension of the kind of nonrecognition and disrespect the bosses have always demonstrated in measuring out rewards to black loyalists."[61]

Call and Post columnist Charles Lucas, Stokes's 1968 Republican opponent, warned the Caucus not to succumb to a "divide and conquer tactic" which "has been the format of the racists and the bigots [and the] old slave masters."[62] He stressed the symbolism of the Caucus's "magnificent" and "dramatic" stand, as "a real test for the maturity of black political forces. . . . To capitulate would be a severe blow to the ambitions of black citizens, not only in Cleveland, but throughout the state and nation. All eyes are on the Twenty-first District Black Caucus." By standing firm, the Caucus "lifted the spirits of thousands of people, both black and white, to learn that it would not be intimidated by dangling congressional positions as a ploy. All can take pride in the guts the Caucus showed. . . . Blacks must no longer be bought off with single-purpose positions at the expense of the masses."[63] When Stokes's path was finally cleared, a triumphant picture with editor Walker congratulating Congressman Stokes highlighted the front page of the *Call and Post*.[64]

The Stokes appointment to the Appropriations Committee was treated as a major victory for the group interests of the black community. In terms of Lou Stokes's representational activity, the appointment would, in time, help him to reach his policy goals. But at the moment, the victory came in the form of symbolic representation, because he and his closest supporters had stood together and had stood tall to achieve an outcome that had strengthened black independence, black self-respect, and black pride within a larger attentive constituency at home.

As a newcomer to the Appropriations Committee, Stokes commented, "I doubt very much that my constituents understand the power of the Appropriations Committee. I have an educating job to do."[65] The best education, of course, is to be able to show that you are responsible for bringing money into the district. But it takes time to figure out how to do that. During the time that I traveled with him, there was mostly frustration.

"I'm having an adjustment problem," he said in 1971. "Oh, are they smooth. They've got lots of stuff hidden away in those bills. I knew I'd get the bottom of the barrel of subcommittees." He acted out Chairman George Mahon asking him to submit a list, looking furtively in all directions, telling "Louis" that he couldn't get him what he wanted, and then putting him on the lowly District of Columbia subcommittee.

Compared with Education and Labor, his new committee "is dull and there's nothing exciting about it—all figures." And its decision processes did not seem very logical. "Everything revolves around how the guys feel," he said. "'Oh, maybe we ought to round the figure off. . . . this bureau always puts yeast in theirs. . . . cut this down a little, but . . . cut out $2,000 here.' There's nothing very intelligent about it." Spoken like a newcomer still sitting "below the salt."

With respect to his inside power, he noted a newfound ability to command the attention of others.

> I had my most fun last year on the D.C. [appropriations] bill. We got to conference and [William] Natcher [chairman of the subcommittee] was wheeling and dealing and cutting down the appropriations. Finally, I had enough of the way he was dealing with the District of Columbia. I said, "I just want it understood that you don't speak for me, Mr. Chairman. I won't go that low. And you can't deal with [Senate Subcommittee Chairman Daniel] Inouye without consulting me. I'm a member of this committee. If you keep that figure, I won't sign the conference report." Four of the Republicans wouldn't sign the report because the figure was too high and I wouldn't sign it because it was too low; so there weren't enough signatures to have a report.
>
> I left and went to Cleveland and the [full committee] chairman called me. "Is it true," he said, "that you won't sign the report?" I said "yes," that I wanted Mr. Natcher to understand that I am no token member of the committee, that I'm not going to sit there and do what he wants. I want to be consulted and listened to. He said he understood. Then Hale Boggs [Democratic Whip] called me and then the Speaker. Then Walter Washington [D.C. mayor] called me! When Walter told me, "We can live with that amount of money," I agreed to sign. But I had to make the point that I was a member of that committee. And I made it.

Symbolically, his appointment to the committee was very important to his supportive constituency, and he was pressing his case on that dimension of representation.

But substantive representational accomplishment still eluded him. "I don't think it's helped any yet [back home]. Maybe that's something that comes with seniority and pork barrel projects. I don't think people in the black community have any idea of the potential that my job has for them—not now anyway." In his 1976 campaign, as noted earlier, he was arguing that his constituents had an investment in his committee seniority and his career. By that time, he had been placed on the Subcommittee on Veteran's Affairs,

Housing and Urban Development, and Independent Agencies. And that appointment had put him on a representational path that would eventually mean very tangible results for his constituency.

THE NATIONAL CONSTITUENCY

When Lou Stokes spoke at the Liberty Hill Baptist Church in 1976, he articulated the concept of a constituency more encompassing than his own primary, or reelection, or geographical constituencies. It was the concept of a national—even international—constituency of black people whose group interests were so much like those of his own black constituents that he felt obligated to act as a representative of the broader constituency, too. Most especially, that obligation touched his fellow African Americans in the United States—people in difficulty, but who could not elect or claim a Representative of their own in the U.S. House of Representatives.

Because of the sheer paucity of black members when he was elected, this obligation was especially pressing for freshman Congressman Louis Stokes. The election of three first-termers in 1968 brought the total to an all-time high of nine. And he interpreted that election as the opportunity for the nine to take action to recognize and work for the national constituency. As he put it to another interviewer in 1972,

> My election to the House, along with Shirley Chisholm and William Clay, represented an historic moment in American politics. It marked the first time in over 92 years that more than eight black persons had ever sat in the House of Representatives. The thrust of our elections was that many black people around America who had formerly been unrepresented, now felt that the nine black members of the House owed them the obligation of also affording them representation in the House. It was in this context that each of the nine of us realized that in addition to representing our individual districts, we had to assume the onerous burden of acting as congressman-at-large for unrepresented people around America.[66]

Out of that realization came the Congressional Black Caucus. And out of the 1968 election came the necessary stimulus. "Without Bill Clay, Shirley Chisholm, and myself," opined Stokes in 1971, "there wouldn't be a Caucus."

The history and the activities of the Congressional Black Caucus (CBC) have been chronicled, dissected, and evaluated elsewhere.[67] My only purpose is to note Lou Stokes's role as a founding father of the CBC and his early immersion in its affairs. He saw himself as an original—if not the main—instigator in its formation. Bill Clay, who has written about its origins, says,

"Stokes and I decided that nine of us . . . constituted a power bloc deserving respect within the institution . . . and we made our feelings known to the other seven."[68] That statement seems fair, given the similarity of views the two men brought to the CBC and to the close friendship that quickly developed between them in the House.

Both men took the most expansive and inclusive view of the black community, one that reached beyond the black-power militants in strategy and beyond their individual constituencies in scope. Clay spoke for Stokes when he wrote that "Black pride is not the exclusive property of any unique faction of the black public. It belongs to all of us as surely as it is our birthright." He praised Carl Stokes as a "consummate professional practitioner" of black politics. And, he reserved his deepest scorn for an early black congressman who was "a disaster for the black community . . . [because] not once during his tenure in office did he identify with any universal cause of black people."[69] They were articulating a view that some scholars have labeled "surrogate representation."[70]

Similarly, when it came to choosing the first chairperson of the Congressional Black Caucus, Stokes rejected out of hand a narrow-gauged senior colleague because "he wouldn't hear of anything black. He's totally out of touch with the present." Both men embraced as the motto of the Congressional Black Caucus: "Black people have no permanent friends, no permanent enemies . . . just permanent interests."

In January 1971 six more newly elected African American members joined the group. And they joined in electing the most acceptable veteran member as their first CBC chairman. A year later, dissatisfaction with the slow pace of CBC activity produced agitation for a more activist chairperson. And, with seniority no longer the key qualification, Louis Stokes was elected the new chairperson. "I gave it a lot of thought before I accepted," he said. "I knew I didn't need any more responsibility. I'm loaded as it is. But the boys talked to me about it, and I knew they wanted to get the thing moving, that it had bogged down. I felt that way, too. I was committed to the Caucus because I knew what it meant for the country and for our historical development. And so I accepted. But I can see already what it means in work."

Staff and workload were uppermost in his mind when we talked. "All the press releases and statements have to come from me," he said. "The television and newspaper people call me and ask, 'What did you mean in that press release on Nixon's trip to China?' No one else can answer that for me. Yesterday, we met from 2:30 to 6:00 on Caucus business. And when we finished, the staff handed me two pages of calls. . . . I don't want my [own] staff here fooling around with Caucus business and neglecting the congressional office business. So I asked for [and got] a Caucus person here in the office, so I can shift Caucus mail and phone calls onto her." One study of the Congressional Black Caucus notes that when Stokes became chairperson, "the Congressional Black Caucus underwent an extensive revision of staff and direction. With one exception, the entire staff was changed."[71]

The implementation of a Congressional Black Caucus strategy for dealing with its broader constituency evolved under Stokes's chairmanship. Marguerite Ross Barnett, in her seminal work on the Congressional Black Caucus, argues that the initial idea of the Congressional Black Caucus as "a single unified group representing a construct called the national black constituency," or as "Congressman at large for 20 million black people," proved "unworkable."[72]

It was under Lou Stokes's leadership that this earliest mission was altered. As chairman, he said in 1973,

> At first, we were unclear about our proper role. Therefore, in the past year, we had to analyze what our resources were, what we should be doing and how best to do it. And our conclusion was this: if we were to be effective, if we were going to make the meaningful contribution *to minority citizens in this country* [italics added], then it must be as legislators. This is the arena in which we possess expertise—and it is in the halls of Congress that we must make this expertise felt.[73]

Four years later, he recalled that, "We started out trying to be all things to all people. We were trying to fill a void nationally. And in doing so, we were trying to respond to every crisis involving blacks nationally. . . . We knew we have to leave civil rights leadership to other organizations and other individuals. We are legislators. . . . We realized we had to break into the power structure."[74]

In Barnett's view, Stokes led the Congressional Black Caucus from its early pressure-packed "collective stage" into a later more realistic and relaxed "ethnic stage."[75] As a speculative matter, his selection and success as chairman may have been aided by the translation of his position as a centrist and a unifier in Cleveland's black community into a similarly balancing position within the CBC.

The Congressional Black Caucus was not a research topic of mine, and I talked with Stokes about it sparingly and intermittently. Thus, I cannot evaluate his performance as a member of it. The Cleveland congressman was certainly a founding father, and his reelection as its chair reflects the satisfaction of his fellow members. He instituted one major, permanent activity, the Annual Congressional Black Caucus Fund-raising Dinner, and it has continued to be the CBC's main financial lifeline ever since. In 1973 his schedule showed him carrying the broad messages of the CBC to ten audiences beyond Washington and throughout the country.

When we last spoke of the CBC, he had just (May 1974) turned the job over to his successor. He was looking forward to devoting a fuller measure— per his own prescription—to his legislative expertise and to his committee work. "It was a relief when I gave that [the chairmanship] to Charlie Rangel. I think I was able to move a few things forward. But there are some things I want to do on the Appropriations Committee. I'm the only black over there, and I'd like to have time to spend on the committee." His success in that venue is another story. But his participation remained crucial to the CBC. Three years later, Barnett named Rangel, Stokes, and Clay as "the most influential members inside" the CBC.[76]

As a final, covering word on his Congressional Black Caucus experience, perhaps it is best to use Marguerite Ross Barnett's summary comment on its earliest period that its "greatest success was the brilliance of political innovation inherent in the decision of black representatives to work together *to represent the interests of the black community*" [italics added].[77] That was the essential goal of Louis Stokes's group-intensive representational strategy. And since he became a founding father of the CBC and later presided over its transition to effectiveness, he would surely feel rewarded by her judgment.

CONCLUSION

Louis Stokes's ultimate goal was to protect and promote the interests of the black community of Cleveland. His supportive constituency, the constituency he perceived and represented, was "the black community." He never doubted that he knew what their group interests were or that their interests and his interests were inextricably linked to one another. The context in which he worked—a 65 percent black constituency—made those identities easy to maintain. Voting in the legislature, for example, was never a problem for him.

His dominant representational strategy was a group-intensive strategy. It was grounded in his policy connections, but it incorporated a large component of symbolic activity as well. In whatever he did, he connected with his constituents as the embodiment of their aspirations—as a path breaker, a role model, and a source of pride for the entire community. Overall, there seemed to be a remarkably comfortable fit between his representational strategy and the strongest desires of the group.

His community-wide connections could not, however, assure the accomplishment of his instrumental goal—the pursuit of a successful, long-term political career. That electoral goal had to be pursued in the competitive context of intracommunity politics, and it required, therefore, a more specialized set of connections. At the beginning of his career, those political connections were cultivated for him and delivered to him by his brother. Without strong ambitions and without having to do much building-block networking, he comfortably claimed his place at the top of the office ladder. His first election—heavy with support from black churches—confirmed his position as a unifying, centrist leader of the black community. And from that position, he battled—as only an African American could—for the empowerment of that community. The instrument of his success in that battle was the Twenty-first Congressional District Caucus. And his leadership of the Caucus both broadened and solidified his community support.

The crucial negotiating-and-learning sequences of his constituency career came from his trial-and-error efforts to transform that bipartisan organization—bequeathed to him by his brother—into the instrument of his own political survival. And he was still working to maintain that rock-bottom connection—"to protect my back" from possible competitors—when I left him in 1976. Nonetheless, he was well fortified by connections of policy, pride, and power at home. That security left him free to contribute fully to the work of his Appropriations Committee, his Black Caucus, and his Democratic Party inside the House of Representatives. "The book" had, indeed, taken shape.

CHAPTER 3
. . . .
BARBARA JORDAN
1972−1973

PIONEER COHORT: DIVERSITY

Two years after I had first met and traveled with Congressman Louis Stokes in Cleveland, I met and traveled with congressional candidate Barbara Jordan in Houston. They were two of the eighteen U.S. House members whose constituency activities I was studying in the 1970s—in the hope of generalizing about their perceptions and their behaviors at home. Stokes and Jordan brought diversity to that group. But neither race nor gender played any part in my generalizations. They were members of the pioneer African American cohort in the House, but I had no intention of writing about them in tandem.

Now, however, I have returned to them as anchors for a research narrative about African American representation in Congress. My travels with the two of them give me leverage for an analysis that is both cross-sectional and longitudinal. First, the Stokes−Jordan differences will help me illustrate and explain the diversity of representational strategies to be found among African American House members. And second, taken together, they will allow some comparisons between the representational activity of this pair of House members in the 1970s and the activity of another pair in the 1990s.

Any comparison between Stokes and Jordan, admittedly, comes with a major caution. My firsthand exposure to Barbara Jordan was limited to one three-day visit in 1972 and one Washington interview in 1973. My ability to make comparisons, therefore, is limited. Also, the Jordan career segment I captured was very different from the career segment I captured with Lou Stokes. He was already in Congress; she was not. But she had been in politics longer than he had. I watched him for six years; I watched her for six months. So I have much less to say about Jordan than about Stokes—and less confidence in saying it.

There is, however, a helpful autobiography that Jordan coauthored with Shelby Hearon and an excellent biography written by Mary Beth Rogers. Both will supplement my firsthand observations.[1] They will allow me to sketch out the events and develop the texture of her political career during the ten years before I arrived. My own observations, however, constitute the centerpiece of the study, and no interpretation will be based solely on outside sources. What follows, then, must be understood as an incomplete picture of Barbara Jordan's representational activity, centered on what I observed and on what we talked about.

As members of the pioneer cohort of African American House members, there were biographical and policy similarities between Jordan and Stokes. In biographical terms, both had been born and raised in the black, segregated, central-city neighborhoods they would eventually represent in Congress. Both had fought similar battles for inclusion in a white-dominated political world. Both sets of parents had placed the highest premium on education as the essential weapon in that battle. The group consciousness of black citizens and the obvious needs of urban black citizens meant that a basic commitment to black interests would be a policy goal for both of them. It also meant that their voting records would be predictably and similarly liberal, reflecting their strong preference for legislation to help their lopsidedly disadvantaged constituents.

The negotiating activities of Louis Stokes and Barbara Jordan with the people of their districts must be placed, therefore, within the broadly similar policy goals and policy constraints fixed by the "group interests" of their black constituents. But within these broad similarities, the two African American politicians I met in the 1970s displayed quite different representational strategies. When we move beyond their common generational, biographical, and policy bonds, we find that Barbara Jordan and Louis Stokes differed in their goals, their careers, their constituency contexts, and their negotiating histories. In David Canon's categorization, Jordan became a "new style" member of Congress—perhaps the earliest one. In contrast to Lou Stokes, she displayed a representational strategy based on racial "commonalities" as well as racial "differences."[2]

PERSONAL GOALS AND REPRESENTATIONAL STRATEGY

When I met her in Houston in May 1972, Barbara Jordan was a thirty-six-year-old Texas state senator campaigning in the Democratic primary for a seat in Congress. Her career milestones were these: she had been born and raised in Houston and educated in the segregated public schools of that city and at Houston's all-black Texas Southern University. She graduated from Boston University Law School in 1959 and set up a private law practice in her Houston neighborhood. Twice she ran unsuccessfully for a seat in the Texas State House of Representatives, in 1962 and 1964. In 1965 she served as Assistant to the Administrative Judge of Harris County. In 1966 she was elected to the Texas State Senate for a two-year term, and she was re-elected in 1968 for a four-year term. Reaching, as she was, from a constituency of 315,000 people to a constituency of 462,000 people, she was still—albeit marginally—in the expansionist phase of her constituency career.

Barbara Jordan's father worked as a union laborer in a railyard warehouse. He was also a part-time Baptist minister. Her family life was lived within what her biographer called "a cocoon of respectability in the heart of Houston's Good Hope Missionary Baptist Church."[3] Her family owned their own home. "We were poor," she said, "but so was everyone around us, so we didn't notice it. We were never hungry and we always had a place to stay."[4] Her father had three years of college at the Tuskegee Institute, and his strong middle-class aspirations included a college education for his three girls.[5] The extended family chipped in to put Barbara, the youngest, through Boston University Law School.

She did not know poverty as starkly as Lou Stokes did. And she first encountered the white world in graduate school instead of the Army. Otherwise, their trips up the professional ladder were similar. At home, both individuals became exemplary success stories.

As of 1972, Jordan's story could be told in her list of achievements. She had been one of only two black women in her law school class. When she passed the bar exam, she became only the third black woman to be licensed to practice in Texas. She was the first African American to serve as top assistant to the Harris County Judge. She was the first African American since Reconstruction to be elected to the Texas State Senate. She had been the first African American and the first woman to serve as president of the Texas State Senate. And she was about to become (with Andrew Young of Georgia) the first African American since Reconstruction to be elected to the United States Congress from the South. The pioneer generation generated "firsts." As in the case of Stokes, Jordan's firsts helped to mark the beginnings of some measurable political inclusion for black Americans in our national political life. Among black people who read or heard about them, their firsts gave each of them symbolic importance as exemplars and agents of political change.

Representational differences between Louis Stokes and Barbara Jordan begin with differences in their goals. In this respect, Barbara Jordan was everything that Lou Stokes was not. She was an ambitious, self-starting, entrepreneurial, natural-born politician. "How long have you been interested in politics?" I asked her early on. "Always," she replied. "As long as I can remember. Judge Andrew Jefferson sometimes says, when we are together on a speaking engagement, that he was responsible for my first political defeat. People sit up and listen. And he says that he defeated me for president of the freshman class at TSU [Texas Southern University]. Actually, I wanted to run for student council, but I found out that a freshman wasn't eligible. I was sixteen, so that was pretty early. And I've been running for something ever since."

The differences in their early career ambitions are reflected in their different career paths. Stokes came to politics sideways, through a career in the law. Jordan came to politics head on, through electoral activity. Stokes had a politically pathbreaking brother to coax him into politics, teach him the ropes, and pave the way for him. Jordan's motivation for a political career was self-generated, and she had to succeed on her own. What Stokes learned from his brother, she learned for herself. She had to fight tough political battles in order to get to Congress; he did not. She had to climb the political ladder step-by-step to get there; he did not. And in climbing, she also had to learn a greater range of negotiating skills in dealing with her constituents than he did in dealing with his.

Barbara Jordan's political career began in 1960 when she went, unsolicited, to Harris County Democratic headquarters, volunteered, and was put to work stuffing and licking envelopes. From that day on, she was a strongly committed Democrat—loyal and partisan to a degree unmatched by Stokes. His threat, during his struggle with Cleveland's white Democratic Party hierarchy, to "tear up the party" would never have occurred to Jordan. Soon, her remarkable talent for public speaking was recognized, and she was put to work talking—"primarily to black groups, political groups, civic organizations, clubs, and churches" throughout Harris County.[6] By the time the 1960 campaign ended, she wrote, "I had really been bitten by the political bug . . . [and] I couldn't turn politics loose."[7] Two years later, at the age of twenty-six, she was running for the Texas House of Representatives.

Of that first race, she recalled, "I had a financial problem. I was only a year and a half out of law school, and that wasn't enough time to get much business or make much money. The filing fee was $500 and that was like $5,000—or more—today. I was just too poor to run. When the Harris

County Democrats [an unofficial liberal and labor group] said they had decided I was the one to run [as the first black ever on their countywide slate], I told them I had no money. They said they would take care of it and they did." When she finished her story, I interjected, "And then it seemed natural to try again in 1964?" And she nodded. "You just keep running. You just keep running. I don't know how you ever get it out of your blood."

"What do you like about it?" I continued. "It's people and the response you can get from them. You can get people excited. That makes you feel good. Then, when you get elected, you try to deliver on all the promises you made. And that's not so easy."

Her obvious ability to get "a response" and to get people "excited" was drawn from a commanding combination of personal attributes. She was an unusually large woman with an extraordinarily rich and resonant speaking voice, and she had a way with language. In the words of her biographer, "The sound of her voice was her supreme gift because, like music, it evoked an emotional response in her listeners."[8] She was a public-speaking champion long before she was a politician. "I was in declamation contests, oratorical contests, college debates, all of them, all through school." She was a self-confident person and she spoke that way. On the campaign trail, she used her rhetorical eloquence to identify herself with her listeners and to draw their continuing support for her representational career.

For three days, I watched her ask for votes and urge her supporters to turn out and elect her. But votes and election were *not* her dominant goal. Winning elections was her instrumental goal, and she was working to win. Her personal gaze, however, was fixed on a goal well beyond that elementary and necessary first step. Barbara Jordan's political ambition was to become an influential player within the legislature. First, in the Texas Senate and then in Congress, her dominant goal was to achieve inside, institutional influence. Therefore, I will describe her dominant representational strategy as an *influence-intensive strategy*.

In her view, the best way to represent her constituents was to become an influential player inside the legislature and, from that position, to gain recognition and to shape legislation in ways beneficial to them. That is the representational strategy I watched her follow on the campaign trail in 1972. And it is what others saw, too, during her six years of public service before that. Her biographer concluded that throughout her early political years, "the significant truths of Barbara's life . . . revolved around her single-minded pursuit of achievement and power."[9] "Jordan," she added, "intuitively understood power and pursued it single-mindedly."[10]

Her only serious opponent was incumbent Texas State Representative Curtis Graves. He was an African American who had been newly elected to the Texas House, in the same year Jordan had been newly elected to the Senate, and whose district was largely enveloped in hers.[11] In a losing campaign for mayor of Houston in 1969, he had captured 90 percent of the vote in black precincts. Early on, I asked Jordan what the main issue was between her and her opponent. "Effectiveness," she answered. "Who can get the most done. That's what I stress everywhere. Blacks can't vote just on the basis of skin color anymore. They have to vote on the issues—and the issue is effectiveness. I'm not saying what I'm going to do when I get to Congress. I'm talking about what I've already done."

"What *do* your constituents think of you?" I asked. "They think I get things done. There was a word in an editorial the other day that sums it up. They called me a 'job accomplisher.' One of the problems I have with my strongest supporters is that they think when I get to Congress everything will change—just because I'm there. I have to tell them that very little will change because of my presence in Congress. If you ask people about me, they all say, 'She's gotten a lot done in Austin. She does things.' But if you ask them what, they wouldn't know. They wouldn't name anything specific. But that's the way they think of me."

The editorial of which she spoke appeared in a local black-owned newspaper, *Forward Times*, which made no endorsement in her race. But they profiled the contestants succinctly. Jordan: "articulate, job-accomplisher, demanding, and a proven disciple of change and progress." Graves: "dashing, flamboyant, outspoken, and willing to climb the steps to the Capitol to decry some injustice."[12] These profiles suggest that the black citizens of the Eighteenth Congressional District faced a very real choice of representational strategies. One was keyed to intra-institutional influence, the other keyed to extra-institutional agitation. *Both* strategies had obviously received winning majorities at Houston's polls. "It's my most difficult race," said Jordan. "It has people confused. There are two well-known black leaders running, and it's hard for many people to choose."

To understand her dominant goal of inside power and her influence-intensive strategy, it helps to recognize her lifelong preference for traditional politics over movement—or protest—politics. She had never been, nor was she now, a civil rights activist. She was a self-conscious beneficiary of the civil rights revolution, but she was far less of a participant in it than was Louis Stokes. By contrast, her 1972 opponent was a prototypical movement activist of the 1960s. His definition of "the" campaign issue centered on the charge that Jordan was insufficiently militant—Aunt Jemima and Uncle Tom, he called her—and, therefore, insufficiently representative of her black constituency.

In rebuttal, she told a reporter, "All blacks are militant in their guts, but militancy is expressed in various ways. Some do it quite overtly, while others try to work their way through 'the system,' trying to bring about change in race and human relations. That's the way I like to work. Disruptive or divisive behavior is no help." [13] From the moment she had arrived in the Texas State Senate, she had signaled her institutionally oriented intentions to her colleagues. "I wanted them to know I was coming to be a Senator, and I wasn't coming to lead any charge. I was not coming carrying the flag and singing 'We Shall Overcome.' I was coming to work." [14] And early on, she told her constituents, too, that "the marching and singing phase of the civil rights movement should give way to calm, realistic progress in the arena of legislation." [15] Those beliefs and choices framed her representational strategy and pointed her toward an influential, inside, institutional career.

PRECONGRESSIONAL CAREER

Barbara Jordan's presentation of self to the congressional electorate in 1972, as someone who would "get things done" depended for its credibility on her six-year performance as a state senator in Austin. As portrayed in her autobiography and in the later biography, her record and her reputation in Austin amply supported her presentation of herself as a "job accomplisher" in the campaign. From the beginning of her six years in the Texas Senate, her goal was to get things done. In pursuit of that goal, she made it her top priority to learn about the people and the procedures of the Texas Senate—a club of thirty, mostly conservative white men who had never known a black colleague. "To be effective," she said, "I had to get inside the club, not just inside the chamber." [16] As a matter of strategic calculation, she set out to win the confidence of some of them and the respect of all of them.

She thought a great deal about how to do it. One prescription, she said, was that "You work and you learn the rules and you keep your mouth shut until it is time to open it." [17] Another was to seek out "those who held the power with their seniority and conservatism. I knew it would be well if I could work my way to them, if they could see me as a legislative member of the Senate [by] doing my work on the committees, asking the right kind of questions that make good law." [18]

Another prescription was to choose a powerful mentor.

I decided that [Senator] Dorsey Hardeman from San Angelo knew the rules better than anybody. I think he wrote most of them, and I had seen him make a fool out of people just by pulling a rule on them. So I had to become acquainted well with Dorsey. In order to gain his respect, I, too, had to know the rules. I used to talk to Dorsey a lot, and I started stopping by his office for a drink in the afternoon. Now, that is really in, when you can do that. One of my friends at that time from Houston, Jake Johnson, who was in the House when I got to the Senate, was looking for me one afternoon and couldn't find me and somebody told him, "Well, you can check in Senator Hardeman's office!" When Jake walked in—Jake was a liberal House member, and Dorsey was the conservative leader of the Senate—there I was, sitting on the couch with my feet on a chair and a drink in my hand, and Dorsey sitting at his desk with a drink in his hand.[19]

Their discussion was about breaking a filibuster.

Later, Representative Johnson himself recounted his surprised reaction in an interview with Jordan's biographer:

Hardeman laid out a series of steps they could take and looked over at Barbara and said, "Isn't that right, Senator?" "Yes, Senator," Barbara said, and then she pointed out some additional parliamentary maneuver they could take. And Hardeman jumped up and said with great enthusiasm, "Oh, *yes* [italics in original], that's right . . ." Here they were planning and plotting, and I realized that not only has Barbara been accepted in the Senate, she's been accepted in the inner sanctum sanctorum. And that's a stunning thing.[20]

"Her path," writes her biographer, "led to the inner circles where key relationships were the tools that allowed deals and law to be hammered out and shaped" (146).

Her first legislative victory came on a fundamental inclusionary issue—the right to vote—when she successfully blocked a conservative bill to impose new requirements for voter registration. The bill was designed to restrict the participation of blacks and Hispanics. "I made a list of ten senators who were in my political debt," she said. "I went to each one and said I was calling in my chit. I needed their votes." Then she confronted the bill's author. "I can count, Barbara. The bill is dead," he said (122). This effort, interestingly, previewed her most important legislative work in Congress—another pioneering inclusionary effort to help her most impoverished constituents retain unfettered access to the ballot.

Her most significant payoffs in institutional influence came when, "In 1969, [her] insider status [as the appointed chairperson of the Labor and Management Committee] allowed her to be responsible for two major changes in Texas law: the state's first minimum wage law and the first increase in benefits in twelve years for workers insured on the job" (146). Both bills provided direct assistance to her needy constituents, both black and white. Both bills "required extensive negotiation, arm-twisting, vote-trading, chit-calling, and the kinds of compromising that only political insiders are capable of managing—indeed, the kind of *effective* [italics in original] deal-making that is the mark of a political leader" (146).

"Of course, I'm a little embarrassed about the amount," she said, in discussing the minimum wage bill afterward. "Only $1.25 an hour and $1.40 after a year. But now that we have a law, we can try to improve it."[21] "It was a major victory," she said, "to get the two words *minimum wage* as part of statutory law in Texas."[22] Legislating, she was saying, is a bargaining process and, therefore, an incremental business. It was a pragmatic business. Establish the legality of your idea first and then work to perfect the details.

With respect to the workman's compensation benefits bill, she followed the same legislative strategy. And it was another legislative landmark—in the sense that it crowned a success after twelve years of failure. She recalled that "some of my [liberal] friends didn't like it because it didn't go far enough. It was a compromise measure. I wasn't happy with it, but I was pleased that we did increase benefits by the amount we did. . . . And, of course, that's the way you do. You compromise."[23] It was, again, a pragmatic, incremental, compromise-oriented view of her legislative work. You get what you can now and come back for more later. It was a view that enabled a liberal to make her mark in an institution dominated by conservatives.

After her first two years, as a show of their respect, Jordan's colleagues unanimously voted her "outstanding freshman legislator." Near the end of her sixth year, she was elected president pro tem of the Senate, third in line for the governorship—an honor that they topped off by making her "governor for a day." On both occasions, she noted that when she came to the Senate, they were "strangers" and that early sentiments of "suspicion, fear, and apprehension" had been replaced by "friendship" and "mutual respect."[24] By Jordan's second term, her biographer writes, "Not only had she gotten *in*, she had become a consummate *insider*. [And] that would set her apart from most other African American leaders in the 1960s and 1970s."[25]

From the beginning of her career as a representative, Jordan's dominant goal had been institutional power. She had achieved that goal inside the

Texas legislature. And her influence-intensive representational strategy had paid off for her working-class constituency—in minimum wage and workman's compensation legislation. On behalf of her constituents, she had become an important inside player. And that was the political persona she presented to her expanded congressional electorate in May 1972.

CONSTITUENCY CONTEXT

The Eighteenth Congressional District of Texas was located in the heart of Harris County, on Houston's east side, and contained the great bulk of the central city. "It's a core district, the core of the city, the pulse of the city," Jordan explained. "If you are looking for diversity, it's there. It's all there. This district represents a concentration of all the problems of America localized into one spot. . . . it has the best of philosophy and the worst of philosophy . . . it has extremes of poverty and affluence [and] a composite of urban problems. . . . it has a great deal of industry, but very diversified." It was, she generalized, "a working-class district." And that last descriptor was her basic perception, the umbrella under which she could conceptualize, and represent, a majority of her constituents.

Her district was a majority minority district, but it was *not* a majority-black district. And therein lies its great difference from Lou Stokes's Ohio district. The ethnic makeup of Jordan's district was 42 percent black, 20 percent Mexican American, and most of the rest Anglo, in other words, white. If eligibility to vote is considered, the district's minorities held an even slimmer majority.[26] Her own estimate was that the district's Mexican Americans would cast from 10 percent to 15 percent of the vote. The overriding consequence of the ethnic equipoise was this: that she could not ignore her white constituents as Louis Stokes was able to do. That contextual difference produced distinctively different connection patterns at home.

The very first thing we did, when we met, was to take a ride through the district. After she introduced herself—"What's your first name? Dick? Mine's Barbara. Barbara, Dick. Now we've got that settled"—she said, "I suppose you'd like to see the district." She asked her top campaign aide to drive and "to be the narrator of the trip." She put me next to the driver, and she squeezed herself into the backseat. She cheered whenever she spied a campaign poster in a store window. "Good for you Club 500!" The easy informality of her approach to the visitor was in the sharpest contrast to the natural reserve of Lou Stokes.

The district tour took us through the heart of her black constituency—

the Fifth Ward on the northeast side of Houston and the Third Ward on the southeast side. We drove by her law office, which occupied the second floor in a small wood-frame building on the main thoroughfare of the Fifth Ward. She described her own Fifth Ward as "low income" and the Third Ward as "middle income," to illustrate the district's diversity. To this she subsequently added the city's "black professionals, all of whom are in my district." The Fifth Ward, once "the largest black area" in the city, was beginning to experience "stagnation and decline"; and the Third Ward was becoming "the hub of black social and cultural life in Houston." [27]

I asked her whether these income differentials had produced "divergent interests" among her black constituents. "No," she said. "And I don't see why they would have." Although she never invoked the idea of "the black community," the underlying notion of a commonality of black interests across economic lines was certainly a congenial one. Later, when a reporter asked her the same question about "divergence," she answered directly: "All blacks are in the race together, and we know that what affects one does have repercussion effects on the other. . . . if the chips were down, middle-class, lower-class, and under-class blacks would, I think, unite together in a concerted way." [28] She understood the idea of "linked fates." But because she lacked a solid black majority, as compared to the 65 percent black majority in Lou Stokes's case, "the black community" was too exclusionary a concept around which to construct her representational strategy.

At one point in the tour, when our driver turned from one busy street into another busy street, Jordan spoke abruptly to her. "Why did you just leave the district?" I was astounded at her recognition of district boundary lines amid such a citified maze. It reflected a hands-on, working knowledge of an urban district that I had not yet seen among urban House members. And it was strikingly different from Lou Stokes's apparent lack of interest in such detail.

There was, however, a good and sufficient reason for her boundary-line expertise. She had drawn those boundary lines herself! She had been made vice chairman of the Redistricting Committee of the Texas Senate and given carte blanche to map a district that would send her to Congress. That prerogative was the direct result of her effective courtship of the lieutenant governor, the presiding officer of the Senate. "Go get your precinct lines set and then we'll build the other Houston districts around what you want," he told her. "You're in charge of creating your own district." [29]

She might have created a majority-black district; but in the line-drawing negotiations, she ceded some black areas to a worried white incumbent [and friend], Democratic Congressman Bob Eckhardt.[30] She even ceded him areas from her own Senate district. In purely electoral terms, however, the district she drew was one that she knew would send her to Congress. And, as a first impression, she demonstrated a good deal more familiarity with its nuances than Lou Stokes ever did with his district.

My notes reacted to what I had seen.

We drove through the neighborhoods of the Fifth Ward—tiny wooden homes for the most part, many one-story wooden on brick pilings, sometimes packed two and three deep in a block so that the house on the street has one or two more houses in its backyard. The streets were—many of them—unpaved, with deep holes in which your axle touched as you rode along. We were not too far from Campbell Street where Barbara lives. The main thoroughfares . . . are paved. But off the main streets, the side streets are not. They are very, very poor people, and their poverty is more visible than it would be if you rode down a street of tenement houses, in say, Harlem. Their streets are not paved because they have no power. They cannot put the squeeze on anyone and don't know how. No one in suburban Rochester, say, would put up with these conditions for a minute. These people do not know how or in what direction to scream. They are the people BJ wants to get out to vote, the people she worries about not voting, and the people for whom she keeps saying she will work and speak.

The visual sights—like nothing I had ever seen in Cleveland—were those of powerlessness.

A subsequent study of Houston's black community corroborated these first impressions. In a book entitled *Invisible Houston,* the author concluded that its black residents were "politically powerless during the height of the city's growth period of 1970–1980. The prevailing sentiment has been 'out of sight, out of mind.' . . . City services in the older minority neighborhoods suffered seriously . . . [and] blacks in their neighborhoods remained invisible."[31] Those unpaved roads in the heart of one of America's largest cities spoke volumes to me about the unmet needs of its black citizens and about their lack of political inclusion. They also argued that political inclusion required that Houston's black citizens have, as their representatives in government, people who could identify with them racially.

When I had toured Louis Stokes's district with his aides in Cleveland, they had described certain areas in terms of prior racial turmoil—pointing out to me "where the trouble was," where a protesting minister "fell under a bulldozer," where offices had to put "iron grates" on their windows, where "the worst streets" in "the worst neighborhoods" were in terms of violence. By contrast, there was no talk of black militancy during my Houston tour. Houston, I learned, did not have a vivid legacy of urban unrest and rioting.

In the words of one historian, "Although many of the social problems that triggered nationwide protest demonstrations and riots in the 1960s were present in Houston at that time, the city's black community remained relatively calm during this turbulent period, with only a series of sit-ins and demonstrations from black students at Texas Southern University." [32] Black militancy seemed further from the surface of Houston politics. And whereas Stokes's connections with the more radical elements of his constituency had stood him in good stead politically, such ties seemed irrelevant in Jordan's case. She seemed not to curry such connections. Her opponent, who openly nurtured them, appeared not—in the 1972 context—to be profiting from them.

During the tour, we drove through one Mexican American neighborhood, but we did not drive through any white areas. Jordan did talk about her white constituents; but she did not discuss the Mexican Americans. In fact, she never articulated any sense that she had ever entertained the idea of an African American and Chicano coalition—nor did she convey any certainties about the Mexican American vote. A contemporary observer described the "Latin American" community of Houston as "traditionally . . . poorly organized and mobilized." [33] I interpreted the choice of our itinerary and the tilt of her commentary as conveying the message that the heart of her black constituency was also the heart of her political support.

My hunch was confirmed when I asked her directly, "Who are your strongest supporters?" She replied, "My strongest supporters are the working class, the blacks, and labor, organized labor. And the people who were in my senatorial district, of course. The Fifth Ward is low income, working class and is my base of support. I grew up there, I have my law office there, and I still live there. The white businessmen who are supporting me now are late converts—very late. They support me as the least of the evils. They are not a strong base of support. They know it and I know it." Again, she described her primary constituency as "working class," a perception that allowed her to count a large component of blacks and a smaller component of whites as reliable supporters.

Her description of her supporters, unlike that of Lou Stokes, involved two groups of white people—members of "organized labor" and "white businessmen." The support of organized labor dated to her first Senate campaign. As she recalled, "They gave me support in name only when I ran [twice] for Representative. But I would say that their strong support started in my Senate race in 1966—in terms of money and votes." They were ideological allies, and her legislative accomplishments in the Texas Senate were targeted to their concerns as well as to the concerns of her center-city black citizens.

White business support came with her congressional contest. Their concerns, directly or indirectly, involved the economic "pillar" of the city—oil, gas, and petrochemicals. "Of the nation's thirty-five largest oil companies," wrote one economic historian, "most have major administrative, research, and production facilities in the greater Houston area. In addition to these giants, there are nearly five hundred other oil and gas companies and hundreds of geological firms, petroleum engineering firms, drilling contractors, geophysical contractors, supply and transportation companies, law firms, and accounting firms serving Houston's oil and gas companies."[34] These industries needed friendly representatives in Congress to help ward off the legislative efforts of frost-belt, consumer-oriented representatives to impose regulations on the industry that had made Houston the "oil capital of the world." White businessmen, therefore, climbed aboard in 1972.

Along with the white businessmen came the Houston newspapers. The *Houston Chronicle* and the *Houston Post*, each with a circulation of about 290,000, were very conservative. Neither paper had ever endorsed a black candidate when the *Houston Chronicle* and the *Houston Post* broke the mold with their 1972 endorsements of "Miss Jordan."[35] There were no countervailing black newspapers to match the *Call and Post* in Cleveland. For her, it was not a congenial media climate in which to work.

Long before either the unions or the businessmen tendered her their support, Jordan had depended on the support of another predominantly white group—the Harris County Democrats. This unofficial club was a crucial organizational element of her constituency context. As described by one political scientist, they were "an alliance of white liberals, unions, blacks, and Mexican Americans . . . grounded organizationally in ideological zeal, ethnic solidarity, money from small contributors and liberal angels, and the efforts of CIO block workers."[36] They were not the official, nationally recognized Democratic Party organization. They were the liberal and labor wing of a badly divided party, a faction whose nominees were strenuously opposed by a conservative faction in the decisive Democratic primary. The Harris County Democrats were the group through which Jordan had to make her political way. They were the group that tapped her, early on, to speak for the Democratic Party and, later, financed her race for state representative—in a countywide, 80 percent white constituency.

From the beginning of her career, therefore, she had to work with, and appeal to, white politicians as well as white voters. She had to work out black–white connections that Lou Stokes never faced. He could ignore the white community. She could not. He could appeal unreservedly to racial identity and racial symbolism. She could not. He could rally the black community to go to war with the Democratic Party. She could not. He could, in short, adopt the black community as the sole object of his representational strategy. She could not.

EARLY NEGOTIATIONS AND EXPERIENTIAL LEARNING

Barbara Jordan and Louis Stokes faced one common constituency problem: that their personal political interests were not the same as the interests of the local Democratic politicians who operated within their districts. For both Jordan and Stokes, therefore, the most important negotiating and learning experiences of their careers resulted from their efforts to cope with this problem. And in neither case were their trial-and-error adjustments easy, smooth, or quick. In both cases, the local parties were white-dominated. So both of their negotiating histories and their experiential learning developed out of their dealings with white politicians.

Stokes's negotiating sequences developed within a partisan and organizational context inherited from his brother—a citywide Democratic Party organization unfriendly to blacks and an all-black counterorganization of which Stokes was the appointed leader. Over time, he learned how to protect and preserve his leadership of his extra-party organization, while at the same time working out manageable relationships with Cleveland's official party hierarchy. Jordan's negotiating experiences, on the other hand, developed out of her search for a personally supportive constituency *within* the Harris County Democratic Party. Over time, she learned how to pursue and solidify her political career, while at the same time developing manageable, working relationships with a key party faction. Eventually, the contrasting negotiating postures of Stokes and Jordan—one from outside the party, the other from inside the party—made each Representative, *the* leading black politician in a major American city.

Barbara Jordan's problems surfaced early, during the "travel talk" of our district tour. And it centered on the "white liberals" who dominated the

Harris County Democrats. In my notes, I wrote: "My first real rapport came when we were riding along and [her campaign aide] was expounding negatively on the 'white liberals.' I said, 'The trouble with them is they think they have the truth.' And BJ almost shouted [for her], 'You're absolutely right! How did you know that?' 'I live with them,' I said."

The next evening at the AFL-CIO candidates' night, the top staffer, who had given me the tour, passed me a note. "The Anglo lady in red and white that just came in is Billie Carr, our great white liberal that is going to save black Houston." And I noted that the aide "echoed this theme at least ten times during the day—her disgust with white liberals who wanted to rush in and tell the blacks how to save themselves." That evening, Jordan's campaign manager dropped in at the headquarters and, in Barbara's presence, ridiculed the League of Women Voters—a white liberal bastion. The next evening, as several of her finance committee members sat around in headquarters gossiping, Jordan admonished, "Now, we don't want to expose Dick to any of these knee-jerk liberals." Barbara Jordan was a liberal, but a "knee-jerk," "white liberal" she was not. It was an important distinction in her thinking and in the thinking of her small "personal constituency."[37]

The same conclusion—and its implications for her constituency negotiations—is suggested by Jordan's biographer and is fleshed out in Jordan's own autobiography. When she first ran for state representative, her main advisor had been a white "liberal lawyer"—a leader of the Harris County Democrats. He was the person who persuaded her to run and the person with whom she worked "most closely." When she lost in 1962, she felt that "[I] had been used to get black people to vote and had not been helped among white voters in return. . . . those fine people, I thought, all the Harris County Democrats, they had me come to their teas and coffees in their area in the southwest part of town, and the people would come to hear me and be very polite. But they didn't give me their votes. The votes were just not there from these fine white people." She kept on, however, laying political groundwork. "I continued to go around and speak . . . and meet people. . . . I made speeches for everybody because I was trying to get myself known locally."[38]

In 1964 she decided to run again, but against a different, more vulnerable opponent—a choice available to her because of the countywide "place system," whereby all twelve Harris County slots allotted to the Texas House were filled by holding twelve *separate*, head-to-head countywide elections.[39] Her liberal lawyer advisor assured her, however, that she could win in a rematch with her previous opponent. So she followed his advice, changed her decision, and lost again.

Afterward, she wrote that, when the advisor called her on election night to say, "'Well, we've got the analysis for you,' I snapped at him: 'I've got the analysis for you. I didn't win.'" For the advisor, it was liberal politics as usual. "The mood, the credo of the inner circle of the Harris County Democrats then," wrote Jordan's coauthor, "could be summed up in the words attributed to longtime liberal spokeswoman Billie Carr: 'It's not always a matter of winning; there's nothing wrong with losing.'"[40] That was *not* Barbara Jordan's credo.

"I did not like losing," she wrote. "I intended to devote my full attention to figuring out a way to succeed. And the first thing I knew was that it was not to let anybody else get inside my head. It was not to let anybody else make the decisions again." "I wasn't going to go to their teas if they were not voting for me at the polls."[41] It was a declaration of independence from her white liberal sponsors. It attenuated her connections with them. And, as such, it was *the* defining decision of her career as a constituency-wide negotiator.

In winning her 1966 race for the state Senate, Jordan gained control of her destiny. But it was the law, not the activity of the white liberal Harris County Democrats that was decisive. In her 1962 and 1964 defeats, the electoral rules—the head-to-head place system and the countywide, largely white electorate—had been stacked against her. In 1965 the state courts—pursuant to Supreme Court one-person, one-vote rulings—ordered the creation of equitable state legislative districts. Jordan found herself sitting in a state Senate district that was based in her Fifth Ward neighborhood and was 38 percent black. Moreover, in her 1962 and 1964 contests, she had carried every black precinct in the new district.

Before she could run, however, she had to do something Lou Stokes never had to do. She had to take on, head-to-head, an incumbent—a liberal, white (and angry) state representative who had been elected countywide and, in a sense, already "represented" the district. She did this, displaying the same strategic insight that Lou Stokes expressed in defense of his Caucus—that no one gave up power willingly and that African Americans would have to, in his words, "seize power." "There are no instances in history," said Jordan, "where people voluntarily relinquish or give you a gift of power. Power has to be seized."[42] As for her own desire for power, she took the straightforward view that "one who feels that power is distasteful and to be disdained ought not to be in politics."[43]

She still needed supportive white politicians and white voters. But this time, the whites she needed were not affluent liberals, but blue-collar workers and organized labor unions. And she quite naturally advocated policies that could unify black and white working-class voters.

A vote analysis after her 1966 victory confirmed two results of her three successive negotiating battles with her prospective constituents. First, she had become unusually popular with the black electorate, having drawn the highest participation rate among registered black voters out of ten Democratic primary contests in the county—a 42 percent proportion, for example, compared to 29 percent in Curtis Graves's state representative race. Second, as the income level of voters declined, her support level increased.[44] A black and white, working-class, low-income coalition undergirded her nearly two-to-one primary victory in 1966 and her unopposed victory in 1968. The white liberals stayed with her, but the terms of their negotiated relationship had changed. This time, wrote her coauthor, she, not they, decided such matters as where to place her campaign headquarters—in her own backyard. And "this time, she didn't send white liberals to make her contacts with the newspapers."[45] In this case, she had learned *not* to do "this time" what she had done "last time."

The necessary condition of Barbara Jordan's election victory, of course, was the change in the election rules. The sufficient condition, however, was her six years of continuous constituency-building activity, through personal appearances, in season and out, during which she built up a strong personal following in the black community and a labor-based following in the white community.

"The political, social, ethnic, and religious organizations which . . . call on her incessantly as principal speaker, honored guest, or particularly in politics—as a fence-mender, fire extinguisher, or pep leader," wrote one local observer, "are so numerous it is doubtful that even she knows them all. Yet she responds to every summons, accepts every invitation that she possibly can."[46] "I know I don't have to accept all these invitations," she said, "but I like to. I enjoy it."[47] Her personal "permanent campaign" put her in a position, in 1966, to accomplish her dominant goal of inside, institutional influence. Whether her ambition would carry her to further positions of influence would depend on her performance in the Texas legislature.

Her declaration of independence from the white liberals had major consequences for her institutional behavior in Austin. When the "strategist of the [Texas] Senate liberals" sought to organize the eleven of them as a group inside the legislature, he noted that Jordan withheld her allegiance. "Barbara kind of held back, right from the beginning," he said. "She would come to meetings and talk, but she always made it real clear that we were not to speak for her." And Jordan's biographer commented, "Jordan made it clear to [this leader] and the other liberals that she would never merely be a part of their group, no matter how philosophically close she might feel to the liberals. After her two losing races for the legislature on the liberal-sponsored ticket, she had decided that liberal politicians would never control her fate again."[48] On the campaign trail in 1972, I was hearing and feeling the reverberations of that critical decision.

CONSTITUENCY CONNECTIONS: THE CAMPAIGN

Given the primacy of every legislator's electoral goals, it is not surprising that discussions with political scientists about representation quickly gravitate toward their election campaigns. It may be the campaign they are currently engaged in; it may be the previous one; it may be their most problematic one. But they cannot entertain the question of linkage very long without referring to some campaign-related activity or influence or strategy outcome. The campaign is the time when their constituency contacts are most concentrated, most emotional, and most consequential. The actual campaign may be only the tip of a representational iceberg, only the culmination of previous efforts. Nonetheless, campaign activity seems to be most memorable and, therefore, the most available experience when answering questions about constituency connections.

My discussion of Barbara Jordan's representational activity is hampered by the relative paucity of firsthand observation. But, given that limitation, it is probably optimal that my one period of observation coincided with a crucial election campaign.

The constituency connections I observed on the campaign trail came from seven of Barbara Jordan's presentations to seven different audiences in seven different settings. They were: three presentations to black neighborhood groups, one presentation to a black high school assembly, one presentation to a racially mixed labor group, and two radio presentations, one an interview and one a debate with her opponent. In the five face-to-face meetings, she was reconnecting with people who already knew her as their incumbent state senator, giving them reassurance and reinforcing their strong support. They were politically involved people and part of her existing primary constituency. Her two media presentations were efforts to connect with a broader reelection constituency.

The emotional highlight of her campaign had occurred several months before I arrived. Former President Lyndon Johnson—whose political goals were very much the same as hers and with whom she had enjoyed "a warm, affectionate, even adoring relationship" since 1968—came to her kickoff fund-raising dinner to offer support and praise.[49] Now, in May, she was nearing the end of her effort—but still running. "You have to like campaigning," she said, comparing herself to other Texas politicians. "I think people know whether or not you like to campaign. Probably, it can be cultivated. But some people come on too much like politicians and that turns people off." From the beginning of her political career, she had tried to speak wherever she was asked. That is what she enjoyed, and that is what I watched her do.

It was a campaign without a written plan. "We don't have any strategy," she said. "I just run. At first, we tried to plan a grand strategy, the group of us, but it doesn't work out that way. I'm not that organized. And the campaign isn't predictable either. Things just happen day-by-day." With respect to her several presentations, the one detectable strategy was never to mention her opponent or to confront any of his charges on her own initiative. It was the strategy of a strong front-runner.

Back in the campaign office, where I helped out off and on, the strategy of playing to her strength among black voters was obvious. The policy on mailing out her literature, for example, made these priorities clear. A letter contrasting Jordan and Graves, together with a sample ballot, listing all polling places, went to the designated "black" precincts on a "get them out at all costs" basis. When they needed emergency help with these mailings, several Teamsters, the source of her biggest single financial contribution, answered her call and came to the office in the evening to help her get over the crunch.[50] By contrast, people in the Anglo precincts received only a copy of the *Houston Chronicle*'s flattering, first-ever endorsement of Jordan. And these letters had been farmed out to a professional firm on a "do what you can before election" basis—very different strokes for very different folks.

In the black precincts, she was behaving in a protectionist manner. Her campaign manager had been organizing black precincts since 1956 and was doing so again.[51] Only in the Anglo precincts, with the *Chronicle* endorsement, were her efforts expansionist. And the assumption was that white voters would prefer her to her opponent no matter what. A white campaigner called Jordan "the universal candidate." "I've never heard her say anything bad about the whites." Even her campaign leaders, who wanted their candidate to ignore the affluent whites, acknowledged that Jordan herself thought it "important" to have "the whites around Rice University" on her side. Her demonstrable ability to work with whites was, after all, basic to her representational strategy.

Office conversation about her opponent, Curtis Graves, centered on his militancy, thus provoking ongoing discussions about a strategy for dealing with him. The tactical question of the moment was whether or not Jordan should go where the largest pocket of militant blacks were located—among the students at all-black Texas Southern University. Her student volunteers argued "yes," that she should "respond" to Graves, who had recently talked at TSU and "cut her up" as a tool of the establishment—as not being sufficiently black. The older campaign group argued that Graves's appearance was not worth a response. "Curtis Graves had a demonstration," said one, "and about fifteen people showed up—Bill Lawson [an activist minister] and six others. There were more newsmen than demonstrators." In the headquarters, this discussion—and its implications for Jordan's nonconfrontational strategy—continued.

Finally, Jordan put the question to her top aide. "Do you think we should schedule something at TSU now that Curtis Graves has been in the pit?" "Maybe," said the aide, "if all the Houston colleges have a joint meeting. Otherwise, I think it will be a big waste of time." This internal debate seemed to signal the presence, in the district, of a more radical liberal political viewpoint. Those who espoused it would, they believed, support Curtis Graves regardless of anything she could do. I do not know what she decided.

Her nonpersonalized, nonconfrontational, properformance campaign strategy fits nicely with David Canon's "supply-side" theorizing and his predictions—first, about the effects of district makeup on who runs for office, and second, about the effects of who runs for office on the election outcome. When two black candidates run, he argues, in a district that is at least 30 percent white, the candidate who campaigns more on the basis of commonalities among blacks and whites will defeat a candidate who campaigns more on the basis of differences between blacks and whites.[52] That captures a lot of the arguments about campaign strategy within the Jordan camp.

In Canon's terms, Jordan, with her "working-class" constituency perception, was the black and white "commonalities" candidate. Graves was the "differences" candidate. Her strategy was to assume that she, as the only commonalities candidate, would capture the white vote no matter what. Therefore, she waged her campaign elsewhere—in the black community. The centerpiece of her commonality campaign was legislative competence and the ability to get things done. In Canon's terms, her strategy—of ignoring the whites and fighting it out in the black community—was the predictably appropriate one. And it had the predictable outcome.

Hers was not a person-to-person, handshaking campaign. I asked her about shopping areas. "I do some of that," she said. "But that kind of campaigning does not come easy to me, just walking up and shaking hands. I always feel I'm interfering. I did do some on Monday. I sponsor a Little League team, and fifteen of them went with me with their 'Barbara Jordan' shirts on. People will take things from children. They would ask people if they would let them put a bumper sticker on their car. *Then* I would go up and shake hands." She was not a natural at close-up retail politicking. Indeed, journalists who watched her often took particular notice of her inability or unwillingness to make "social chat" or to "get out and press the flesh." [53]

She did, however, convey the strong sense to her constituents that "she is one of us." But she did it at a distance by speaking to groups. That was her obvious political strength, and that was the kind of campaigning she really enjoyed. From her earliest days in politics, she had always talked to any group that asked, on almost any subject they wished. "I speak in a church every chance I get. I've been averaging five each Sunday—in and out." "How do you choose what groups to speak to?" "Numbers count for a lot of it," she answered. "But if some of your strongest supporters ask you to come, well, you just have to make that one—like the people in Settegast. . . . If there's time, you try to make them all." The meetings she "made" when I was there were as follows:

SETTEGAST

One evening after an 8:30 meeting with the AFL-CIO, she drove across the city for forty-five minutes to the small outlying community of Settegast—an area that had been in her state Senate district, but which was *not* in her new congressional district. It was a trip motivated by past attachment and not by future calculation. "Settegast is a low-income community and has some of my very strongest supporters," she explained. "And they vote out there. I hated to lose them, but [in the redistricting] I let Bob Eckhardt have whatever he wanted."

It was very likely, she said, that the meeting would be over by the time we got there. But when we arrived, at ten o'clock, the group [about 20] was still there, waiting. "We knew she would come," said the moderator. "She said she would, and that's why we've been keeping the meeting going." When she spoke, Jordan told them that "the worst thing" about the redistricting was that Settegast was not in her new district. There was a murmur of surprise— which she quickly squelched, "I'll still be your representative. And I want you to think of me, always, as your Representative. I belong to you." That was the essence of her very brief talk. Like Louis Stokes and his "national constituency," she was reaching out—in a smaller way—as a "surrogate" representative to people who were like her but lived beyond the district.[54]

"I'm in the fight of my life," she told them. "And when I get there, I'm going to work hard for you. I'll be a congressman [sic] you can be proud of." Black interests and black policy connections were assumed—not articulated. The talk was about personal connections, about her close identification with her listeners, about connections based on loyalty, pride, and trust.

"Did you see their faces light up when I said I would still be their representative?" she said afterward. And she added, "When you see people that enthusiastic and that devoted to you, you know how wrong Curtis Graves is when he goes around saying that I'm not with the folks. Of course I am. I can feel it in a meeting like that." After the meeting, a man came up to me and said, "I could listen to her talk all night on the subject of mumblety-peg. She speaks so beautifully. And the thing is, that whatever she says—it's believable. She's believable." Despite the fact that she was not their formal representative, I took the people of Settegast to be a perfect surrogate for her political base—the ordinary black citizens of Houston. And she was their trusted, "believable," and reassuring representative.

PRECINCT WORKERS: THIRD WARD

The next night she met with more of the same loyal, "fight, bleed, and die" supporters. They were twenty members of the Democratic Committee of the 193rd Precinct in the District's Third Ward. My notes describe the setting as "a large, old ramshackle house that once was an elegant mansion. We sat in what probably was the living room—broken venetian blinds on the windows, high ceilings with flaking paint. The front door was nearly all down to bare wood. Yet the brick building sat on a large lot and had a large porch. Her talk was a good rousing pep talk to Democratic precinct workers . . . evoking ties of sentiment and asking for [their] hard work for the future."

She began by assuring them that, notwithstanding the new district lines, they could still vote for her. Then she moved to the historic significance of their vote. "This can be a real breakthrough for Texas," she began. "Not in over one hundred years has a black person from the South sat in the House of Representatives . . ." To which a woman up front quickly added, "and *never* a black woman." Everyone nodded and several repeated, "Yes, never a black woman."

As she made her personal appeal, there was perpetual nodding and agreeing. "I could lay out my record, but I know I don't have to. You know I've worked hard. ["Yes, yes."] You know I've gotten the job done. ["Yes, yes."] You know the bills I've passed. ["Yes, yes."] You know I've done my best for you. ["Yes, yes."] I want you to help me." ["We'll help you."] "I'll do a good job for you. I'll make you proud of me. I'll work hard. You know me. You know I've worked for you. I might not always have been right," she added, "but I've done my best. I've spoken out for what I thought was right. . . . I'm not going to Washington and turn things upside down in a day. I'll only be one of 435. But the 434 will know I'm there. . . . You don't want someone who just talks; you want someone who will get the job done."

She closed with a get-out-and-work pep talk. "Mrs. _____, do you remember how we sang 'I'm glad I made it' in 1966 [her first victory]? Well, it's been a long time since we've sung that song. But with your help, we'll sing it again on May 6. . . . I know a lot of people want to help me and want me to win. But they don't count ideas and thoughts—they count *votes*. So work this precinct and do the block work and motivate the lazy folks, the people who don't want to vote, who can't come to the precinct meetings. Motivate them!"

The meeting slowly unraveled into discussions about who had authority to invite her to their church next Sunday and what was the most advantageous placement of lawn signs. After a couple of parting, one-on-one discussions, we left. These people, I noted, "were clearly her people." And she was every inch "their representative"—doing a good job as "one of us," a much-admired person and an important source of black pride. Again, black group interests and black policy connections were assumed, and the personal connections—candidate outreach and supporter trust—were asserted and strengthened.

PHYLLIS WHEATLEY HIGH SCHOOL: FIFTH WARD

Phyllis Wheatley was Barbara Jordan's high school, the pride of the Fifth Ward, where she had been a champion orator and debater, president of the Honor Society, and "Girl of the Year." There was an extra reason for audience hero worship when she returned "home" to speak to a senior-class assembly. Jordan spoke directly to the students, using her own career to inspire them. She was a celebrity. As with Lou Stokes, there was evident "black pride" in her celebrity, and she was taking advantage of it.

> When I was first elected to the state Senate in 1966, do you think that those men wanted me, welcomed me? They did not. They were scared to death that this black woman was going to come in and mess up their playhouse. And I did! [Cheers!] One of the most conservative old senators wouldn't even speak to me—not in simple sentences with a subject and predicate. If he had to speak to me, he would come over and grunt—or groan. And I was supposed to make sense out of what he said. That was 1967. Now, two months ago in 1972, I was elected president pro tem of the Senate, the highest honor the Senate has in its power to bestow, and third in line for the governorship. If Governor Preston Smith and Lieutenant Governor Barnes were to die tomorrow, Barbara Jordan would become the governor of Texas! [Cheers!] Who elected me to that high post? The same men—thirty members of the Texas Senate—in secret Democratic caucus. Eight other senators were eligible, but they chose me, unanimously. And one of them got up, seconding my nomination, spread his arms wide, looked across the chamber and said, "What can I say? Black is beautiful." [Cheers!] That's what happened between 1961 and 1972. And that's why I say, get out there and work! Change their minds, work on their attitudes, on their psyches. Chip away at their minds, little by little.

Her theme was that students need faith in themselves and confidence in themselves and that, though their life would be hard and there would be a great deal of racism to overcome, they could succeed. And she told them that when they did, "America will be for you the land of the free and the home of the brave, . . . you can recite the Pledge of Allegiance and mean it, . . . [and] you can recite the Declaration of Independence and have it apply." She concluded, "Don't let me down."

In this presentation, as in her first two presentations to an all-black audience, the symbolic connections that derive from descriptive representation, racial identity and racial pride, were evoked as the underpinnings of her constituency relationships. So long as she was seen as a leader who was also "one of us," it would be *assumed* that her actions in the legislature were taken in pursuit of their interests.

Questions from the Wheatley audience centered on their upcoming choice at the polls. Jordan was asked why her old Senate district had been changed from a black- to a white-dominated seat—one implication being that she had traded it away in exchange for her congressional district. Curtis

Graves was making that case. She denied it, and she explained the change as a result of the enemies they shared.

> There was some racism involved, but it was mostly economic. The big corporations, the oil and gas and insurance companies, were afraid because this year the Texas Senate came within one vote of passing a corporation tax—a tax on their big profits. So these big men, these big businesses were so frightened they decided to redistrict the Senate to make it more conservative. The reason was money—the green folding stuff. That's why the blacks got redistricted out of a seat in the Senate.

She also said that Graves had once told her that he had no interest in the state Senate seat.

Other questions revealed some confusion among a black electorate faced with an unprecedented choice between two such high-level elected black officials. To those worriers, she answered, "Black people have to grow up. You can't cop out on the race issue anymore. White people have been running against each other for a hundred years. Black people can expect to do it more and more. And this means we will have to confront the issues and talk about the issues." And that, in fact, is just what Jordan did in her three other presentations to voters.

ORGANIZED LABOR: HARRIS COUNTY

Because of her strong prolabor record in the state Senate, Jordan had won the endorsement of Harris County's COPE—the Committee on Political Education of the AFL-CIO. She went, with the other endorsees, to acknowledge labor support and solicit their continued help in the campaign. It was the only one of her face-to-face meetings with a racially mixed group. "If organized labor, which is so helpful and important financially" asks you to come, she had said, "you have to make it." Organized labor was an integral, active part of her reelection constituency and, as such, basic to her representational calculations—more so than organized labor ever was to the calculations of Lou Stokes.

Her presentation had the same themes as the others, "I'll work hard for you, . . . I'll be a congressman [sic] you can be proud of." But the representational connection between herself and this group was substantive, not symbolic. She spoke less in the language of personal and emotional ties than in her first three talks and more in the ideological and quid-pro-quo language of bread-and-butter electoral and legislative politics. "I'll work for you and your interests. I'll be your voice," she began. "You know from my record that I support labor. I am your friend. Ninety-four percent of the time you are right. On the 1 percent [*sic*] when I think you're wrong, I'll tell you." Whereupon she blasted the Nixon economic policy as "bad for you because corporations are making it at the expense of the ordinary working person."

Then she turned to the exigencies of the moment. "Send me to Washington," she said. "You've got to get me there. You know I will work hard. I'm asking you for a promotion." And looking ahead she said, "The Texas delegation needs Barbara Jordan. I'll be the best congressman in the Texas delegation. I'll be a congressman you can be proud of." Every one of these themes drew enthusiastic applause—so much so that the next speaker publicly bemoaned his bad luck at being slated to follow her at the microphone.

"Well, now you've seen organized labor—all of it," she said as we left. "They've been a big help. In the beginning, in 1962, they were less than enthusiastic. But since then, they have been fine supporters, strong supporters." I asked her whether any of the other labor-endorsed candidates could bring votes to her. "None of them can help me, but I can help some of them. I'm more help to them than they are to me." It was a mutually beneficial constituency connection.

She volunteered that her interests and the interests of the AFL-CIO might not always coincide—that they had privately asked her for a commitment, whereas she wanted flexibility.

> The state chairman was there, and he asked if I would be a member of the local welcoming committee for Hubert Humphrey when he comes to Texas. I don't want to commit myself. I don't have a [Democratic presidential] candidate. But labor loves Hubert Humphrey. Oh, how they love him! I shudder to think of a rerun between Humphrey and Nixon. But if he gets it, I'll be in there with all the rest. I'm going to be at the convention, and I'm a member of the credentials committee. I want to be free in making decisions there. Once you commit yourself, people put you in a slot and you're isolated. You lose your freedom to move inside the party. I want to keep that freedom.

She was doubtless expressing another strategic lesson of inside, institutional influence: if a project is not your own, do not commit too early. She did not, in the end, support Humphrey.[55] But the explication of her dilemma had come from a strategic politician whose first thought would be to maximize her own influence within almost any organization of which she was a part.

She also hinted at a second problematical commitment within the Democratic Party. One of the speakers had drawn cheers when he said he had opposed "the dirty thirty" in Austin. After the meeting, she explained that the label referred to a group of liberal, reform-minded Texas legislators who had attacked other Texas public officials for their involvement in a bank scandal. "Newspapers called them the dirty thirty, and they were proud of it," Jordan said, with what I noted as "disdain." "They took it as an honor, got together, and endorsed candidates of their own—candidates who promised reform and who, if elected, would eliminate all scandal from Texas forever and so forth." One of the "dirty thirty" leaders, it turned out, was now the Democratic candidate for governor, a woman beloved by the Harris County liberal Democrats. And Jordan, true to her early lessons, had balked at endorsing her.

The Harris County Democrats, I heard later, had pressured Jordan. They told her that, at best, they were going to remain neutral in her race against Graves but that they would oppose her outright unless she gave her endorsement to the gubernatorial candidate. Jordan finessed her dilemma by endorsing "the entire [county] ticket."[56] Two years later, when asked whether she would support the same woman for governor, she said, "I'm not supporting anybody for any race except Barbara Jordan for reelection. . . . I have a rule of thumb. When I am a candidate and I am on the ballot, I stick to my own campaign."[57] The independence lessons that she had drawn from her experiences in the early 1960s still shaped her constituency negotiations in the 1970s.

AFRICAN AMERICAN RADIO STATION

The most policy-oriented of all her encounters during my visit was her radio interview at the tiny, fourth-floor alternative radio station, Pacifica. She was interviewed by the dashiki-dressed proprietor of an African American clothing store. Anticipating a session dominated by her opponent's more militant viewpoints, she predicted, as we rode the creaking elevator, that "I'll get cut up." This event was a prime example of her readiness to speak wherever she was asked. It promised no electoral benefits.

The host invited her to name "the issues in the district." With explanations, she cited three: the economy (inflation, prices, and taxes), health care (the delivery of health care to the poor), and jobs. Among Houston's black activists—many of whom, such as the aforementioned Bill Lawson, were vocal Graves supporters—institution-building in the black ghettos was a primary theme.[58] The interviewer pressed her on questions of community control of local institutions, such as police and schools. They jousted back and forth. To his suggestion of a local "vigilante" police force, she demurred in favor of a Julian Bond proposal that black citizens work together and organize themselves to help get criminals off the street. To his suggestion of local control of schools, she asked, "Where is the money going to come from? I'm going to take a good hard look around to make sure we have the financial resources before I endorse community control of the schools."

But she ended on a preemptive positive note by asserting the "need for community control of cultural activities." "Nobody else can control black culture, because nobody else has it," she said. "Only we have it. It's uniquely ours and a source of our pride. Only we can produce its beauty, and only we know its substance." The interviewer then took a couple of listener calls. A Mr. Martinez complained about escalating charges for employment assistance, and he ended with praise for Jordan, saying, "I would lay down my life for her."

We left. She was not "cut up"—just bewildered. "I couldn't understand where he was coming from. I couldn't figure him out. Of course, nobody is listening. I could have advocated communism on that program." With respect to the schools, she added, "People wouldn't know what to do with the money." Then, a touch of whimsy. "What was that man's name? Mr. Martinez? Didn't he say he would lay down his life for me? Let's find Mr. Martinez. We've got to find Mr. Martinez."

Of greater contextual interest to me than the radio program itself was its venue in the black-owned Atlanta Life Insurance Building, which we entered through the Temple Barbershop on the ground floor. We stopped to talk with the barbershop's owner. "The shop," I wrote in my notes,

> is operated by George Nelson, an old man. It was piled with papers and litter. An old, toothless crony was sitting in there gossiping with Mr. Nelson. It was the exact antithesis of any barbershop I have ever been in. The creaky elevator outside was operated by some relative of Mr. Nelson's. [Her greeting was the same one she used with everyone, "Are you all right?"] BJ asked Mr. Nelson what he'd heard, how things were going. It turned out that George Nelson is a member of Jordan's Campaign Finance Committee. I saw him at the campaign office twice—once stuffing envelopes and once conferring with the committee. He's the source of her strength—black, independent, loyal, elderly, and community-minded.

The Finance Committee members I eventually met, chosen "for the most part" by the candidate, were: a male M.D. as its chairman, the Temple Barbershop owner, a male pharmacy owner, a female beautician, a female school teacher, a female retiree, a male member of the International Longshoremen's

Association—all black—and a white male lawyer. George Nelson and his colleagues, I assumed, were prototypes of her strongest connections in the black community.

CIVIC IMPROVEMENT ASSOCIATION: FOURTH WARD

Before I ever saw the two candidates together, the differing thrusts of their campaigns were clearly visible in their literature. Barbara Jordan's financial advantage—she spent $55,000 and he spent $5,000—was reflected in the contrast between her slick professional, multicolor foldout with eleven pictures, and Curtis Graves's self-typed, black-and-white mimeographed, one-picture, one-fold flyer.[59] Her brochure and her mailer highlighted her influence-intensive representational strategy with such language as "effective," "leader," "getting things done," "get the job done," and "get needed legislation passed." His flyer used words like "shamefully inadequate," "crying need," and "mess" to highlight local problems such as health care, housing, and welfare. And he promised to "stand up for you and fight" against "the money manipulating Texas Democratic machine" and "the uncaring downtown powers." He saw her as the handmaiden of interests outside the black community. She saw him as an ineffective loudmouth unable to deliver any help to the black community.

My one brief glimpse of Curtis Graves came during a candidates' night meeting sponsored by the Civic Improvement Association and held at Rose of Sharon Church in the Fourth Ward. Jordan made a short, uneventful, and nonmemorable appearance, after which I listened to Graves pose his basic question to the thirty or so prospective voters in attendance: "Do you want your leaders picked for you by outsiders or do you want to pick them for yourselves? Think about it." Unable to make an issue out of Jordan's qualifications for the job, he was making another familiar all-purpose charge—that she was "out of touch" with her constituents.

"What did you think of him?" she asked afterward. "He's trying to paint you as an outsider," I replied. "That's one of the things he's trying to do," she agreed. "But it's ridiculous. Anybody can see that. I don't have to answer that. Maybe I'm giving people too much credit. Maybe I'll be sorry. But I don't think so." "When he spoke," she continued, "I kept trying to catch his eye. I tried, but he wouldn't look at me. He's shifty-eyed." I asked her where his support was coming from. "I don't know, and that's what bothers me. Every day, he says something, and I think the campaign is lost. I guess he has pockets here and there."

I knew from a conversation with her two top campaign staffers that they could think of only one precinct that Graves could conceivably win. It was, they said, a Catholic-dominated precinct made favorable for Graves, a Catholic, because he was being helped by the church and by a precinct leader who had been turned against Jordan by "the white liberals." But Jordan would have none of this outspoken optimism. When I mentioned a recent poll showing her at 50 percent, Graves at 10 percent, with 40 percent undecided, she clammed up: "I don't have much faith in polls." Entering the debate, therefore, she seemed confident, yet fearful of overconfidence.

RADIO DEBATE

On the last afternoon of my visit, the two candidates squared off in a KXYZ radio debate.[60] In her responses to her opponent's attack, Barbara Jordan highlighted and clarified her idea of representation.

Her opponent's debate strategy was to go on the attack immediately, stay there, and, thus, control the debate. He began by emphasizing the need for a "super-congressman" who "cares about the problems in the district," who will "really service people who have not gotten services" in housing, zoning, and health, who will be "totally controlled by the [black] community"—in short, "a person with guts, who will speak up and not someone whose voice has been compromised at every corner."

Jordan chose to stress the diversity of the district and broaden the frame of reference. "The people who operate downtown Houston don't live in the district," she said. "The people who do live in the district need a voice that can span the diversity of the Eighteenth District. . . . Moreover, this election will be a real first for Texas, and eyes will be focused on it. It's very important that the person elected express the problems and work for their solution."

Graves persisted, "The question is, who will control the voice and the action of the first black congressman? Either they can choose a person who has been compromised and who has accepted money from the conservative wing of the party, or they can choose a free voice. . . . I don't think that can be said of the person the establishment has decided to run in the race." When Jordan protested the idea that she "could be bought," he interrupted. "There's a history. When your people carry [conservative gubernatorial candidate] Ben Barnes signs through supermarkets, that's a history of selling out the black man. People are tacking up your signs and Ben Barnes's signs—the same folks. What's cooking?"

The moderator asked each candidate where their money came from. Graves: "The vast majority of my money comes from black sources, black physicians, dentists, and businessmen." Jordan: "The largest portion of my money has come from organized labor." The rest has come from a "broad spectrum . . . eight pages of contributions," she said, by ordinary people giving as little as "fifty cents."

The moderator asked Graves whether he was "a rabble-rouser." Graves cited a number of his protest activities, saying after each one, "If that was rabble rousing, then I want to be called a rabble-rouser. . . . When 'the man' couldn't think of anything to call Adam Clayton Powell, he called him flamboyant and controversial. I don't mind being called flamboyant and controversial."

Jordan countered by posing a different question—her framing of the representational question: "Do you want someone who does the talk and stirs the pot and then, after the pot is stirred, leaves it? Or do you want someone who gets in there to see what solution can be worked out, what legislative result can be produced?" Her mailer to black precincts had levied a harsh attack on Graves's ineffectiveness in Austin—one bill passed out of forty-three proposed—but she eschewed explicit attacks in the debate. The best kind of representation, she was saying, would come from the accomplishments of an institutionally influential representative.

"Everything in this town is cranked up," Graves asserted. "The conservative Democratic Party, the corporations, the establishment are cranked up to elect Barbara Jordan. That's what's coming down, and the black community should know that." Jordan acknowledged seeking endorsements but said that voters "will decide in the quietude of the voting booth. . . . they will not be swayed by the endorsement bag."

Graves charged that, from her Senate position, she deliberately drew a congressional district with a large group of whites in it—a district that gave whites the balance of power—when she could have drawn a majority-black district. She answered, "We [she and Bob Eckhardt] were trying to draw a district in which a black could be elected. The district does *not* have whites as the balance of power. Mexican Americans have 10 to 15 percent of the vote. It was planned to pass muster in the courts, to make sense in the federal courts. . . . you've got to understand, it was not something I drew up and said take it or leave it. It had to be passed by the Texas Senate and the Texas House."

The combatants ended with their respective campaign themes. Graves asked, "Do the people of the Eighteenth District want a congressman who is controlled from within the community or [one] controlled from without?" And he said, "I will go to Washington uncompromised." Jordan noted that "Approximately 10 percent of the black population is unemployed, compared to 3.5 percent of the white population. We have talked more about blacks because their problems are worse, but white people should ask themselves the same question. The issue is, which of the candidates can represent the interest in the issues? Who can get on a committee, help draft and redraft legislation, persuade, cajole, and push forward the legislation?" It was a clear statement of her influence-intensive representational strategy.

"How did I do?" she asked on the way out, "a little too namby-pamby?" I said, "If you think you are well ahead, you were right not to get into charge and countercharge with Graves, which would only have given him publicity." She agreed that her nonconfrontational strategy was "deliberate," with the clear implication that my conditional premise was correct.

In the real world, the attacks of her opponent and the debate itself had zero impact. Barbara Jordan seemed to be about as solidly connected to her district by background, by policy, by her previous performance, and by constituent pride as anyone could be. Nine days after the debate, she effectively won election to Congress by winning a whopping 81 percent of the primary vote—including 90 percent of the black vote.[61] Asked to interpret this result, she said, "It shows that black people want representatives who get things done."[62] Her constituents had approved her influence-intensive representational strategy. The expansionist days of her constituency career were over.

INSTITUTIONAL CAREER AND REPRESENTATION

EARLY DAYS: THE INTERVIEW

When Barbara Jordan went to Washington, she took with her all that she had learned about goal seeking in Houston and Austin. And she intended to follow the negotiating practices that had brought her success there. She continued to believe that the best way to represent her constituents was to become influential inside the legislative institution. My postelection talk with her in January 1973 reconfirmed the dominance of her influence-intensive representational strategy.

When we met in her Washington office, Congresswoman Barbara Jordan had been a member of the House for four weeks. I congratulated her on her November election victory. "You were in on the making," she said. And "the making," it turned out, had been valuable preparation for our conversation about her institutional life. It was, however, our second and last encounter. I was never able to follow the congresswoman around at home or to ask her any of the questions I had put to Louis Stokes—questions about her votes, her legislative activity, or her constituency-related activities involving explanation, trust, or contact. Nor could I trace any subsequent developments in her representational-cum-governing relationships during the six years of her tenure.

A brief description of our early conversation, however, will strengthen the basic "findings" of my campaign-time visit to Houston. It will demonstrate how much of the strategic candidate in Houston remained within the strategic congresswoman in Washington. That linkage, in turn, lends credence to the notion that studies of institutional activity can be enriched by studies of constituency activity.

In answer to my standard "How's it going?" opening question, she immediately zeroed in on her primary concern with "getting things done"—in this case with a Democratic Congress facing a recently reelected Republican President. "It's all right, but it's nothing I'd want to do for the rest of my life—being a member of the United States House of Representatives," she began. "It's the worst of times to be a member of Congress, with everyone worrying about who has the power and about the confrontations we're supposed to be having. The old men are frustrated. They don't know what to do, and they won't do anything. Nothing will be done. And I don't see how anything can be done. [A brief discussion of the defense budget followed.] But I'm off the hook. If the leadership can't figure out how to deal with the president, then a freshman certainly can't be expected to."

One early action she had to take—an action crucial to her opportunity to "get things done"—was to secure a committee assignment. "How did you do it?" I asked.

I got out the book and looked at each committee and its jurisdiction to see which one I wanted. A number of people called me to ask me to go on Education and Labor. But I dismissed Education and Labor completely. They said there was no Texan on the committee. But there was nothing else I could add to it. There are several blacks, and the committee is loaded with liberals. So what if a person from Texas was added to the list? Then people told me that the committee's legislation is always written on the floor and never accepted—it's so lopsided. That's another reason why I didn't want that committee.

Being a lawyer and having been on the jurisprudence committee in the Texas legislature, I was interested in the Judiciary Committee, with civil rights, constitutional amendments, the administration of criminal justice. So I wrote a letter to my zone representative, Omar Burleson [Texas], whom I had never met, and one to Wilbur Mills [Chairman of the Com-

mittee on Committees] expressing my preference. Then, to weld it together, I called Lyndon Johnson and asked him to call Mr. Mills and
Mr. Burleson to put in a word in my behalf. And he did. When I went to
visit the chairman of the committee [Peter Rodino], I learned that his best
friend was Jack Valenti from Texas. So I called Jack Valenti, and he called
the chairman asking him to help me.

I just brought all these things together [arms sweeping inward in hugging motion]. I understand that when the committee met—it's supposed
to be secret, but I heard—when they got to the Judiciary Committee with
its five vacant spots, Wilbur Mills opened the discussion by saying, "Now
what are we going to do *after* we give the first spot to Barbara Jordan."
[Smile!]

In this story, her careful pursuit of inside power (compare her sophisticated
assessment of the Education and Labor Committee to that of Stokes), and
her skillful use of powerful people to help her achieve it, seemed like the application, in a new setting, of a proven pattern of behavior she had learned
inside the Texas Senate. So skillful, indeed, that Peter Rodino wrote that it
was he who invited her to become a member of his committee and claimed
her, therefore, as his "protégé."[63]

Equally familiar was her performance in the organizational meeting of
the House Democrats. There, in a major reform effort, the party voted to
subject each committee chairman—one by one—to the approval of the
party's membership. She was "happy" she said, "to be in on" a reform she
knew she was "for." But when it came to the actual vote on each one, she said
that she did not know how to vote. "So who did you talk to about it?" I asked.
And she mentioned, in order, "Bob Eckhardt, whom I trust and with whom
I almost always agree, Tip O'Neill, and Wilbur Mills."

Bob Eckhardt was the fellow Houstonian with whom she served in the
Texas legislature and with whom she negotiated their new congressional district boundaries. Tip O'Neill was the third-ranking member of the Democratic leadership. And Wilbur Mills was the most powerful Democratic committee chair in the House. In Austin, wrote her biographer, "it was second
nature for her to look for and align herself with those who had power."[64] On
Capitol Hill, too, hers was not a random choice of mentors. Her choices
were totally consistent with an early contemplation of inside influence.

Her reaction to other early choices was similarly selective and strategic.
She had, for starters, clearly planted her roots among her Texas colleagues.
"We meet for lunch once a week," she said, "and I've enjoyed that very

much. Anything they think I might want, they are only too happy to do. One of the members, Ray Roberts, said to me I was the best thing that had happened to the Texas delegation since he'd been there. 'Since you've come,' he said, 'we are looked upon very differently. We are held in much higher regard.' So I feel that I'm a helping hand in this delegation. The only one I don't have rapport with is O. C. Fisher. He's sour. Some people are just sour and he's one of them." "What about George Mahon?"(the most influential member of the delegation), I asked. "I like him. He's nice." (His opinion of her was that "I've been here forty years, and I've never known anyone to capture so quickly the response of the House.")[65]

Toward other informal institutional groupings that beckoned, she had adopted a cautious "wait-and-see" approach. One was the liberal Democratic Study Group (DSG), which had spearheaded the committee reform. She attended their December organizational meeting. "There was one very revealing vote," she recounted. "They voted against having a freshman on the DSG executive committee. These great opponents of the seniority rule, these great advocates of opening up the system wouldn't let one freshman sit on their executive committee. I thought that was very revealing. It all depends on where you sit. One of the members called me afterward to explain his vote! He assured me that he had nothing against freshmen, and he went on and on with all of his reasons. I said, 'You don't need to explain to me. I know there are always "reasons."'"

As a result, she said, "I haven't paid my dues yet. I'm going to go to a few more of their meetings and see whether it's the kind of group I want to be connected with. Until then, I'm withholding my dues." Similarly, she withheld her allegiance from a freshmen group being organized by other liberal newcomers. "Barbara Jordan is very cautious about joining," said one organizer of the group. "We've been a lot more active on reform in the DSG than Barbara Jordan and those cats." It was almost as if she was rehearsing the lessons of her negotiating history with the "white liberals" of Harris County.

After her DSG discussion, Jordan continued her many assessments, saying "and the [Congressional] Black Caucus is just as bad. They have long meetings. And they've decided they don't want a freshman as one of their officers. They feel that we should wait and learn our way around. Not one of the three of us [Jordan, Andrew Young, and Yvonne Burke] is considered qualified." Her conclusion was clear, but left unsaid.

Back in Houston, I had asked her whether she knew the members of the Congressional Black Caucus (CBC). She said she knew "most" of them and had attended their "workshop" on "Strategy for the '70s." But she was critical of their decision to exclude Shirley Chisholm from that panel because of her presidential campaign. "Shirley was right. She should have been on the panel. They muffed that one badly." [66] And she noted, too, that at the recent CBC-sponsored all-black convention in Gary, Indiana, "the Black Caucus lost control of the convention before it even started." Hers was a mixed review of the group.

In Washington she was not rushing into their embrace. Later accounts of her campaign for a committee assignment suggest an early reason for her reluctance—the intervention of the CBC in her quest for a congenial committee assignment. "They had taken it upon themselves to look after me," she wrote. They "had decided that they would ask me to request the Armed Services Committee." The goal of the CBC was to spread their members across the greatest range of committees. Lyndon Johnson, she wrote, convinced her that Judiciary would be preferable to Armed Services. His message: "You don't want to be on the Armed Services Committee. People will be cursing you from here to there, and the defense budget is always a sore spot and people don't want to spend the money. You don't want that. What you want is Judiciary. If you get the Judiciary Committee and one day someone beats the hell out of you, you can be a judge." His argument, she wrote, "made sense." [67] To someone making a personal calculation about influence, it did. To someone thinking of the CBC as an influential collectivity it might not have. CBC intervention in her decision making and her rejection of their committee recommendation was not the most auspicious beginning of an institutional relationship.

Everything Jordan said in this interview was consistent with someone following an influence-intensive representational strategy, someone who believed that the best way to represent constituents was to achieve influence inside the institution of government. Her choice of influential mentors and her pursuit of a committee assignment reflected the same power-seeking strategy she demonstrated in her Texas legislative career. In her cautious approach to the DSG, the liberal freshmen, and the CBC, she showed her determination not to replay her history with the white liberals of Harris County. The contrast between her ready attachment to the Texans in Congress and her uncertain attachment to the other groups was rooted in her nose for power and her determination to position herself in ways that would help her get things done.

While she made decisions that affected her pursuit of inside influence, she also made decisions affecting its intended beneficiaries at home. She had no intention of letting her institutional activities crowd out her constituency activities. "So far," she offered,

> I've made it back to Houston every other week. And I intend to keep that up. Some congressmen get up here and haven't the slightest idea what's going on at home. They may get reelected, but they become permanent residents of Washington, D.C. I don't want that to happen to me. I'm too important to the people of my district to come up here and stay. I want to go back and let them see me. So I'm keeping the Lyons Avenue [law] office open in addition to the office in the federal building. A lot of people still call the Lyons Avenue office. Last weekend, I spent half the time at the federal building and half the time at Lyons Avenue.

Her longtime personal secretary, she said, was serving half time at each place in order to manage the arrangement.

In keeping with her Washington ambitions, she had filled her congressional staff entirely with people who had Capitol Hill experience and connections. "I wanted people who knew their way around here. It's bad enough having a congresswoman who doesn't know her way around here, without having a lot of other Texans trying to find their way around. I'm the freshman in the office." It was an arrangement that left her in total control of all constituency-sensitive decisions, while expanding her sources of Congress-sensitive information.

Her congressional staff was chosen for its Washington experience. The selection process had begun early, she said, at Harvard University, where she, along with three other newcomers, had been invited to a postelection seminar. The seminar "gave me confidence that I could do the job. It was a nice transition, but I was commuting between Texas, Washington, and Boston, and I really couldn't afford the time. So I cut off one week." The director of the seminar was a congressional staffer, and Jordan set up shop in his Capitol Hill office at Thanksgiving time and began screening and interviewing the "three hundred to four hundred applicants." She leaned heavily on the top assistant of a fellow African American House member, Bill Clay, for her top appointment. "Bill Clay is a good congressman, and he has the kind of administrative assistant I want. So I asked him to help. I thought that anyone Clay's AA thought was good would be just what I wanted." This exercise was totally forward looking, bearing no trace of the election campaign she had recently won back home.

I raised the subject of her October election campaign against her Republican opponent. "There was no campaign," she said. "I spent $150—50 for posters and 100 for refreshments. I went wherever I was asked. And I went whenever I knew my opponent would be there, because I thought I would stand to benefit by the contrast. But nothing happened. Nobody was interested. Everyone thought I had been elected. I had to identify myself as a candidate."

Then I asked her about Curtis Graves. "Has he come to rally round?" "I have no relationship with Curtis Graves," she answered. "I've had absolutely nothing to do with him since the primary. I wouldn't go to him. He would never come to me. And I would not want him to rally round. I like it the way it is. I understand he's working up here at OEO (Office of Economic Opportunity). But I don't want to have anything to do with him. He's a nonbeing—just a something out there—as far as I am concerned." My notes described her icy reply as "controlled animosity." But it was an emotion she had held in check during my campaign visit. Spoken now, in her D.C. office, it indicated how totally she had closed the book on the campaign and had immersed herself in the career beyond. There were many links, of course, from her campaign to her legislative life, but that would be more my concern than hers.

Just before I left her office, there was one fleeting intimation of what her future career might be like. The phone rang. Her face wrinkled. "Congressman who?" she answered. As he talked, she reached for her orientation handbook to see who he was. She listened, then said, "Well, I'll let you work on me a little." When she put the phone down, she adopted a vintage southern drawl as she fumbled for his name. "Ah know he's from South Carolina. Ah never will remember the names of all these guys. But 'William Jennings Bryan Dorn,' Ah'll probably remember that. Ah suppose if Ah can carry a little light to South Carolina, Ah ought to go, don't you?" Her reputation as a speaker and her symbolism as "the first black woman" had already made her a star attraction beyond Texas—to whites as well as to blacks. The phone call signaled an end to my visit.

"So, do you have any overall impressions of this institution?" I asked. "I'll save my overall impressions till later," she said. "I haven't been here long enough and we haven't gotten into the substance of things." She spoke with the experienced caution of someone who intended to make her mark later, when "the substance of things" reached the agenda of the House.

EARLY DAYS: THE RECORD

Published accounts of Barbara Jordan's early days in the House dovetail nicely with both the tone and the substance of my interview. Jordan's first speech on the House floor, for example, flowed directly from her initial expression of pessimism, during our interview, concerning the ability of the House, as an institution, to "get things done." "In the ninety days that I've been in Congress," she declared in April, "I find that Congress is having difficulty finding its back and its voice." She helped organize a set of speeches by freshmen members who, she said, "do not expect powerlessness of Congress as an institution." And her own speech argued that President Nixon's impoundment of funds was a usurpation of congressional power.[68]

Also paralleling our interview was her "wait-and-see" stance toward the institution as a whole and her careful concentration on the building blocks of influence inside the House. In her autobiography, her first observation about that institution compares it to the Texas Senate and focuses on her personal prospects for inside influence: "I was coming from a 31-member state Senate into that 435-member House of Representatives," she wrote. "It became obvious to me that it was going to be difficult to make any impact on anybody with all of these people also trying to make an impact" (180).

Accordingly, her initial preparations were modest but basic. "The first thing was I would have to get in good with my colleagues from Texas. I would be the unique new kid on the block and I wanted to work comfortably with them" (180). The delegation had broad and effective contacts inside the institution, and she had a fine working familiarity with Texas politicians. They were her natural, constituency-related support group. And, as reported in our interview, her connecting activity was well underway.

"Next," she wrote, "I gave some thought to where I should sit on the floor of the House. My conclusion was: you can hear better on the center aisle, and you can catch the eye of the presiding officer better on the center aisle, as you are in his direct line of vision. So I decided that is where I would always sit, leaving one seat next to me on the aisle vacant, for those people who would want to stop and visit from time to time" (180–81). Later accounts emphasized her diligent attentiveness to floor business—during which time "the vacant seat" invited her colleagues to drop by and help her develop personal relationships. For someone whose dominant goal was inside influence, these calculations signaled an attentiveness to stepping-stone detail.

Taken together, these two early choices—harmless as they might seem—had repercussions inside the institution. Both choices—her fellow Texans and the aisle seat—ignored once again the expectations of her African American colleagues in the CBC. "I was accused of not wanting to sit with the liberals and the Congressional Black Caucus people, who sat to the far left," she wrote, "but that place near the center aisle seemed the most advantageous to me" (181). One CBC colleague noted, "Barbara's attitude was that she was a

Texan. Her closest colleagues were the Texans. She never sat with the rest of us" (185). In combination, her early choices signaled a distancing from the CBC that, her biographer says, "set her on a collision course," "ruffled a few feathers," "raised a few more eyebrows," and caused "resentment" and "periodic carping" among its members" (178, 179, 230, 248). Also, "It was well known that when there was a conflict between a meeting of the CBC and the Texas congressional delegation, Jordan always chose Texas" (230).

Jordan's decision not to link her legislative fate to the Congressional Black Caucus had been previewed in our interview. But what explains that decision? What explains why, by contrast, Lou Stokes should have thrown himself so completely into the life of the CBC—using his African American colleagues to help him get his committee assignment, helping to organize them into the formalized CBC, and then becoming its leader? The answer is threefold: his goals, his context, and his learning experiences.

Lou Stokes's personal goal was to protect black group interests, his context was a majority-black constituency, and his negotiating lessons had come from within his all-black organization. It was natural, therefore, for him to think in group terms inside Congress—to turn to his fellow African Americans in Congress for assistance, to join them in building an all-black organization and to find a collegial home inside that organization. The CBC was the institutional embodiment of his constituency home, "the black community."

Barbara Jordan's personal goal was to achieve influence in the legislature, her relevant constituency context included whites, and her negotiating lessons had taught her the perils of depending on organizations with their own agendas. In all these ways, her strategic calculations differed from those of Stokes. Her preference for Texas over the CBC was in no sense directed at the CBC. It was a reflection of her wariness of all informal groups lest they compromise the individual maneuvering room and the independence she deemed necessary to pursuing inside power.

To be sure, it was also a preference for the group of Democrats that her Texas legislative experience taught her would be most helpful in achieving her goal of inside influence. Her Texas colleagues kept her mindful of the black and white nature of her own supportive constituency, and they were minimally constraining in terms of a policy agenda. Given her personal goals and her pattern of legislative success in Austin, the all-white Democratic delegation provided her with a perfectly natural source of collegiality inside Congress.

Both Stokes and Jordan behaved in a path-dependent manner in their inside choices. He, following his local Twenty-first Congressional District

Caucus experience, was attracted to his fellow African Americans. She, following her local legislative experience, was attracted to her fellow Texas Democrats. As one observer noted, she "preferred a role independent of the [Congressional Black] Caucus," while he, on the other hand, became one of its three "most influential members."[69]

As her term progressed, Jordan's strategic calculations about keeping her independence extended her wariness of the CBC to wariness of the informal organization of congressional women. "I don't participate in the activist part of the feminist movement," she said.[70] And Washington commentary on this subject had a familiar ring: "The women set up an informal caucus and tried to have lunch on a regular basis, but Jordan did not always attend."[71] "Her relationship to the newly formed women's group in the House is . . . a sometime thing."[72] "She has little to do with the Women's Caucus, and has stayed away from a meeting of women representatives called to agree on a woman candidate for the Steering Committee." "She doesn't need us," said one of the women, "after Jordan herself (with her ties to the leadership) got the job."[73] Thus, she had benefited from a major DSG-sponsored reform without wholeheartedly embracing that group either. A later headline in the *Washington Post* read: "Black, Women's Groups Complain as Eloquent Texas Goes Her Own Way."[74]

"I am neither a black politician nor a woman politician," she told an interviewer in 1975. "Just a politician, a professional politician."[75] "Professional politician" was the familiar stance she had taken in Austin. Both there and in Washington, that calculated self-image must be understood as a residual effect of her trial-and-error learning experience early in her career. The lessons she learned in campaigning continued to have a major effect on her in governing. She viewed the CBC and the Women's Caucus and the DSG, I would argue, as analogous to the "white liberals" of Harris County. Her early negotiating history remained with her to the end of her congressional career. As she put it later, "In my time in Congress, I had tried to build support across the board so that I would not have to rely on that band of liberals that I had relied on in 1962 when I lost. I had tried to expand this because I wanted conservatives and business types to become supportive of Barbara Jordan and not just to tolerate her."[76]

In that same spirit, one of her earliest decisions—one not touched upon when we talked—involved her negotiations with her late-blooming, white-businessmen constituency at home. She agreed to vote with them on their topmost legislative priority in return for leeway, for "wiggle room" on all other business-related votes. "When Jordan first went to Congress," writes her biographer, "she held a meeting with key Houston bankers and industry leaders and asked them, in her most direct and forthright manner, 'What is your bottom line? What is the vote you most want from me?' They told her, 'deregulation of natural gas.' She promised them they would have her vote on that issue."[77]

Two people who worked with her explained, "It was the one thing the oil and banking people really wanted from her, and because she gave it to them, they left her alone on other votes." "She voted against the business establishment on a number of things, but she gave them this vote on natural gas. She realized that her core constituency was the Fifth Ward, the black community, but she was also very aware that she represented downtown Houston" (230). One of her African American colleagues reacted to these votes with the sweeping comment that "We just never feel Barbara's heart is with us. She's first and foremost voting the interests of Texas" (220). As a summary description of her voting behavior and her legislative activity, however, that last comment is more a reflection of unmet expectations than a matter of accuracy.

Whenever Jordan perceived that her relevant constituency on a matter comprised only African Americans, she acted as they prescribed—even if her actions hurt her larger alliances. She did this most notably when she voted against her white Texan friend, Robert Strauss, as chair of the Democratic National Committee—in response to black opposition to him (180–83).

In her first major legislative effort, she initiated in subcommittee and shepherded through the Judiciary Committee and the House a provision of the Voting Rights Act of 1975 that protected the voting rights of Mexican Americans by giving them new Justice Department protections. It was an inclusionary effort that paralleled her first legislative victory in Austin. Because the provision meant bringing Texas procedures under federal surveillance for the first time, she had to battle conservative Texas interests in the process. The legislation was designed to help the poorest among her working-class constituents, and the relationships she had built with various House (and Senate) colleagues helped her to do it.[78]

Indeed, her view of the proper activity of the CBC was also the same as that of Lou Stokes—even though he developed it as an insider and she spoke as an outsider. "As members of Congress," she said,

we are legislators and we ought to remember that is our role. . . . I have told my Black Caucus colleagues that we cannot try to be the Urban League, the NAACP, the Urban Coalition and the Afro-Americans for

Black Unity all rolled into one. . . . There are bills which come up and which affect black people directly, and in my judgment, the Black Caucus ought to be looking for those pieces of legislation and seeing to it that amendments are offered which would change the impact, if that impact would be negative or adverse to black people. (177–78)

It was another statement, albeit in lecture form, of her devotion to the incremental process of negotiation and compromise in the legislature. And it reflected the course she took in her Voting Rights amendment.

Lou Stokes found a legislative home inside the Black Caucus; Barbara Jordan did not. The explanation for the difference, I have argued, is grounded in the differences in their personal goals, their constituency contexts, and their negotiating histories.

As for her continuing personal constituency connections, Jordan seems to have carried out her stated intention in our interview to return to Houston twice a month. Her office records for 1973 showed twenty-three separate trips home and a total of eighty-four days spent there.[79] These records say nothing about office appointments with individual constituents. They do show forty scheduled events, or about two per trip. This observable record of events looks very much like that of Lou Stokes in both numbers and type, with half of her appearances featuring the congresswoman as the main speaker. In the first five months of 1974 her trips home declined slightly to less than two per month, and total days declined from forty-two for the same period in 1973 to twenty in 1974. For someone without competition at home, and for someone seeking inside influence, her trips to the district, time spent there, and visibility to her constituents there do not seem out of the ordinary.

What is extraordinary about this newcomer's schedule, however, is the sheer range of her scheduled appearances outside of Houston. Her office records for 1973 show twenty formal speeches given outside of her home district—as many speeches, indeed, as scheduled inside her district. Four of those were in Washington, three in Texas, and the other thirteen in eleven different states. Similarly, in the first four months of 1974, her schedule called for ten major extra-constituency events. Her brief telephone conversation during our interview, with her South Carolina colleague, hinted at this burgeoning nationwide appeal.

Jordan's biographer sums up her first two years in the House with two observations:

During her first two years, Jordan focused her entire attention on the work she felt she was sent to Washington to do: building relationships, voting her constituency, and getting things done.[80]

In 1975, although a national arena seemed to be opening for Jordan, her orientation, views, ambition, and patterns of thinking and acting were still rooted in her desire to be a Texas insider, to be "let in" by those who held power in Texas. It was as if all the national attention were simply one more tool to pry open the door to enter the room and be admired by the men who—outside of public view—wielded political and economic power at home. Early in 1975, she felt close enough to that power to re-mark, "I think I'm about to crack it."[81]

She had adhered to an influence-intensive representational strategy; it had dominated her political life, and it had brought her early success at home and in Washington. More than that, I cannot say.

POSTSCRIPT

Barbara Jordan's death in January 1996 produced an outpouring of praise and remembrance. But there was almost no mention of the part of her life I have written about here—nothing about her 1972 campaign and virtually nothing about her early electoral and legislative life. It was her elo-quence, not her strategy, that stirred the memories.[82]

In the years following my narrative, Barbara Jordan became a national hero, the most celebrated and admired elected black politician of the twen-tieth century. Her fortuitous placement on the Judiciary Committee—and the eloquence of her rhetoric concerning the Constitution and black people, during the Nixon impeachment hearings—propelled her overnight into the national spotlight and into a warm and widespread multiracial embrace.

She had made the jump from local to national politician faster than any African American had ever done—with the possible exception of Adam Clayton Powell. And her reception was more positive than his. In June 1976 she ranked seventh in a list of prospective vice-presidential candidates (ahead of eventual nominee Walter Mondale!) in a national poll of likely voters.[83] A month later, she captivated the Democratic National Convention as its keynote speaker.[84] Six months after that, she ranked as the fourth most admired woman out of eighty-six listed possibilities in a national poll.[85] Her future, it was said, had no limit.

In 1978, at the end of three terms, she retired from Congress and from politics. At that point, the firsts of her early career had been sublimated by the firsts of her impeachment performance and the firsts of her post-impeachment career. When she retired, her representational reach had transcended her Houston constituency and her national black constituency, too, as a keeper of the national moral conscience. "I felt more of a responsibility to the country as a whole, as contrasted with the duty of representing the half-million people in the Eighteenth Congressional District," she said. "I felt some necessity to address national issues." [86]

Her valedictory comment on her congressional career carried the same theme. It began by citing her accomplishments for "my constituency in Houston." But it quickly expanded to a statement of "my greatest single accomplishment" as "representing hundreds, thousands of heretofore nameless, faceless, voiceless people." [87] That larger accomplishment would transcend the local constituency. The accomplishment, and the career that went with it, is the subject of another story, far beyond the reach of this one.

CONCLUSION

Barbara Jordan, like Louis Stokes, had two personal goals—one instrumental, one dominant. Her instrumental goal was to get elected and reelected to legislative office. Her dominant goal was to become an influential player inside the legislature to which she had been elected. She believed that the best way to represent her constituents was to get things done on their behalf inside the legislature—first in the Texas Senate, then in the U.S. Congress. To that end she worked "single-mindedly" to maximize her inside, institutional power. Her dominant representational strategy was an influence-intensive strategy. Influence was her goal whether she represented a majority-black state Senate district in Austin or a racially mixed congressional district in Washington. It governed her electoral connections and her reputation at home.

Her supportive constituency—as she perceived it, connected with it, and worked for it—was a black and white "working-class constituency." The black constituents were her reliable "fight, bleed, and die" political base, and the whites were a necessary added ingredient. Because of the makeup of her district, and because of the imperatives of influence-seeking in a white legislature, Jordan could not adopt—as Stokes did—exclusively African American perspectives on representation. Jordan's entire political career was spent cultivating connections with her white—as well as black—constituents.

While she enjoyed considerable leeway in her voting inside Congress, it was not as complete as that enjoyed by Stokes.

Unlike Stokes, who negotiated with the local party from the outside, she negotiated with the local party from the inside. Unlike Stokes, too, she was given no reputational head start. The political career that took her to the top of the elective office ladder was lengthy and difficult, and it required that she work tirelessly at face-to-face, ground-level activities—a never-ending round of speech making in her case. Her most crucial negotiating experiences took place early in her career as she learned, by trial and error, how to navigate independently of the white liberals of her district. The tangible pay-off was her subsequent electoral success, upon which she built an influential legislative career in Texas. When I left her in 1973, she was calculating to follow the same path inside the House of Representatives.

The large purpose of the Stokes and Jordan narratives has been to propose the usefulness of constituency-centered, observational research in studying the representational activity of members of Congress. The specific purpose has been to use a constituency-centered set of ideas to explore the representational work of two African American House members. Their racial heritage, their early personal circumstances, the aspirations of their constituents, and the timing of their political ascendancy bespeak strong commonalities. Both claimed important firsts in the inclusionary struggles of their race in the post–civil rights era. Both were pioneers. And both did the work of pioneers, charting and conquering new territory—at home and in Congress. Their similarities of accomplishment, time, and place were sufficient, certainly, to justify this pairing.

Within the full set of ideas proposed for constituency-based studies, however, the two narratives exhibit a lot of variation. In the goals they sought, the contexts they had to interpret, plus their negotiation-and-learning experiences, Stokes and Jordan differed. Both their similarities as African Americans and their differences as negotiating politicians are equally necessary for understanding their representational strengths, their strategies, and their success.

CHAPTER 4
. . . .
CHAKA FATTAH

1996 – 2001

THE CONTEMPORARY COHORT

The twelfth and last member of what I have designated the "pioneer cohort" entered Congress in 1974. Harold Ford's election brought to eighteen the total number of African Americans in that body. Twenty years later, after the election of 1994, their number had doubled to thirty-six. Of the earlier eighteen, only six remained. My curiosity about the newcomers, about their representational experiences and their outlooks, triggered two new explorations.

Because of his early exposure on national public television and because of the accessibility of his district, I was attracted in 1995 to first-term Democratic Representative Chaka Fattah of Philadelphia. I began to visit with him there in 1996. Two years later, when Louis Stokes announced his retirement, the opportunity presented itself to examine, in the same Ohio district, the succession from a member of the earliest cohort, to a member of the latest cohort. Representative Stephanie Tubbs Jones, Stokes's Democratic successor, took office in 1999. Early in 2000, I began to visit with her in Cleveland.

For purposes of comparison, I have designated the more recent arrivals as the "contemporary cohort." Because of the exceptionally large influx of new members in the post-redistricting year 1992, it seems reasonable to take that election as the starting point for members of the more recent cohort. Of the sixteen newcomers, fifteen had prior electoral experience. The Joint Center for Political and Economic Studies, a major African American think tank, marked the "dramatic" increase by devoting a book-length study to the new group.[1] Chaka Fattah and Stephanie Tubbs Jones easily fall within the post-1992 group. In the year 2000 the "contemporary cohort" numbered twenty-six African American House members. These two members are in no sense representative of that contemporary cohort. Because they work in two northern cities—Philadelphia and Cleveland—they certainly cannot be representative of the fifteen African American newcomers who, through 2000, had come from the South (see table 2).

TABLE 2

AFRICAN AMERICAN MEMBERS OF CONGRESS: 1992–2000

Contemporary Cohort	Year Entered	Year Left
Eva Clayton (D/N.C.)	1992*	
Sanford Bishop Jr. (D/Ga.)	1993	
Corrine Brown (D/Fla.)	1993	
James Clyburn (D/S.C.)	1993	
Cleo Fields (D/La.)	1993	1997
Alcee Hastings (D/Fla.)	1993	
Earl Hilliard (D/Ala.)	1993	
Eddie Bernice Johnson (D/Tex.)	1993	
Cynthia McKinney (D/Ga.)	1993	
Carrie Meek (D/Fla.)	1993	
Melvin Reynolds, (D/Ill.)	1993	1995
Bobby Rush (D/Ill.)	1993	
Robert Scott (D/Va.)	1993	
Bennie Thompson (D/Miss.)	1993	
Walter Tucker III (D/Calif.)	1993	1995
Melvin Watt (D/N.C.)	1993	
Albert Wynn (D/Md.)	1993	
Chaka Fattah (D/Pa.)	1995	
Jesse Jackson Jr. (D/Ill.)	1995	
Sheila Jackson-Lee (D/Tex.)	1995	
J. C. Watts Jr. (R/Okla.)	1995	
Elijah Cummings (D/Md.)	1996*	
Juanita Millender-McDonald (D/Calif.)	1996*	
Julia Carson (D/Ind.)	1997	
Danny Davis (D/Ill.)	1997	
Harold Ford Jr. (D/Tenn.)	1997	
Carolyn Cheeks Kilpatrick (D/Mich.)	1997	
Barbara Lee (D/Calif.)	1998*	
Gregory Meeks (D/N.Y.)	1998*	
Stephanie Tubbs Jones (D/Ohio)	1999	

*Off-year election because of a House member's retirement or death.

My picture of Chaka Fattah is drawn primarily from our six days of shared experiences and conversations in Philadelphia—in June 1996, October 1996, June 1998, June 2000, and April 2001. When we met, he was forty years old and nearing the end of his first term in Congress. His career milestones were these: born, raised, and educated in Philadelphia; attended public schools, Philadelphia Community College, the Wharton School of the University of Pennsylvania, the Fels Institute of State and Local Government of the University of Pennsylvania (earning an M.A.); the Senior Executive Program, Kennedy School, Harvard University; administrative assistant in city government; Pennsylvania state representative, 1982–1988; and Pennsylvania state senator, 1988–1994.

In some respects, his precongressional career outline resembles that of Louis Stokes and Barbara Jordan. His early community service reminds us of Stokes; his layers of prior legislative experience resemble those of Jordan. But, taken as a whole and treated developmentally, his public life and his representational activities were markedly different from theirs—sufficiently so to encourage the continued pursuit of my twin themes of change and diversity among African American House members.

In sharp contrast to both Stokes and Jordan, Chaka Fattah cannot be treated in terms of his "firsts." He was not the first African American elected to the Pennsylvania House of Representatives or to the Pennsylvania Senate or to the Congress—not from his state and not from his constituency. When I mentioned the imposing string of firsts racked up by members of the pioneer cohort, Fattah said with emphasis, "That is the last thing we would want to hear now. We hope that time has passed. It would be very unfortunate if we were still celebrating firsts." His comment clearly places him in a different cohort.

Chaka Fattah is the fourth African American elected from Pennsylvania's Second Congressional District. Robert Nix served from 1959 to 1980, William Gray served from 1981 to 1991, and Lucien Blackwell served from 1991 to 1994. Fattah elaborates his idea of firsts by describing the change in constituency expectations in the quarter-century separating his career from that of Robert Nix: "Congressman Nix was the first black congressman to be chairman of a House committee—the Post Office and Civil Service Committee. That was a great accomplishment at the time—first black chairman. It was his claim to fame. Now, I'm the top Democrat on the Postal Service Subcommittee and no one ever mentions it." When he compares himself to his predecessors, Fattah self-consciously places himself within a contemporary cohort of African American politicians.

He also differentiates between the background experiences of the two cohorts: "Most of the early generation of African American congressmen came out of the civil rights movement—or the church," he says. "Most of the generation now, though they hate to say it, have the orientation of career or professional politicians. They come out of local government. I'm doing what I decided to do early in life. I'm doing what I trained myself to do. . . . There is a different level of preparedness from Nix to Gray to myself. Bill Gray prepared for the ministry, but I prepared for politics."[2]

Outside observers, too, found a more contemporary pattern. In their 1995 analysis of the Congressional Black Caucus, Richard Champagne and Leroy Rieselbach single out its "newer, less senior" members as "a new breed of pragmatists who have become issue activists and coalition builders eager for influence." Current CBC members, they say, "Often seek policy influence more as individuals than as a collectivity." And, while "they still feel an obligation to represent the national black population . . . [their] strategies seem clearly tipped toward ordinary congressional routines and away from symbolic politics."[3] These distinctions help explain Chaka Fattah's personal goals and representational strategies.

PERSONAL GOALS AND REPRESENTATIONAL STRATEGY

Chaka Fattah was born into an intensely community-minded and community-involved family. "My father and mother run the only urban boys' home [House of Umoja]in the country.[4] [It's] a place to live for young men who are delinquent or dependent or both. They have several row houses in west Philadelphia." "So I grew up in a home where there were always thirty or forty people around," he added. "Maybe that's why I feel at home in politics."

Earlier in their lives, both parents had multiple community attachments. His mother had once been an editor of the *Philadelphia Tribune,* the oldest black newspaper in America, and later she became vice president of the Philadelphia Council of Neighborhood Organizations. His stepfather had once run the Hartranst Community Center in North Philadelphia, and later he had become a teacher, pursuing an advanced degree when in his sixties. His brother still runs a food kitchen for the destitute—Fattah's Food for Thought—which serves "thousands of people each month." Chaka Fattah's entire family was deeply involved in the business of helping others less fortunate than they. With considerable understatement, the congressman says, "I grew up in a home where being involved in community life was a norm."

Helping others through community activism can easily morph into helping others through political activism. And it seems to have done so in Fattah's case. With a story that begins with his own neighborhood organization—the Winnfield Resident's Association—he traces just such a sequence.

My family was very much involved in efforts to deal with youth gang violence. The Winnfield neighborhood was a substantial, integrated, middle-class area that felt exempt from young gang violence. Then one weekend, there were two killings, one in retaliation for the other. My father and I set up meetings between the two groups. There was a picture of me in the *Philadelphia Inquirer*. I was a teenager—sixteen or seventeen. We facilitated a dialogue.

We also fought to close the bars in the area, and I marched in those protests. Ann Jordan was a leader in the Association and she ran against the Speaker of the [Pennsylvania] House. I helped her. She lost. Then we tried to get rid of the ward leader. I got involved in that, and after an eight-year fight, we won. Those committee membership fights were hand-to-hand combat. Then there was a creek that ran under part of the area and there was a settling problem with some of the foundations. When I worked at city hall, I helped work on that problem. I had a history of involvement there by the time I ran for state representative.

He developed a taste for politics and political ambitions early in life. One busy day, when the oil gauge in his car started blinking, he threw up his hands and only half joked, "I don't know anything about cars. I don't know anything except politics. That's all I've cared about since I was a kid." Taste and ambition have combined to propel him steadily up the electoral office ladder.

In this respect, he is very much like Barbara Jordan and very much unlike Lou Stokes. We had known each other less than twenty minutes when Fattah offered his first self-description. "I'm a career politician," he said. And the supporting record is ample.

He was only twenty-one—and not quite eligible to serve—when he and a friend ran a citywide campaign "as a team," to fill two vacancies for the job of City Commissioner. They lost; but Fattah, encouragingly, finished fourth in a field of twenty-two. Four years later, at the barely eligible age of twenty-five, he defeated an incumbent to win election to the Pennsylvania House of Representatives. He was the youngest ever to serve there. In that campaign, he recalls, "no one knew who I was. They couldn't even pronounce my name."

After three terms in the House, he sought and won election to the state Senate. In that case, he challenged a twenty-year incumbent and drove him from the race. As Fattah told it,

The senator had a shrewd strategy. Every election year, he delayed announcing whether he would run or not, so people would wait. Then, when it was too late for anyone to organize, he would announce for re-election. In 1988, while he delayed, I started running. . . . We rented the old civic center and packed it with my supporters. We announced it on the radio—a big opening campaign celebration. It was not quite show-biz, but we had fifteen speakers. I announced my candidacy. We had raised $12,000, and we spent all of it in the first week creating a big splash. Then on the first day petitions could be circulated, we held a breakfast for all the volunteers. . . . He did not react publicly to any of it. But a few weeks later, he announced he would not run. I called it a preemptive strike.

The local African American paper, the *Tribune,* he recalled, "thought I was too pushy, that I should wait my turn." He was a young politician in a con-siderable hurry.

In 1991, during Fattah's first term in the state Senate, the incumbent con-gressman, Bill Gray, unexpectedly resigned, and Fattah jumped into the spe-cial primary election. The Democratic Party organization, however, had al-ready endorsed their own candidate—a veteran labor leader and city councilman. Fattah ran as a Consumer Party independent and lost.[5] His op-ponent, Lucien Blackwell, went to Congress. As Fattah recalled, "It was a twenty-eight-day campaign and the organization was able to slot their can-didate before I got started. Since I had said I was going to run, I felt I had to. I promised in the campaign that if he won, I would not challenge him in the next election. I thought that whoever won should at least have one full term. I gave him that one term. Then I challenged him and won." "My whole ca-reer is one of winning against incumbents," he says.[6] His elective office his-tory presents an ultra-classic picture of progressive ambition.

The fact of his ambition, however, does not tell us about his motivations and his goals—about why he wanted so badly to be in politics. Very early in his life, the sheer allure of politics may have been paramount. "I remember driving to Washington with my mother," he recalls, "to watch her testify at a congressional hearing on gang violence run by John Conyers and Louis Stokes. That experience inspired me to go into politics. And it had nothing to do with policy." As the story of the Winnfield Resident's Association makes clear, however, his actual involvements were, from the outset, policy involvements.

From his earliest days in office, his dominant goal as a legislator has been to participate in making public policy. "I'm dedicated to legislation," he says when discussing his state legislative activity.

I want to be an intricate part of the policy debate. Some people are content to criticize other people's policies. . . . I want to be at the table when policies are being made. I do what you have to do—the grunt work beforehand. As a freshman state representative, I helped get a small group to meet together to do something about the poor economy. We called it "Penn Pride." We worked all summer and produced a package bill, The Employment Opportunity Act, to uplift the state's economy. Some of my colleagues wondered why we would do that—in summer. But I thought that's what a legislator is supposed to do.

As a freshman member of Congress, he articulated the same goal.

I hope that my distinction—not my legacy, I'm too young to speak of that—will be as a legislator. That is my intention—to be able to draft bills, to focus on public policy. I hope my accomplishment, my achievement, will be in legislation, not in how high a position I reached. It wouldn't matter to me what position I had if I got two or three bills passed. Very few people actually drive the policy machine. I want to be one of those people. I don't care about the trappings or the perks, except as they help me to legislate in Congress.

His goals are dominantly policy goals. When he emphasizes his "level of preparedness" and his "training for politics," he means preparedness and training for policy-oriented politics. I will describe his strategy, therefore, as a dominantly *policy-intensive representational strategy*.

This same "policy-intensive" label has been applied usefully to other House members in other constituencies.[7] In Fattah's case, however, an extra measure of intensity should be added. For he is not simply goal oriented, he is goal driven. He is not just policy oriented, he is policy driven. He is not just legislatively oriented, he is legislative-product driven. He is always thinking about establishing and pushing policy goals and legislative goals. He views every situation as a challenge to overcome, and he constantly puts himself to the test.

Unexpectedly faced with minority status in the U.S. House, he told a reporter in 1995, "The question is, how can I be successful in this environment? It's the most difficult challenge I've ever had to face."[8] In our first visit, he defined his test this way: "What is it you want to do with the position? I'm young and just beginning. Many elected people don't spend time solving problems. They spend time on the next election or on politics. . . . I don't want to spend time increasing my vote. Anything beyond what I already have is ego. What are you getting accomplished? That's the question." Five years later, after he had won a coveted position on the House Appropriations Committee, he expressed the same sentiment. "My goal is not to be on Appropriations. My goal is to be a legislator." Later, I will trace his efforts in pursuit of that goal.

CONSTITUENCY CONTEXT

Chaka Fattah represents a 100 percent urban constituency in a major American city. The district, he says, "is urban, economically and ethnically diverse. It is 60 percent African American. I have—not the poorest section of the city—some of the poorest. I also have some of the most affluent parts of the city, both black and white. And I have more medical colleges in my district than any district in the country." Except for the last, those several characteristics would lead us to expect his constituency context to be broadly similar to those represented by Louis Stokes and Barbara Jordan. That is the case.

As an older, northern city struggling against the tides of urban decline and suburban dominance, Philadelphia resembles Cleveland more than it does growth-minded Houston. Because it is much larger than Cleveland, however, Philadelphia's socioeconomic stabilization and turnaround problems seem less tractable than those of Cleveland. A *Forbes* magazine study of job trends, 1991–1996, in thirty-six metropolitan areas found that Philadelphia topped the list in the severity of its job losses.[9] The sheer scope of Philadelphia's urban problems has been described up close, personal, and in detail by Buzz Bissinger in his mayor-centered book *A Prayer for the City.* The citywide context of Fattah's congressional constituency—"a dying and obsolete city"—is vividly portrayed in that superb study.[10] Indeed, the author and the congressman have nearly identical pictures of the city. For Fattah, that picture is the backdrop against which to examine his own policy goals, the policy views of his constituents, and his policy efforts as their representative.

Like Cleveland and Houston, Philadelphia has a large African American population. Similarly, too, the boundary-drawing process has placed the largest number of them in a single congressional district. The Philadelphia congressman calls his district "the historically African American Second District." And a large African American majority has been its main characteristic from its beginnings. The *Almanac of American Politics,* in its first 1972 edition, labeled the district simply as "Philadelphia's black district."[11] When Robert Nix became its first African American Representative in 1958, the district was 50 percent black. That number has changed with each decennial redistricting; but the defining characteristic has not. After the 1960 census the district was 59 percent black; after 1970, 65 percent black; after 1980, 76 percent black. After the 1990 census, and through the 2000 election, it was 62 percent black.

The district's racial makeup is a faithful predictor of its partisan makeup. The 1972 *Almanac of American Politics* described it as "consistently Philadelphia's most Democratic district in statewide elections." [12] For the eight presidential elections between 1968 and 1996, the district's Democratic vote—with a low of 75 percent and a high of 91 percent—averaged 84 percent. In 1996 Fattah's district gave President Clinton his fifth-highest vote margin.[13] In voting for Congress, only the Democratic primary matters. Since Fattah won there in 1994, he has been unchallenged in the primary and been elected by margins from 86 percent to 100 percent. "People tell me," he says, "that I have the safest seat in the country." It would be a challenge to find one safer.

Describing his geographical constituency further, he says, "Forty percent is west Philadelphia, 40 percent northwest Philadelphia. And that's the district. The rest is just spicing." He estimates that "the spicing" includes "south Philly, north Philly, center city, and Yeadon [in an adjoining county]," each of which makes up 5 percent of his geographical constituency.

West Philadelphia is Fattah's home area. He describes it as "black, poor working class to middle class." It has been a prototypically declining urban area. Between 1950 and 1990, it lost a third of its population; in 1990 it had over four thousand abandoned structures, and 12 percent of its available housing stock was vacant.[14] During a ride up Market Street, the main artery connecting center city to "west Philly"—with the elevated transit line rumbling overhead—I watched people shopping in small clusters of stores. The clusters were separated by even larger clusters of boarded-up stores and homes, all thickly laced with graffiti. The omnipresence of urban blight bespoke the inequality of resources and the policy needs common to the poorest black communities—jobs, housing, health, schools, and safety. In all these respects, the need for government assistance was observably stark and serious.

The other 40 percent of "the district," northwest Philadelphia, he describes as "black and white, middle class to wealthy." Separated from west Philly by the Schuylkill River, it has a large white population—some of it, as in Chestnut Hill, upper-class Republican. The area has also been a destination of choice for many upwardly mobile, middle-class blacks leaving the west Philly ghetto by "jumping the river" into places like Germantown and

Mt. Airy.[15] Congressman Fattah's "strongest support" came from Mt. Airy. "It is thought to be one of the most successful models of racial integration in the country," he says. "It is a very active part of my constituency—filled with civic groups of all sorts. It has the highest income of any place in my district except center city. They vote independently and progressively. And they are very comfortable with a congressman like me."

The Second Congressional District contains, therefore, a measurable element of white, liberal Democrats, with whom a broad-gauged and policy-oriented African American House member can work easily and on equal terms. The presence of this element in Fattah's district brings distinctive characteristics to its politics. Such, at least, is the view of the congressman himself.

Each of Philadelphia's two main congressional districts, he says, has a distinctive character. He begins a description of his district by contrasting it to the adjacent First Congressional District—and its best-known former congressman. "It is not a coincidence that the First District sent Bill Barrett to Congress," says Fattah.

> He was a ward leader from south Philadelphia. The nicest thing you could say about his legislative interests was that he did not have any. Every night he came home and went to the clubhouse and people came to see him. He would see them all and sit there till the last person had been seen. I grew up in that district. I remember my grandfather going to see him. His business was constituency service. His interest was in political patronage and jobs. . . . The congressman there now, Bob Brady, is also the party chairman. He focuses on the needs of the local constituents. To that degree, the First District has a character that goes way back.

On the other hand, he continued, "The Second District has been the centerpiece of independent politics—not just black politics, but all politics, liberal white politics. The party people here are not interested in street money; they are interested in the editorials in the *Philadelphia Inquirer*. People in the district are more independent-minded." In 1994 he campaigned there with a set of policy papers on key issues. Whereas the west Philadelphia segment of his constituency was tied closely to the organizational politics of the Democratic Party, the northwest Philadelphia segment—typified by Mt. Airy—leaned away from the party and toward issue-based politics.

When I asked him whether he perceived his congressional district to be homogeneous or heterogeneous, he parried, "I think that there is a harmony of spirit in the district." That "spirit" added an issue-oriented, liberal, white element to his basically black reelection constituency. Neither the Stokes nor the Jordan districts had anything comparable during my time with them. Even controlling for time differences, the white constituents in Fattah's district worked to mitigate the kind of racial divide that existed within Lou Stokes's district and to mitigate the kind of liberal divide that existed within Barbara Jordan's district.

The congressman thinks of himself as a particularly good fit for the diverse district he describes. It is not surprising. As a member of the state Senate, he helped draw up the redistricting plan that the courts accepted in 1991. "I drew up the plan for the historically African American Second District," he says. "I had more to do with it than anyone, except the courts. The district I have is the district as I wanted it—hook, line, and sinker. It was even more of what I wanted than I expected to get."

He summarizes his constituency relationship as "comfortable."

It is an easy district to represent—for me. That's because of where I've been and what I've done. I was born in south Philadelphia and moved to west Philadelphia. I went to school here—to community college and to Penn. It is not possible to represent the district without paying a lot of attention to the University of Pennsylvania. It is the outstanding institution of my district and the biggest employer in my district. When I go to speak there, to the young Democrats, the Law School, Wharton [business school], I'm not intimidated. I'm at home.

Lucien Blackwell never went there. And they felt ignored. He didn't feel comfortable in some of the areas in the northwest section, so he didn't go there either. He had a very successful career as a labor leader. No one could talk to poor people any better than Lucien Blackwell. But that's not "the district."

For me, the district is uniquely easy. I went to the community college. It has branches and it educates more people than any institution in the district. I'm on their Board and I'm tuned in to what they do. I can talk with the environmentalists in the northwest section about their interests. And I can talk to the CEOs in center city. Those are the groups that Lucien ignored. It's the comfortability of it. I think that's the best way to put it—it's a *comfortable fit* for me.

"Lucien Blackwell," he added, "could not have lasted in this district for long. But if Lucien had been in the First District, he might have been there forever."

His biracial political support, together with his own policy goals, combine to give Fattah more of a citywide presence than either Stokes or Jordan seemed to have. As one possible explanation, his is the only district of the three that contains the seat of city government—city hall. And he seems more conscious of the city as a working context than the others did. When he articulates his view of his representational job, he speaks of "multiple levels of representation." And he mentions the district needs first, followed by the city and its needs—the airport, for example, as well as race relations. In his office, he was on the telephone with the mayor. "I worry first about my district," he says, "but then about the whole city. I'm influential in the city because of the prominence of my position." And he added, typically, "It's a challenge every day to figure out what a congressman can do. It's a very political city."

At a massive AFSCME rally in front of city hall, in support of a collective bargaining agreement for one of its unions, Fattah inveighed, "Let the word go forth that Philadelphia is a union town, that we have to stand up for our rights. In the shadow of city hall, those who believe workers will be pushed aside are wrong. They hurl insults at one of the strongest, most progressive unions in our town. . . . When you are struggling to win, we all stand together for the working people of Philadelphia." And he said afterward, "At the rally today, I knew a whole bunch of people from a whole lot of associations all over town. I had a whole lot of different connections—positively convoluted." "My strength is in the district," he says, "but I'm comfortable in the city. For many problems, we are one and the same."

Because he found common ground with antiparty reformers and intellectual liberals who looked to the *Philadelphia Inquirer,* and because he has a citywide perspective, I expected him to take more of an interest in the citywide media than either Stokes or Jordan. And that is noticeably the case. Where Stokes sensed media antagonism and Jordan experienced media neglect, Fattah sees fair media treatment.

The city's two major newspapers are the *Inquirer* and the *Daily News,* with daytime circulations of 400,000 and 160,000, respectively. "I've been treated very well by the *Inquirer,*" he said in 1996. "They have supported me every time. The *Daily News* has been good to me. They opposed me once [against Blackwell], but they have supported me since. On a scale from one to ten, I'd give the *Inquirer* a ten and the *Daily News* an eight. Neither of them has ever attacked me. I've led a charmed life with the media." He was quick to add, however, "The publicity I've gotten at home has been earned publicity. I don't get puff pieces. When I was in the state Senate, the city went broke. I got a group of businessmen together to raise $34 million to save the city.

Then I got my name on the front page. I earned that publicity. It's the only kind I get."

A third paper, the *Philadelphia Tribune,* the nation's oldest black newspaper, with a three-days-a-week circulation of 110,000, supported his opponent, Lucien Blackwell, in both their contests. Calling it "an advocacy paper," Fattah said that while he was frequently mentioned in it, they took no interest in reporting or interpreting his representational activities.

Thinking back to Lou Stokes's intimate dependence on his city's African American *Call and Post,* Fattah's dismissal of his city's *Tribune* suggests a rather different media mix—more favorable citywide and, therefore, much less dependent on black community outlets. Fattah's own citywide view was matched by the media's perception of him as a meaningful player in citywide politics. In 1997, for example, he was listed by the *Philadelphia Weekly Magazine* as one of five mayoral possibilities.[16] It was a different media perception than existed for Stokes or for Jordan.

That difference may be explained also by the change in race relations that occurred in the period between the pioneer cohort and the contemporary cohort of African American House members. Both Lou Stokes and Barbara Jordan had to fight the first, pathbreaking inclusionary battles with their white communities. That included battling with their white-dominated newspapers. Chaka Fattah, on the other hand, did not. His predecessors had fought those battles for him.

Still, he was receiving some favorable media treatment on his own. When we met, he had already been listed as one of a nationwide "Fifty for the Future" in *Time* and as one of six "rising star" House and Senate Democrats in the congressional newspaper *The Hill.*[17] I've gotten some exposure in the national media," he said, "I've been on McNeil-Lehrer nine times, and I just finished one of those two-hour sessions where people sit around and discuss issues. This one was on the American family. It's playing in Washington and PBS this weekend. There are congressmen from Philadelphia who have been here sixteen years and have never been on national television. I have no problem with the media."

The congressman did, however, have at least one problem at home. His three district predecessors may have helped by breaking down racial barriers, but they bequeathed him a local complication that did not face either Stokes or Jordan. They had set a standard. In practical terms, the Philadelphia media would begin by measuring and judging Chaka Fattah by the success of his predecessor, Congressman Bill Gray.

A third generation minister, Bill Gray had become much respected in both black west Philadelphia and biracial northwest Philadelphia. In his twelve years in the U.S. House of Representatives, he had risen faster and further in terms of his position there than *any* African American ever had—eventually becoming both Chairman of the House Budget Committee and, as Democratic Party Whip, the third-ranking member in his party's leadership hierarchy. As a public figure, Bill Gray had reaped much favorable publicity nationally. He had resigned to accept the nationally prestigious position as President of the United Negro College Fund.[18]

None of this was lost on the newcomer. When we first met, he spoke of Gray as "my predecessor—well, my real predecessor, in spirit anyway." And he took pains to point out that despite "one brief moment, . . . Reverend Gray has been very helpful to me. He held a fundraiser for me the other night in his home. *It was the passing of the baton.*" Later he referred to the event as "the passing of the mantle"—which he was only too eager to accept—albeit provisionally. To someone who continually set challenges for himself, it was another one he confidently accepted. Citizens typically hold two kinds of expectations of their House members, he told an interviewer in 1996. "They either expect greatness or they don't expect much. I prefer," he said, "the burden of high expectations."[19]

It was not a burden easily or quickly lifted. Two years later, a lengthy profile in the *Inquirer* opened with the inevitable comparison: "Chaka Fattah is finding out that Bill Gray is a tough act to follow. . . . [He] knows that three years into his own tenure in the House, he has a long way to go before he reaches Gray's status." The congressman asked only for time. "Bill Gray was, indeed, a very prominent figure, but . . . you can't compare Bill Gray to me after thirty-six months," he said.[20] The constituency context in which he began included the shadow and the burden of Bill Gray's legacy.

ELECTORAL CONNECTIONS

By the time we met in 1995, the expansionist stage of Chaka Fattah's electoral career was over. He had been elected to Congress and, barring the unforeseen and the unimaginable, was assured of reelection for as long as he wished. Most of the district-level activity I observed, therefore, was protectionist. He was maintaining old connections, not negotiating for new ones. In order to understand the source and the strength of his connections, however, it is helpful to take note of his earlier expansionist activity—especially his 1994 primary victory. When African Americans run for Congress in majority-black districts, their only serious electoral challenge is almost always their first Democratic primary. If they are victorious there, they will rarely face a credible challenge thereafter. That was Fattah's situation when we talked about his electoral connections.

As he saw it, he had spent twelve years "growing the district" from 60,000 as state representative to 200,000 as state senator to 580,000 as a member of Congress. In every case, he began by mounting a primary challenge to the candidate of the Democratic Party organization. In 1982 he defeated a white incumbent state representative by fifty-eight votes to become the first black representative from that west Philadelphia district. In 1988 he induced a twenty-year black incumbent state senator to retire in the face of a Fattah primary challenge. That Senate district expanded his territory into the northwest area. In 1992 he suffered his only primary defeat—in the special election for Congress. It was a race he did not expect to win. He remained, however, in the state Senate. And in his 1994 Democratic primary battle with the incumbent congressman, Fattah reversed the outcome.

In his losing 1992 primary, he recalled, the party-backed candidate also exploited favorable voting mechanics. "Blackwell was expected to win because the mayor, the president of the city council, and most of the ward leaders were behind him. And we had the one big lever in the voting machine. With one throw of the lever, you could vote the entire Democratic ticket. Since there were only two races on the ballot, it would have been foolish for most people not to throw the one big lever." But whatever the outcome, he added, "everybody's expectation was that no matter who won that off-year primary, the loser would run again."

The 1992 primary had been a three-way race. "Everybody expected that John White would come in second and would run in the next primary and win. He was the protégé of [resigning congressman] Bill Gray. He was a city commissioner and had an independent profile like mine. I was the stepchild in the race. John and I made a deal—that whoever came in second to Blackwell in the first race would be the nonparty candidate against Blackwell after his first full term. To everyone's surprise, I finished second, and White dropped out of politics." Of his personal pledge to give the incumbent that one full term, he commented, "It was a foolish thing to do."

Attesting to the importance of his prior experience in "growing the district," he emphasized the electoral advantage gained through his position in the state Senate. "My advantage first over White and then over Blackwell was that I knew every inch of the Second Congressional District—because as a state senator, I drew the lines. I could walk my way through every ward and precinct map and see where White's previous strength had been and Blackwell's previous strength had been. I could remove some of their better areas and keep all of my best areas." And he added, "The irony was that when I had finished drawing the lines, Blackwell had a much better chance of winning in the First District than he did in the Second District."

On more than one occasion, he commented on the crucial advantage he gained from his accumulated knowledge of the electoral terrain. "People thought that I would do well in the mostly white, upper-income parts of the district but that I would not do well in the row houses of west Philadelphia. That's what they thought. But I knew I would do well because I had represented the people there. I won a smashing victory in every part of the district." And again, "The so-called experts said that because I was a policy wonk, I would be strong among white liberals, but that Blackwell would win in west Philadelphia. On election night, KYW was on the air saying that Lucien Blackwell had won—that I had carried the northwest area and he had carried west Philadelphia. I heard it on the radio as I was driving to my victory party! I won every ward in the district—even Blackwell's own ward. That tells you how wrong people's perceptions were. The point is, I do well everywhere."

To emphasize the word "everywhere," he described a successful effort to cultivate a most unlikely element of his northwest segment. "I feel comfortable," he began, "even in Roxborough. It's a white, ethnic, working-class town, typical of the [Frank] Rizzo [tough-talking, law-and-order, former mayor] base in the city. When I ran [in 1994] there was this columnist on local politics in the old *Roxborough News* saying, 'How could anyone with the name Chaka Fattah get elected from Roxborough?' I read it as a challenge. So I went to a Polish American club in the Polish area of the town. I rolled up my sleeves, walked in, and ordered a round of beers. Then I played a favorite game—I forget the name of it—over in the corner. I bought a few rounds, played a few games. That was the beginning, and I carried Roxborough in the [1994] primary. You can win anywhere—if you present yourself in that place." How he would fare in that town against a white candidate is, of course, another question.

He described his winning primary campaign, also, as an organizational achievement.

We ran a textbook campaign. There wasn't one thing we did wrong. We did no TV. We relied on radio—white radio, black radio, talk radio, rock radio. We were always on the radio. We did direct mail. We walked door-to-door, not just Mitch [an aide] and me—which the press focused on—

but hundreds of other people walking in the neighborhoods. And we had phone banks. We didn't get money from the normal Democratic supporters, but we nearly matched him in money. He was, maybe, 85 percent PACs and 15 percent individual, and we were the reverse. We got a lot of thousand dollar checks.

His 1994 primary victory was a convincing biracial, antiorganizational victory. It registered his electoral connections and sealed his incumbency.

POLICY CONNECTIONS

NEIGHBORHOOD IMMERSION

When Lou Stokes thought about the constituents he represented and for whom he worked, his covering conceptualization was "the black community." He never doubted that he was referring to the vast majority of Cleveland's African Americans, and he never doubted that he knew what their group interests were or how best to pursue them. He was, of course, one of them. Moreover, his reputation among the city's black population rested upon his leadership effort in the U.S. Supreme Court in securing the most widely held of all the group's interests—their political inclusion by means of racial representation in the United States Congress.

The idea of the black community identified for Lou Stokes his reelection constituency. Within that circle, he further identified his primary constituency—the black ministers and the Twenty-first Congressional District Caucus. Beyond that, however, there was little intracommunity differentiation. He was not, as I have shown, very active in, knowledgeable about, or connected to the workaday world of his constituents. He operated at a distance from and on a plane above—as part leader and part symbol. The idea of "the black community" worked well for him, but it was a distinctively broad and unrefined perceptual screen through which to conceptualize his representational relationships.

I have rehearsed these constituency perceptions of Lou Stokes in order to contrast them with those of Chaka Fattah. The Philadelphia congressman rarely if ever uses the term "the black community." And that is not because he is any less cognizant of the hard-core policy agenda of his African American constituents. He does not use that broad reference point, because he has been, throughout his career, deeply involved in the everyday lives and problems of his black constituents. In thinking about the people he represents, therefore, he operates with a detailed and fine-grained perceptual screen.

Chaka Fattah's perception of his constituency is very different from that of Louis Stokes. Where Stokes saw the whole black community, Fattah sees individual black neighborhoods. The district's neighborhoods are the building blocks of his representational relationships, and the cement in each building block is public policy.

The easiest way to support this generalization is to listen to three excerpts from his travel talk.

> They say Philadelphia is a city of neighborhoods. That's true. *My district is a district of neighborhoods.* I know them because I've been involved with them—the Haddington Leadership Association, the Winnfield Residents' Association, the Point Breeze Association—dozens of community organizations, youth organizations. I know a lot about them because I go way back with them. My association with Legal Services goes way back to the sit-in in west Philadelphia. I worked with tenant associations, like the Stubbs Association. I understand the pulse of the neighborhoods.

> Philadelphia is a city of neighborhood organizations. I have been active in these organizations in a variety of roles—some of which I took on as a teenager, some as an adult. There are a thousand community organizations in the city. And I have worked with more of them than anyone in the community. I've spent years dealing with the small minutiae of these groups. And that goes way back to jobs I held in city hall. I remember once when the power company turned out the lights in one of the city parks. The people came to me. I asked PICO to turn the lights back on. They said, "No, we can't do that till they pay their bill." So I worked it out that the power company lent the park people money so they could pay to have the lights put back on.

> I helped Haddington Leadership to build the second shopping center in their area. I was involved in citywide gang meetings where they negotiated peace treaties. I helped bring dropouts together. It's a district of neighborhoods with similar issues whether it's Overbrook State or Landsdowne South or the Action Council.

Whereas Lou Stokes deputized a staffer to identify and describe his various neighborhoods for me, Fattah talked about them and their problems as the basic underpinnings of representational discourse.

Chaka Fattah's numberless neighborhood involvements are, at bottom, policy involvements. And they rest on a broad underpinning of policy agreement. Of all the neighborhood policy problems he has attended to throughout his life, the one that engaged more of his precongressional efforts than any other was public housing.[21] Indeed, a story is told that, at the age of fourteen, he helped his parents engineer their initial purchase of the west Philadelphia row houses that became their House of Umoja. "I've been in more community meetings, toured more abandoned houses and vacant lots, and participated in more community clean-ups than a whole host of elected officials put together," he says. Riding along, he points out housing clusters for which he obtained funding in the state Senate. "That deal fell apart and I rescued it at the last minute. . . . There isn't an affordable housing project anywhere in the city that I haven't been involved in. We started rehabilitating a row of old mansions when I was in the state legislature, and we've been doing them one at a time ever since."

As a state senator, he recalled, "I attacked the Housing Authority for rehabilitating the high-rises, and I called for rehabilitating old homes instead. I was one of the first people to condemn the high-rises—as inefficient and wrong. And I called for the reform of the Philadelphia Housing Authority. It shocked people." He spun out the facts and figures of his investigations that were supported policies emphasizing investments in older homes. "We put a system of dots showing where the literacy groups went to teach people to read. And we found that the closer you got to the high-rises, the fewer dots there were. The high-rises weren't safe, and the community groups that wanted to help the poor wouldn't go near them."

He held a press conference on the subject that attracted a burst of citywide publicity. "The papers loved that story," he said in 1996. "It was an issue you could get your arms around. Seventy percent of everything I do *now* has to do with education issues. But if you ask people what they know about me, 80 percent will say the housing issue. It's the most publicity I ever got. But I earned it, too."

Chaka Fattah's constituency relationships resemble the activism of the helping professions. His pattern of involvements was doubtless influenced by the community-regarding activities of his parents. He emphasized the informality of his neighborhood relationships. "I feel so much at home [in the district] that it's like I'm not the congressman. My son and I ride our bikes up and down these streets. . . . I don't make a point about being called 'the congressman.' People call me 'Chaka.' They don't call me 'the congressman.' I'm not interested in the trappings. My interest is in policy." He readily admits that his constituents do not always see him in such an informal light. As a diagnostic matter, however, it is hard to imagine such an immersion-centered comment coming from his Cleveland counterpart.

The two House members faced different circumstances. Lou Stokes fought the great overall war to gain inclusion, while Chaka Fattah was fighting the endless, incremental battles to redeem inclusion. Their contrasting representational relationships did flow from their differing personal predispositions. But importantly, too, differences in their representational performance resulted from their different placement in the history of African American politics.

The Philadelphia congressman practices representation by immersion. "My politics grows out of the neighborhoods," Fattah generalizes. "And I call my politics 'empowerment politics,' not party politics. When I first went into politics," he says, "I had a big interest in world politics, but the longer I've been in politics, the more I've moved toward issues sorts of groups." When asked, "Who are your strongest supporters?" he moves directly to those "issues sorts of groups." That is, he locates his primary constituency among the policy-oriented groups with whom he works.

In 1966 he answered that his "strongest supporters" were: "The antidrug groups—there are forty of them—and the liberal groups that are concerned with education, literacy groups. Liberal isn't exactly the right word—people active in community organizations like the people concerned with affordable housing." Two years later he spoke similarly. "The most important people to me are not the elected officials, but the people who are actually involved in the community. Talk to anyone in Philadelphia who has anything to do in affordable housing and they will have a connection to me—the Enterprise Fund, the Germantown Foundation. I've been involved in antidrug efforts—the "Drug Free in '93" campaign. There are layers of people involved in efforts to improve the life of their neighbors. Not all of them are charitable. Some are self-interested, like the Neighborhood Crime Watch. But the result is that you get to help others. The base of my support is in all these groups."

My first morning in Philadelphia was spent observing some of those street-level connections at a Community Volunteer Appreciation Fair "hosted" by the congressman. It was a daylong event where representatives of fifty-six different local organizations were scheduled to display materials, hold workshops, and recruit. At their plenary session, Fattah spoke to a dominantly African American gathering of about two hundred people, and he presented awards to one hundred volunteers.

As we entered, he said, "I meet a lot of these same people when I go places.

In the beginning, it dawned on me that more or less it's the same group of people. They are the fabric of the community. I didn't start this program, but I could see that, as a public official, I had a unique opportunity to spotlight the contributions of volunteers. So I've been doing it for a number of years. . . . Without them, it would be impossible for the institutions of the community to operate. They deserve recognition, and I want to give it to them. We will stay longer than we will anywhere else today. This meeting is a priority for me."

The mood was upbeat, and so was his short talk. "Volunteers make the everyday things that happen, happen. . . . We did not meet to talk about what's wrong and what did not happen, but to see what's good and what is happening. . . . As a state representative, as a state senator, and now as a congressman, I've worked for affordable housing, and I know that none of it would have been built without volunteers. . . . The great lesson of life is that we grow by helping others." Among the others, he gave awards to individuals from his parents' House of Umoja and from his brother's Fattah's Food for Thought. We spent a couple of hours there while people talked with him and he visited exhibits. Many were, I have since concluded, his strong supporters. Doubtless, many were nonpolitical. But, in general, they fit his self-described mold. On the way out, he noted as a matter of fact that "several [party] committee people were there."

These multiple, overlapping neighborhood involvements give him a depth of constituency immersion that is remarkable and—in my experience—unique. Part of the immersion grows out of the extensiveness of his neighborhood connections and the diversity of his policy connections. Part of the immersion, too, derives from the longevity and the continuity of his efforts.

As he did in his talk at the volunteer fair, he often emphasizes how long he has already been in public life and how crucial that has been to his current constituency connections. "People know me from years of activity with various community groups. Everything I'm doing now I've been doing for years."

All the major players in the district know me personally. That's because I've been around so long—six years in the assembly, six years in the Senate, and now two years in Congress. Bob Haskins, whom you'll meet at the bank—he and I have known each other and worked together in various projects for fifteen years. People know that I've taken the lead on drug-free schools, high-rise housing, putting together $34 million to save the city. Bob knows how much I work in the community.

Indeed, "Because of my involvement, people expect more out of me than they do out of the ordinary run-of-the-mill figure in town." His expectations for the future are similarly optimistic—and realistic. "It's been a ten-year project for me so far," he said in 1996. "I think I'm living off past accomplishments now. I'm in Congress, but I'm in the [Democratic] minority. However, I think I can work through the [Democratic] administration to shake loose a few dollars."

His extensive street-level policy attachments probably have eclipsed other likely elements of reliable constituent support. One such would seem to be the black ministers of the district—a group that was so pivotal a part of Lou Stokes's primary constituency. Whereas Stokes always put them front and center, spontaneously, in any discussions of his political support base, Fattah did not. And the contrast was striking.

When asked, Fattah responded positively—but with varying enthusiasm. In 1998 he answered my question about "the importance of the black church" as follows: "The black church is central in urban politics. I have always enjoyed the support of the influential clergy. They were one of the established groups that went with me over the incumbent. They are invited everywhere in the community. And that goes back a long way to the time when they were the main source of strength for black people. They are an important support base." A couple of years later, however, he answered a question about "the support of the ministers" differently. "I meet with them twice a year. Yes, they are supportive. But many of them supported Blackwell in the campaign. Naturally, I am in closer touch with some than with others. But I meet with all of them twice a year."

In October 1996 I went to one of his semiannual meetings. His top staffer advised me beforehand that sixty ministers would be there. Indeed, his office had already cancelled this meeting once, to accommodate the ministers' schedules. In a church basement, place settings were laid out along all four sides of a large square of banquet tables. But only six ministers came. So we huddled in one corner. It was an election year, and a recent rash of black church burnings nationwide had become a major community concern. Those were, indeed, the two topics of the discussion. But the tiny turnout did not reflect a strong, enthusiastic, and reliable constituency.

The minister who hosted the meeting did most of the talking and questioning. He seemed very supportive. "He's the operator, the leading politician among the ministers," said Fattah. "He's very knowledgeable about politics. He's good at it. . . . He's been very helpful to me." No doubt, other black ministers are individually helpful to him. And doubtless, too, some of their help gets registered through their involvement in his neighborhood projects. At best, however, they can be considered as one among many supportive groups, with none of the primacy that Lou Stokes attached to them in Cleveland. Fattah campaigns in black churches—as all black House members do. But the "thick and thin" supporters of his primary constituency are identifiable more by their leadership in the neighborhoods than by their involvements with the black church.

One group whose electoral support may best be identified by their extra-church activity is African American women. The relevance of that group emerged when I asked which of the several politically oriented meetings he had participated in during one of my visits was "most important" to him. He chose his appearance before a group called the Coalition of One Hundred Black Women. He explained,

> If you divide the people of the district into four quadrants—male–female and black–white—the best voters, the ones most likely to vote are black women, *by far*. In my primary race, we targeted black women more than any other group. We sent them mailings; we knew they were the group that would respond. We did well among men, but we paid most attention to the women's vote. And it worked. The women in this group—The One Hundred Black Women—are business and professional women. They are a real force in the community.

His reception before the group, which was screening candidates for endorsement, was warm, friendly, and mutually congratulatory. In thinking about his most supportive constituents, activist black women—working in the neighborhoods in support of various grassroots policy concerns—may be as close to the congressman's hard core as one can get.

His choice of constituency connections, and his neighborhood immersion, comes from a desire to help others. On the political level, that desire translates into a problem-solving view of politics. "Politics is multifaceted," he says. "At a general level, what people want is a fair set of rules. At another level, what they want is to have the rules broken or bent to solve their problems. Politics is the interaction between these two levels. People want me to react to their problems in ways useful to them. As Jesse Jackson says, 'People want help at the present point of difficulty.'" In the neighborhoods, Fattah works "at the present point of difficulty." As their representative in the Congress, where "you have to think bigger than your district,"[22] he works at devising "a fair set of rules." To both tasks, he brings a ground-level assurance that he is solving real problems for real people.

ROLL CALL VOTES

Policy representation, as conveyed by his votes in the House of Representatives, poses no problem for Representative Fattah. Like Lou Stokes, Chaka Fattah had to wrack his brain to come up with any roll call vote that he either worried about or had to explain to anyone.

"Ninety-nine percent of my votes are easy," he says.

> I feel quite capable of representing the people of my district. I was born in Philadelphia. I was educated in Philadelphia. I went to public school in Philadelphia. My kids went to public school in Philadelphia. My family runs a community program. I went to community college. I've served on boards of trustees at local colleges. There aren't many institutions I haven't been at—one, two, five times. Take Henry Middle School, where we just went. I have been there at least three times in the last five years— to the tree-planting ceremony, to the opening night of their musical play, and today. And that's one out of hundreds of schools.

He is comfortably immersed and hugely confident where the policy aspects of his representational relationship are involved.

The result is a markedly liberal voting record. On the basic liberalism–conservatism scale pioneered for political scientists by Keith Poole and Howard Rosenthal, Fattah's votes—like Stokes's votes—place him as one of the most liberal members of the House. When the roll call votes of all 435 members were ranked from most liberal to most conservative for the entire 104th Congress (1995–1996), there were only twenty-three members more liberal than he.[23] And near the end of that Congress, he commented, "I have not cast any votes that I have been criticized for. I've led a charmed life—so far." He maintained that identical, very liberal ranking for the next two years. In both years, his ranking and that of Lou Stokes were extremely close; both were securely rooted in the most liberal group within the Democratic Party.

When, after some difficulty, Fattah did come up with a couple of problem votes that he had to explain, they were—as they had been for Stokes—foreign policy votes. In particular, they were votes involving Israel. Both congressmen had Jewish supporters who were reliably supportive of their liberalism but needed extra reassurance on Middle Eastern policy.

In center city, Fattah pointed to a cluster of high-rise apartments. "Those high-rises have a lot of elderly voters—middle class, mostly Jewish. . . . [In 1994] I did very well among Jewish voters here. Lucien's supporters thought that my name would cause them to vote against me. [N.B.: It may sound Arabic, but it is Swahili.] That's what they thought. They were wrong. When I was in the state legislature, I represented Overbrook, a heavily Jewish area. And I did well there." During his first term, he recounted,

> I was invited by a Jewish group to come talk about the problem between Jews and blacks. I told them I didn't know there was a problem, that this was the first time I had ever talked about such a problem. I said that the people who were working together to solve problems were too busy to have a problem and that those who weren't working wanted to make it harder for those who were. I worked on scholarship problems with Marcine Mattlin and on housing problems with Jonathan Saidel.

The one vote he did have to explain to his Jewish constituents was on foreign aid:

> I voted against the first foreign aid package that came to us when I got to Congress. It had money in it for Israel, which is a number-one priority for Jews. Before I even knew what they were going to do, I suggested a meeting so that I could explain my vote. When I explained that the money for Africa had been cut out, they said they understood. I voted for the final bill when it came back from conference with the money for Africa restored. And we had no problem.

Aside from a vote on Bosnia, where he changed his vote, and up until the year 2000, that early foreign aid vote was the only problematic vote he could recall.

In June 2000, however, we met in the aftermath of his most problematic vote. And it had been doubly difficult because his indecision on the matter was widely watched. It was the vote to grant Permanent Normal Trade Relations (PNTR) to China. The proposal would replace the annual review of our China trade policy with a permanent decision to grant that nation our best terms on tariffs and market access. As a trade issue, PNTR cross-cut foreign policy and domestic concerns; it was universally considered to be one of the Clinton administration's most important initiatives and was extremely divisive. As one Philadelphia reporter saw it, "President Clinton, big business, and free trade advocates, eyeing 1.3 billion potential consumers, want Fattah to support China trade. Labor groups and human rights advocates want him to oppose it." But Fattah was not an easy sell: "I voted for annual trade relations with China for the last six years," he said. "The reason that I have difficulty now is that this decision is permanent." [24] His "difficulty" persisted until the time of the vote.

As decision time drew close and the outcome remained in doubt, the "undecided" House members drew the maximum of attention from the protagonists, the vote counters, and the media. Fattah was one such undecided member. Five days before the scheduled vote, President Clinton came to Philadelphia to speak on education. Fattah recalled, "The President took me on Air Force One so he could needle me. He took me in his limousine so he could needle me. He came to the ceremony so he could needle me." "The President of the United States is always convincing," he told the press, "but as of yet on this issue I am not sure it's where I'm at."[25] Three days later, he was one of sixteen remaining undecideds. On the day of the vote, both NPR and CNN followed him around. He would not declare, but he enjoyed the attention. "This is what you run for," he told NPR. "The chance to be an impact player."[26] In the end, he had no impact. The measure passed, but he voted against it.

Because he voted with the great majority of House Democrats, with their leaders, and with most of organized labor, the conventional explanation would focus upon the strength of these two basic components of his supportive constituency. But he had voted before as a free trader. As he put it afterward,

> I voted every year to give most favored nation to China. We trade with everybody else. The European Union trades with them now. Why not just do it? Doesn't it make sense to get it over with and not drag it out year after year. People in my district, Cigna [insurance] and Boeing [aircraft] have jobs because of trade. . . . Cigna broke with the [Republican] Party and supported me to the maximum in 1994. Besides, all the unions are not being hurt. There's a rule about voting that you should take your position early and stick to it. That way, you won't get many questions. On China, I equivocated all over the place until the last minute. As a result, I got a lot of questions, mostly "Why did it take you so long to make up your mind?" It was my hardest vote.

In a conventional sense, his policy decision would not qualify as a constituency-dictated decision. Yet it was a constituency-based decision because, as he explained it, it became a minority-rights decision. As such, it was grounded in the African American heritage he shared with 62 percent of his constituents—and with all African Americans beyond. There was simply too much about China for him, as an African American, to swallow. He recalled a friendly relationship with a Chinese embassy official years before. When Fattah had remonstrated with him about the harsh treatment of

African students in China, he was told by the official, "It is none of your business." "I never forgot that message," he said.

And he discussed his vote calculation.

I voted to support divestiture in order to pressure South Africa on a human rights issue, and I looked at China the same way. If I could exert leverage on behalf of human rights in South Africa, why shouldn't I exert leverage against child labor, intellectual property and human rights in China. It was a tough vote. When you approach these votes, you are thinking about everything. At the end of the day, I decided it was better to do it year by year, that it wouldn't make all that much difference at home, that I didn't want to put the stamp of approval on the regime in China, and that I couldn't forget that conversation I had with that Chinese friend long ago.

His vote was constituency based. Narrowly, that constituency was the Second District of Pennsylvania. Broadly, however, it was that *national constituency* of African Americans—beyond the district of any one member—a surrogate constituency of which each black House member often considers himself or herself to be a representative.

At this level of their representational responsibilities, there is a seamless link between Chaka Fattah and Louis Stokes. As Fattah once recalled, "When I first came to Congress, Lou Stokes said to me, 'There are forty million African Americans, but there are only forty of us who can do what we do—write bills, pass amendments, and vote. If we don't do that, we do a disservice to the broader constituency we are responsible for.' And I have been dedicated to that idea." Less than ten minutes after we first met, Fattah had said to me, "You've studied Lou Stokes? I know Lou Stokes. He's a good guy." And a good cohort-to-cohort mentor, too, perhaps.

SYMBOLIC CONNECTIONS: THE DEWEY STREET AWARD PROGRAM

While Chaka Fattah's policy connections have been paramount in his representational strategy, he knows—as every representative of a historically excluded minority knows—that his racial identity is the essential underlying connection with his African American constituents. In conventional terms, substantive connections have driven his representational activity, but his descriptive connections have legitimized his representational activity.

The behavioral aspect of descriptive representation, as noted earlier, is symbolic representation. Among his African American constituents, Fattah is viewed as a representative of his race. His achievements, his inclusion, his influence, is also their achievement, their inclusion, their influence. When he speaks and acts, he embodies their past, present, and future, their history and their hopes. And he does so to a degree and with an immediacy that is not duplicated between white House members and their white constituents.

The congressman conveyed his understanding of his relationship to his African American constituents this way: "There have been about ten or eleven thousand people elected to Congress from the beginning," he said. "And of those, only one hundred have been African American. That any of them should have been elected is a matter of wonderment. Because so few have done it and because there are so few other offices possible, being the congressman is considered the pinnacle of political success. Because of that, my constituents hold me in esteem—almost reverence. When I come into church, for example, people stand up." He is a symbol of their aspirations, their struggles, and their progress.

While he did not use the word *trust* in discussing his symbolic connections, he did use the word *leeway* to describe the favorable consequences of his symbolic activity. "I am the highest ranking African American elected official in the city and the highest ranking African American elected official in the state, and that gives me a higher standing in my district. Because of that, people give me added leeway in what I do here and what I do in Congress." Here, leeway assumes trust. Doubtless, too, his neighborhood immersion has generated that trust among his constituents.

The most memorable and instructive example of Chaka Fattah's symbolic connections was a talk he gave in 1996 to the African American residents of Unit North Block of Dewey Street in west Philadelphia. We were in his native habitat, and he explained it to me as we drove along endless streets of row houses.

> The block organization is the smallest level of community organization. Some neighborhoods will have 90 percent of their blocks organized. Others will have 40 percent. They are not overtly political. They are organized to cope with community problems. But the organizers are the people who are active politically and otherwise in the community. The group we are meeting with now sent me an invitation ten months ago—maybe a year ago. So you can see how well organized they are.

The event was the Scholastic Achievers Award Program organized by block residents to celebrate the recent graduations of six young people from the block—one from elementary school, three from high school, and two from college. A dozen or so other school children from the block were also in attendance. It was a remarkable grassroots event with atmospherics to match. My notes convey context.

[North Dewey Street] was a narrow side street, blocked off at both ends by police signs. It had solid brick row houses on both sides, two stories, with front porches, a few awnings. The curbs were painted white; there were big wooden tubs of flowers along both sidewalks. Many of the doors and grillwork were decorated. It was treeless. A couple of colored flags flew from light poles. There was no American flag in sight. It must have been like a thousand other side streets in Philadelphia, except that it was a neat, clean, cared for, and watched-over street—a family street—of people trying to raise children to follow the right path.

Midway down the street, in the center of the street, about fifty chairs had been placed in a kind of circle. They were partly shaded by five beach umbrellas. There was a podium and loudspeaker. There were about twenty children and ten adults, and the female master of ceremonies had just begun when we got there. We had a prayer from the preacher, the singing of the Negro National Anthem, a "follow your dreams" talk by a uniformed woman from ROTC . . . then CF talked and we left.

An interesting thing about the setting—on Saturday afternoon—was the predominance of women. Among the thirty people sitting at the ceremony were three men—the reverend, CF, and an old man. [Nine of the eleven speakers listed on the program were women.] On the porches and on the nearby sidewalks were people watching the proceedings and clapping at appropriate moments—maybe twenty-five more. Of these, I saw only four other men. . . . Throughout the ceremony, little kids rode bikes, walked around, and got "shooshed" by adults—mostly women. Several women, including one of four featured women speakers, had white Muslim headwear. The people who brought me a chair, ice, and water and who righted the umbrellas and the potted plants when they tipped over were women. The ones who tried to get the tape deck to work for them were women. The three speakers who had the kids write down "what you want to be when you grow up" and "what do you like to do most"—to try to get them to think very broadly and imaginatively about their careers [and they did!]—were women. They had organized to help kids think about education. They were articulate, enthusiastic, and warm.

The congressman's talk began by congratulating the honorees, extolling the value of education for his listeners, and emphasizing the importance of personal determination. Excerpts:

> People here asked me a year ago if I would come. There was no way I wouldn't be here. The people who asked me were betting on you—that you *would* graduate, that you *would* cross the finish line—and you did. . . . The only way we'll be strong is if our children get an education. . . . [Some people] start out at things and don't always finish them—because finishing is often a difficult course of action. . . . [Some people] make excuses for why they don't get things done. . . . [You must] start out and keep on going—see it all the way through even though the going gets tough. . . . My grandmother was ecstatic when I was elected to Congress. When she was young, she wasn't even allowed to vote.

In the heart of his talk, he used his personal experience, as a role model, to emphasize the importance of persistence in getting an education and in reaping the rewards thereof.

> I went to the best high school in the whole world—Overbrook. When I showed up, the counselor put me into the wood shop. I asked her why, and I told her I didn't want to go to the wood shop. She said, "We took you out of the academic program. Maybe you should go on the auto track." I said, "I want to go to college." She said, "You're not college material." This woman did not know me. She didn't know anything about me, and she had already made a decision about me.
>
> I finally got put on the academic track. When I got into community college, I went back to see that counselor. Then when I got into the University of Pennsylvania, I went back to show her again. When I was at the John F. Kennedy School of Government, at Harvard University, I wrote her a postcard. And when I got a graduate degree from Penn I went back and she had finally retired from Overbrook—thank God. . . . Education is a lifelong effort. Wilson Goode [former mayor of Philadelphia] was sent to the wood shop, too. . . . People are always giving our young people the message that they can't do something. Sometimes it comes from your own home: "Boy, you can't do nothing." . . . A kid's hat may be on backward, but his head is straight."

He ended by emphasizing the importance of self-esteem as the underpinning of persistence in getting an education. Again, he spoke as a role model. Excerpts:

Life is not fair. We all know that. But you should be fair to yourself. . . . Set your eyes on the prize you want. . . . When I ran for Congress, every elected official and the whole establishment lined up with the other guy. I got no big names, no big money. And I got elected by the highest margin of any of the new members of Congress. I didn't let anybody else count me out—no counselor at Overbrook can tell me what I can be. . . . Every person has a brand name all to themselves. What God gave each one, he gave to nobody else, and if people don't develop that God-given ability, we'll never know what they could have done if they had done their absolute best. . . . There's a big difference between working at McDonalds and owning McDonalds. . . . Don't get sidelined on the dirt track of life. Get on the main line. Achieve against the odds. And never, never forget this: do your absolute best.

It was an inspirational talk from an African American success story to his African American reelection constituency.

He spoke as one of them, from among them, as someone who understood their circumstances because he had lived those circumstances. He did not promise these constituents any policy efforts in Congress. Nor did he come to deliver tangible benefits to their neighborhood. The connections he made were symbolic connections. To call it constituency service would be totally off base. He offered the children and their parents only advice, persuasion, and a role model, urging upon them the lessons of his experience: set your goals; get an education; stick with it in the face of daunting obstacles; you can do it. I had not heard him talk about education before. But that large policy subject was to become the centerpiece of my later visits to Philadelphia.

ORGANIZATIONAL CONNECTIONS
AND EXPERIENTIAL LEARNING

The most visible of Chaka Fattah's negotiating and learning experiences at home have been those involving Philadelphia's Democratic Party. From a long-run viewpoint, his career has coincided with a trend that political scientists have long highlighted—a steady decline in the relevance of political parties, particularly urban machines, in the selection and election of candidates for office. As Fattah himself puts it, "Parties aren't as strong as they used to be. Candidates are stronger than parties." The Philadelphia Democratic Party is no exception. Nonetheless, the citywide organization does exist, and it still retains a recognizable influence in the choice of many local candidates.

Reflecting on the course of his career, Fattah commented that "there are bookmarks and signposts and directions that come from past experience." Two of his lessons were: first, that it is prudent, at some point, to negotiate with the party and, second, that there are times and ways to negotiate. This section traces the experiences that led to these lessons and the consequences for his representational activity at home.

When he undertook his first campaign for the job of Philadelphia City Commissioner, he rejected the idea of organizational help altogether. He depended, instead, on his own entrepreneurial talents. As he described it,

> Everyone said we [he and his running mate] were the smartest and most capable candidates ever put forward for the job. The [three] commissioners control the electoral process. We had studied it and knew all about it. Both newspapers endorsed us. We were twenty-one years old, just two kids running against some heavy hitters. We didn't win. *And my learning curve began there.* I learned that you couldn't make speeches if no one was on the phone to take the requests. I learned that you can't compete and build an organization at the same time. I learned that organization comes first.

It was his first learning experience. "Something I've learned over the years," he now generalizes, "is that the candidate is not as important as the organization."

Having been taught, by defeat, to appreciate the need for organization, he was determined to remedy that deficiency before he ran again. He did not, however, turn to the Democratic Party organization. He built, instead, his own independent, personally loyal organization. "When I first ran for state representative," he recalled, "I was challenging the party leadership. I didn't belong to any organization." At every key point in the advancement of his career, he used his own organization to run against the Democratic Party and its officially endorsed candidate. In every case, except for the 1992 congressional primary, he was successful.

As he moved up the elective office ladder, he expanded his organization to meet the growing challenge—from the four wards of the state representative, to the eleven wards of the state senator, to the twenty-four wards of the House member. Talking about his 1994 primary victory, he said, "Everything we did in 1994, I had been doing in all my previous races. We just grew the campaign. There's a big difference between organizing sixty divisions [for state Senate] and six hundred divisions [for Congress]."

The bedrock for each election campaign and the continuity from election to election has come from a personal organization. "My organization," he said in 1996,

> is made up of people who have been with me since I went to the Pennsylvania State House. My chief money-raiser today is the same man who was my chief money-raiser when I first ran. We went to high school together. It used to be car washes and chicken dinners. Now it's thousand dollar checks. To understand my organization, you have to go way back to when I started in politics.

"I have learned," he adds, "that you build your organization before you run for office, not as you go along. Candidates don't win elections; organizations win elections."

While his organization triumphed over the party in that first legislative race, the residual clout of the party organization was not lost on the winning candidate. "On election day, when I ran for state representative," he recalled,

> the party turned out the vote. In this ward [twenty-four], my opponent beat me in some divisions [precincts] 400–2, 300–4. The machine controls the vote. Next election, when I was the party candidate, I won those same divisions 400–2, 300–4. Black, white, Irish, Jewish, Italian, it doesn't matter. If you're the party candidate, the machine will produce the vote. If you want to challenge the party, as I did, you'll have to build up your margin in other places.

His initial triumph over the party and their support for him in the next two elections testified to their basic weakness. Once beaten at the polls, the party could not retaliate.

As the newly elected state representative, Fattah decided to intervene in a tight intraparty contest over Thirty-fourth Ward leadership. He swung the leadership election to a white man—one with whom he subsequently developed a mutually beneficial working relationship. A reasonable guess is that this early negotiation may have opened his eyes to the possible benefits of sometimes working with—not always against—the Democratic Party. Six years later, however, he reasserted his independence by forcing a party-supported, incumbent state senator out of the Democratic primary—which he then won unopposed.

In 1992 and 1994 he ran once more against a party-supported candidate—this time for Congress—in the Democratic primary. There was, however, a noticeable change in his discussion of the two races. Of his 1992, losing effort, he said, "Lucien [Blackwell] was in party politics. He was a ward leader, a leader of black ministers, a labor leader. That was his strength. I ran against the party. I was opposed by the mayor, the party organization, and the entire Democratic establishment. . . . Eighty to 85 percent of the party people voted against me." He did not fear the party. Nonetheless, after the primary, he began to see the wisdom of coming to terms with it. And he began to build his own connections within the party.

He took a different tone, therefore, in discussing his 1994, winning campaign.

> When I began, I wanted to just run right over the party. But I learned that you can't do that, because people pay attention to what the ward leaders and the committee people say. In any election, it may be 10 percent or 20 percent or 30 percent. But they listen. So we took as our goal [in 1994] to have 50 percent of the ward leaders with us by election day. Of the other 50 percent, we let half go and we attacked the other half. We wanted to let people know that we had an organization that could attack a ward and take it over. By election day, we had elected new committee people in six wards and a new ward leader in each. Since then, I have tried to develop a dual competency—to work on policy and to work within the party instead of running against the party.

In 1998 he commented, "Many of the party people in the wards are part of my organization now. If our organization couldn't win, we would mix and match—some community people, some party people—and control the ward that way." He explained, "I learned that it's easier to reach out. . . . For some committee people, it may be just a matter of putting them on your mailing list or inviting them to a summer picnic. Now, I have a better relationship with the party. I've learned it's easier to create bridges."

One such bridge is his easy working relationship with the party chairman—the very same Thirty-fourth Ward leader whom he had helped to power years before. "The other day I had breakfast with the party chairman at the Holiday Inn on City Line Avenue. We talked in a leisurely way for two hours. It was at my suggestion. That two-hour talk was worth more than anything else politically." "We are personal friends," he says. "We may not always agree, because our jobs are different. His job is to keep the party afloat. My job is keeping my career afloat." And the congressman concluded with the comment, "We talk about the issues; but it's not the issues that count. It's personal relationships." That attitude may signal yet another lesson along the road to a negotiated coexistence with the citywide Democratic Party.

Personal relationships have not, however, altered his organizational independence. "There are only two organizations in Philadelphia—the party and mine. People who want to buck the machine, for whatever reason, now come to me." He speaks, now, from a position of established organizational superiority: "Our organization is called The Fattah Organization. It is a very significant organization. It was built from the ground up. It is strictly a political organization—to get me elected. It wages political combat, and it wins most of the time. It is the strongest, most feared organization in the city [smile]. The only rival organization is the party. If there are thirty-three contests, the party will win most of them. But if it's head-to-head in one contest, we will usually win." "My organization," he added, "is the reason I never have to worry about an election." His comment made me think of Lou Stokes's insecurities and of his expressed need to "protect my back." So I asked him, "Have you ever had any trouble inside the organization, any rivals?" "No problems, ever," he replied. He had not been challenged in a primary. And his next three general election margins would register 88 percent, 87 percent, and 98 percent.

Chaka Fattah's current relations with the Democratic Party are strictly protectionist. During the 1996 campaign, I observed one such connection, at a ward committee meeting in north Philadelphia. It was the poorest section of his district, and politics there was still controlled by the Democratic Party organization. His appearance exemplified his maintenance-related party activities.

The setting (according to my notes) was "a cramped, dingy club room" in "a broken-down, graffiti-riddled, boarded-up, run-down neighborhood."

You go up a couple of steps, a man opens a beat-up door and you enter a narrow room—two folding chairs on either side of a narrow aisle. There are about six rows of chairs, then a lectern, then at the end, a large desk. The ward leader sits at the desk and speaks from the lectern. It is poorly lit. There is no food. They are passing out sign-up slips for a Ward Twenty-eight bus ride. There are about twenty black people in all—mostly women plus a couple of kids.

Soon after I sit down in the back, a TV reporter comes in to interview two women near me. He asks the first woman, "Are you supporting Clinton?" "Yes." "What has Clinton done for you?" "A lot. We have pavements and things. But there's a lot of things we don't have." He moves to the second woman, who says of Clinton, "He's the best for our people. We really don't have any choice." Soon, the interviewer leaves. The ward leader, sitting behind his desk, asks the first interviewee, "What did he ask you?" "He asked me what Clinton had done for me," she answers. But under her breath, she mutters to the people around her, "He's done shit." They laugh. "And what did you tell him?" asks the leader. She demurs, "I just told him." Then she speaks again to the people around her. "He's done nothing for me. But everyone else lies to the TV, so why shouldn't I. I don't even have a job."

When the congressman arrives, everyone claps. My notes describe "a rousing, up with Democrats, down with Republicans, no holds barred, rock 'em, sock 'em, get out the vote, vote the straight ticket, smite the enemy speech." He calls himself "your representative." And he begins by identifying with them. "I started out as a committee person, so I know the work you do and how important it is." Then he turns to a litany of policy areas where a Republican presidential victory would put African Americans at risk—Supreme Court decisions on redistricting and affirmative action, congressional decisions on economic and social issues. Excerpts:

> You know they tried to shut down the government and they tried to cut Medicare, Medicaid, student loans, job training, affordable housing. They turned the common people against them because of what they tried to do. . . . [Newt Gingrich] is the Speaker, but he's not speaking for the poor. He's speaking for the rich. . . . He led the most vicious attack on working people in the history of this country. [His] was an agenda against everything we want to see in our community. . . . [Clinton] is the lesser of two evils. But he saved Medicare. . . . The Democrats are not perfect, but they are a lot better than what the Republicans have offered up. . . . The number one priority is jobs, jobs, jobs. [When he says this, the group repeats that with him several times.] . . . We need to punish the Republicans for what they tried to do. No Republican should get any vote where people are alive and live in our community. There are no exceptions. Across the board, cut them out for every office. Vote straight Democratic.

He ends by portraying himself, again, as "your representative": "If I zigged when I should have zagged, let me know. Your leader is carrying your pail of water to the table. He calls me all the time on your behalf." There were no questions, and he did not linger.

The contrast between his vigor and their "dispirited" demeanor served as a reminder—to an outsider—of how much the most needy and impoverished African American citizens rely on the active work of their government and on the active participation of their representatives in Congress. It was a reprise of the reaction I first had during a ride on the unpaved streets of Houston's Fifth Ward twenty-five years before.

As we left the Ward Twenty-eight club room, Fattah commented, "These are the foot soldiers of this party. They do the work. This is where the rubber meets the road, so to speak. I try to visit all twenty-four ward committees. I'm now halfway through." And we took off for a second ward meeting. There, the ward leader doubled as Philadelphia's Democratic Party chairman, and he dominated the proceedings. In that setting, the congressman spoke only half-a-dozen sentences—in praise of the chairman. In both ward-level contexts, he was doing routine maintenance work, working for himself, for the Democratic Party, and for its organizational goals.

Four years later, he talked about organizational maintenance in the absence of a challenge. "My organization has been in a period of self-correction, because we have had no one to fight since my [1994] primary." Some "self-correction," he said, had been achieved when the 1999 Democratic mayoral candidate asked him for organizational help. "Everyone thought he would lose. . . . And afterward, when people spoke confidentially, they said our organization won the election. It was the kind of race you want your organization to be in on. It was a test. If you don't test it, you won't have an organization worth its salt. It takes a lot of time and effort. When people move off the scene, you have a fleeting organization. I've learned over the years that so long as my organization is strong, I can focus first and foremost on my legislation." The mayor's campaign had been beneficial for his organization. A year later, in the context of a citywide, attorney general's race, a *Daily News* reporter wrote, "Fattah is widely believed to have one of the best get-out-the-vote operations in the city . . . the 'filet mignon of Election Day operations.'"[27] His candidate lost. His organization was, indeed, in a period of "self-correction," and he was, apparently, still learning.

For all three of the House members I have discussed thus far—Stokes, Jordan, and Fattah—the most consequential of their constituency-level negotiating and learning sequences centered on their battles within their own political party. Each of these black Democrats did battle with a longstanding, white-dominated, and mostly urbanized Democratic political organization. All three negotiated, over time, a customized relationship that put them in Congress and kept them there. My preoccupation with these three different negotiating sequences should not, however, cloud a broader similarity: that the battle of African Americans for political inclusion in a white-majority world continues to have a substantial organizational component.

PERSONAL CONNECTIONS

Congressman Chaka Fattah's personal connections in his district rest upon his neighborhood involvements. Those longtime relationships have provided him with a layer of personal connections of a sort that I found notably lacking during my rounds of constituency activities with Lou Stokes. On the other hand, there was no single stand-out personal relationship in Fattah's constituency life to approximate that which the Cleveland congressman enjoyed with his brother Carl or with the influential newspaper publisher W. O. Walker. Further, the Fattah organization is spread across manifold electoral units and neighborhood groups and not concentrated in a single organizational vessel like Stokes's Twenty-first Congressional District Caucus. In short, and at first glance, Fattah's personal relationships with his constituents seem to be distinguished more by their ubiquity than by their intensity.

The Second District is easily accessible from Washington—one hour by air, two hours by train. According to his 1995 schedules, the congressman made that trip fifty-one times in that year, and he spent parts of 140 days presenting himself to his constituents. Listed on his schedules for those event days were 380 separate events. Chaka Fattah came home, that is, almost every weekend and made an average of three and a half separate personal appearances per day in the district. On all counts, his first-year schedule at home was more extensive and more intensive than the one I examined of Louis Stokes.

My visits reflected that difference. During my five visits and seven days in Philadelphia, I accompanied Fattah to nineteen events, for an events-per-day average twice that of my events per day with Stokes. And while I have no reason to believe that my visits to either district produced an accurate sample of either member's personal appearances, one apparent difference in their presentational patterns seemed noteworthy. While Fattah gave more public talks—and more often than Stokes—he made relatively fewer command performance–type speeches before large audiences than Stokes. Relatedly, Fattah had none of the one-speech days that bulked so large in my Stokes visits.

Classifying home events is difficult and, at best, suggestive. It is hard to know, from a printed schedule, the purpose of the event or whether the congressman actually did it. By the roughest of estimates, therefore, a typology of his scheduled events indicates that the largest number of Fattah's personal activities were his 135 "attend" or "stop by" community events. For about one-third of these, the congressman participated in a non–speech making way—receiving an award, installing officers, presiding, introducing, or welcoming. The other two-thirds—which made up about one-quarter of all his scheduled events for 1996—seemed to be of the "do it if you can" variety. In those cases, I cannot know for certain whether he eventually showed up or not.

The second most frequently scheduled "events" were about one hundred visits in his district office with groups or individuals. They are the most directly personal of his home connections. Without details—who, what, why—further delineation is impossible. But the subject matter of these visits was far more group-related than individual-related. Ranking third in frequency were sixty-five community events for which he is identified as "keynote speaker" or is given some other clear indication of a central role. The two remaining recognizable types of personal connections on his schedules are thirty-seven party-related meetings and twenty-four media appearances.

The remainder mostly come from time devoted to specialized one-day forays—four school visits, four beauty parlors, four picnics, four town meetings. Each of these sets was highlighted on the schedule as part of a designated "Visibility Weekend." There were six such designated weekends during the year. Some were ordinary; others seemed to emphasize certain activities—office visits in a couple, keynote speeches in another, media appearances in another. While patterning was flexible, their very designation as "Visibility Weekend" called attention to the importance of keeping in touch.

My visits provided examples, but no sample. I was present at: six "attend" events, three of which provided for a minor participatory role; zero district office meetings; five "keynote" speaking events; eight party-centered events; and no media appearances. Proximity to election day heavily influenced the makeup of my event days in his district.

In his eyes, that would be atypical. "I try to combat cynicism," he says. "People say to politicians, 'I only see you at election time.' I try to be around more often when there is no election—the reverse cycle. And I try to go to places at my suggestion, not theirs. People like it a lot better when you come to them on your own, without an invitation." Later, in the same 1996 interview, he commented, "I was more successful [at personal contact] when I was in the state Senate than I have been since I have been in Congress. There are more people and less time. I've done 75 percent of what I need to do in the district. The important thing is not be reactive, but proactive. I've been a little more reactive and little less proactive than I want to be." On the evidence of his schedules, his success cannot be confirmed.

In matters of direct one-on-one constituent service, Fattah's correct but unenthusiastic approach seems very close to that of Lou Stokes. "Anyone who wants to see me, can see me. They will be told that there are other people in the office who can help them. But if they want to see me, they can. It's much better to go too far in this direction than to go too far in the other direction and have people calling in to talk shows saying, 'I tried to see my congressman, but he wouldn't see me.'" He gets satisfaction, he says, from being able to help "a client"—as he and his staff call them—but he feels the effect is negligible. "When you do something to make another person happy, it makes you feel good. But in the largest scope of things, where politics is concerned, it is meaningless. If I help 1 percent of my 580,000 constituents in some way, it is a drop in the bucket. It makes no difference. It really doesn't help me." It is, as he knows, however, preventive maintenance.

When I asked him directly what his constituent clients thought of him, he called in his top constituent-service staffer and, briefly, stepped outside his office. Our conversation went like this: "What do his constituents think of him?" "They are comfortable with him. They think he's knowledgeable. They know that he keeps company with kings and queens, but they think of him as a home boy. He talks to them on their level. He cares. . . . They say, 'I knew him when he was a little boy.' Or, 'He visits my church.' Their church may not be in his district, but we serve them anyway. . . . They are very needy people, elderly and worried about taxes." "Do they call to give their opinions on what he does?" "Yes, they do. They say, 'I like what he does. He's got guts.'" "Do they know that he works on education?" "Yes, they like what he does on education." "Where do they come from?" "All over—Yeadon, west Philly, Germantown, Darby."

When the congressman returned, he asked her, "Do they call and ask about issues?" And she replied, "You know what? Not much." I got no sense from these exchanges that he was in close personal touch with his constituent-service operation. "He's not a constituent-service congressman," said one observer. But his staff seemed to be doing its job, and the tenor of my conversation with his staffer seemed routinely favorable to him.

When he spoke positively about his personal service to individuals, he spoke about that which was connected to his network of personal contacts in the community.

Most of what people think about and talk to me about has nothing to do with the federal government. It's the Al D'Amato thing—potholes. Most of the help I give people comes because of the network of people I have met and worked with during my career. That woman we met today with the dangerous middle school building. I can help her because my former chief of staff is on the city school board. I'll call her and ask her to go to the school and help them. With a problem of state licensing, I contact the man who took my seat in the state Senate. The man who is the small business person for the mayor was my first campaign manager. One of my former district aides is now on the city council, and I can go to her for help. I helped a woman's son get into a special post–high school program the other day because I'm on the board of trustees at the school and I play golf with the director of the program. She thinks I did it because I'm a member of Congress.

The congressman has no doubts about the importance of these piecemeal person-to-person activities. "In the end, most people support you for reasons that have nothing to do with anything you put in your job description. The only question is the degree to which you will expend resources doing this kind of work in the constituency."

His immersion in the city and its neighborhoods clearly equips him admirably to do this kind of work in the constituency. But just as clearly, it is not his personal passion. He rations his personal resources of time and energy so that he can devote them to policy making. My guess is that a preponderance of the one hundred personal connections he made with visitors to his district office in 1995 were of two sorts: with people already in his personal network or with people who have particular policy interests. The first group helps with political preventive maintenance, giving him "leeway and flexibility for what you want to do elsewhere." The second group helps him to identify problems and discuss solutions that he can deal with "elsewhere."

INSTITUTIONAL CAREER AND REPRESENTATION

POLICY MAKING AND THE REPRESENTATIONAL CYCLE

Chaka Fattah's life inside the House of Representatives has been driven by his policy interests and by the challenges confronting a policy-driven member of the minority party. His policy interests are those that have grown out of his neighborhood experiences at home, about which he would "have to think bigger than your district." During my two 1996 visits, his policy enthusiasm focused on a complex plan to revitalize the nation's largest cities by increasing their borrowing authority and by attracting private investment in redevelopment projects under the Community Development block grant program. His legislative vehicle was entitled "American Cities Investment Act."[28]

In that context, he articulated his policy goals and his policy-intensive representational strategy. "Something is going to happen in big cities," he said.

> It may not be in the next Congress or the next. But sometime it will have to be addressed. For years, I've been working to put myself "in the room" when that happens. I even got criticized in the state legislature, "Why are you so interested in national problems? Why don't you just take care of your district?" I think I have a creative, radically different approach for putting together the fiscal resources necessary to revitalize big cities. I've been spending time building support for the bill.
>
> There's a big difference between those who can recite the problems and those who can solve the problems. And if you look at who leads and who follows, you see there's a lot of room for people like myself on the solution side. There's not a lot of competition. . . . There are no other proposals like mine. There are other people working on the same problems, but it's a very small number at the table.

He seemed to be adapting to his minority status. Among the five names he mentioned "at the table," three were Republicans and two were Democrats. "It took Jack Kemp to open up the debate on urban issues," he said. "On policy, I work with Republicans." It was the challenge that motivated him. "You don't get rich when you rise to a high position. I've risen as far as most. The question is: What do you do when you get there? What do you want to get done?"

When I returned two years later, the congressman had hit his policy-making stride. His cities investment project had been set aside. He was fully engaged in a policy area where his immediate prospects were considerably brighter—higher education. His prospects had brightened for three reasons: education had been his most enduring policy interest, he was a member of the relevant House Committee on Education and the Work Force, and the Democratic administration had raised education to a top priority. Experience, jurisdiction, and timing, therefore, were on his side. But the idea, the drive, and the skill were his. And he was gaining legislative traction.

He began, he later explained, with an unusual measure of self-confidence.

Some big pieces of my [new] job I was comfortable with. I was very comfortable as a legislator. I knew how to draft legislation, conduct a hearing, and get a bill passed into law. One of the beauties of being in Congress is that you can take that kind of experience and become a leading person in a field—even though you have had no experience in that field. You learn the substance of the issue as you go along. On my Government Affairs subcommittee, I became a leading person on the Postal Service . . . about which I knew absolutely nothing when I came to Congress. . . . I knew how to pass legislation and I could do it for the Postal Service.

On my major committee, Education, I had plenty of experience. In the state House of Representatives, I was a member of the Education Committee. In the [state] Senate, I was chairman of the Education Committee. I sat on the board of trustees at two colleges. I was a representative on the State Board of Education. I traveled to every hick town in Pennsylvania, talking about education. I did not have a lot to learn when it came to passing education legislation.

In the end, events supported that self-assessment.

His idea was to develop an "early intervention" program that would, "increase the access to higher education for very-low-income children for whom the opportunity to attend college is not even on the table." The analytic base was the finding that "high achieving students from low-income families are five times as likely not to attend college as high achieving students from high-income families."[29] Education for low-income students, he said, "is about empowerment. It is about bringing those who have been marginalized into the mainstream. It is the way in which people who have been written off can be written back in."[30]

Under his legislation, middle school students from low-income families would be promised college tuition aid if they met certain performance standards all the way through high school. And colleges would provide extensive mentoring throughout the period. Sixth grade students who enrolled in the program would be given, each year, a "Twenty-first Century Student Certificate," reminding them of the financial help that was waiting for them upon their high school graduation. Schools, colleges, and private groups would form partnerships to apply for and administer the grants. The plan was modeled after several privately financed programs that had been successful in steering low-income students to college.[31] And, as a bonus gift to him from the media, his proposal had quickly been labeled—at home and elsewhere—as "the brainchild of Chaka Fattah."[32]

He introduced the first version of the legislation in February 1997. One year later, his policy leadership was authenticated when President Clinton presided over a nationally televised ceremony in the East Room of the White House to put the administration stamp of approval on Fattah's "High Hopes for College" initiative.

On stage, and on C-SPAN, were the president, the vice president, the secretary of education, and the Representative from Philadelphia. The vice president called Fattah the "driving force" behind the program. The secretary placed him "at the forefront of the effort." The president described him as a man "for whom this has been a life passion" and promised that "under the leadership of Congressman Fattah, we will make it work." In thanking the president for his support and his encouragement, Fattah recalled that during the recent State of the Union address, "the president pointed at me" when speaking about college for low-income students.[33] Few members of the House, majority or minority, early or late in their careers, ever receive so strong a public presidential endorsement—both personal and programmatic—as Fattah received from President Clinton that March day.

In April the bill passed his House Education Committee as the "High Hopes 21st-Century Scholarship Initiative." After easy passage in the House and Senate, and in the conference committee, it was signed into law in October. When it emerged, the title had been changed from High Hopes to Gear Up (Gaining Early Awareness and Readiness for Undergraduate Programs). The Gear Up program was allocated $120 million for the next fiscal year, with a provision for $300 million over three years. It was a major personal and policy accomplishment for its author—the more so because he was in the minority party when he did it. Back home in Philadelphia, it lifted, decisively, the burden of Bill Gray's legacy.

The congressman's reconstruction of strategy and events tells us something about his policy-making perspectives and talents. Several excerpts follow:

> *Early strategy:* There were two major turning points: getting the White House on board and getting the bill out of [the House] committee. And they were equally important. Failure at either point would have cost us the bill.
>
> *White House:* Several times I went over to the Education Department to talk about the idea. One day I had a conversation with a staff member there . . . whom I had known in Philadelphia. I asked her who I could talk with in the White House. Just to show you that when big things

happen, it's the little things that count, she told me that I needed to see [Presidential Assistant] Gene Sperling—that though his job was the economy, his real passion in life was education for poor kids. . . . He and I talked half-a-dozen times over the next year. I don't call it a negotiation, because in a negotiation, you have to give up something. . . . Our meetings empowered and enhanced the program. . . . we increased the emphasis on mentoring and broadened the eligibility requirements. [During the East Room ceremony, the president praised Sperling for his work on the legislation.]

The President: I talked personally with the vice president and the president. . . . He was primed for the idea, because last year's budget had a lot of higher education in it. But the reality of those programs—tax credits and scholarships—was that the beneficiaries were middle-class and upper-class kids and not low-income kids.

The president countered by saying that the Pell grants had been increased—which they had been. And that is still the basic program for low-income college students. The point I made to the president was that my program is a departure from the norm in conventional financial aid programs [because those programs] leave out all the kids that dropped out along the way and never thought they had a chance to get to college. The idea is to take the present financial system and use it as a motivator—to give students the knowledge that they can do something with their lives. It's a different approach. It motivates the students to work and the teachers to get involved.

The House Committee: I needed Republican votes. But the first thing I did was to get all the Democrats to support it. My political philosophy is that you get the Democrats first and then the Republicans. . . . In the committee, [Republican] Mark Souder [who had visited the Fattah family's House of Umoja in Philadelphia] spoke in favor of it.[34] I also got [Republicans Joe] Scarborough and [David] McIntosh. . . . When Scarborough voted "yes," I knew we had it. I had been working on him for a year. [The vote was 24–19 in favor, with five Republicans voting "yes."] [35] It was a moment of great drama in the committee.

House Committee Chairman: I kept working on Chairman [Bill] Goodling. He never fully embraced it, but I was able to moderate his opposition. He was not as aggressive as he could have been. I've been out to his district almost as much as I've been in mine. I went to two hearings he held there—the only Democrat to do so. I took an interest in what he was doing. I did everything I could to wear him out—or build him up. [Goodling voted against the bill.] Afterward, he allowed me to add my name as a sponsor of the entire Higher Education Bill. Usually it's only the chairman and ranking member. It signified that I was the author of thirteen pages. I thought it was a pleasant departure from the norm.

The Republicans: I tried to convince my conservative colleagues that mostly it's the kids' failures that cost us money—crime, teenage pregnancy, etcetera. Here's a program that doesn't cost you a dime unless it works. . . . If you look at [Newt] Gingrich's book, where he talks about the change from a welfare society—which I don't think we have—to an opportunity society, if you think broadly about the idea of opportunity, that's what this bill is all about.

Strategy: The White House agreed that we would not politicize High Hopes. It was not listed in the Democratic agenda. The White House made no comments when it passed the House. . . . That has a lot to do with the smoothness in getting it where it is now—in the Senate. . . . As we moved along, there were all kinds of chances to compromise, to cut deals, to have pilot programs. I used to be called the best vote counter in the state Senate. My philosophy is get the votes and, assuming you have the votes, go forward.

Senate Chairman: I called [Republican Senate Labor and Public Welfare Committee Chairman Jim] Jeffords to suggest we get together before the Senate took up the bill. He asked me, "Are you going to bring staff?" I didn't know him. I had never met him. I thought, "That's a funny question"; but I took a guess and said, "No." We agreed to meet, and when I got over to his office, he said, "Let's get out of here and just walk."

We walked and walked, all around the Capitol. He said that he had read my legislation and that he agreed with everything I said. In fact, he said that he had been interested in the same thing and that he had put a provision in the previous higher education legislation providing for grants to states to help kids move to college—a competitive grant program, authorized at 3 million but never funded. He also said that the Republicans were opposed to starting any new education programs and that he would be very uncomfortable supporting any new program such as High Hopes—even though he agreed with the idea.

Well, I'm not dumb. He didn't say it, but I knew what he was saying. So I said, "Let me go back and work up some language, and I'll get back to you." We went back to the previous authorization legislation and, sure enough, there was his little program. So we devised a single program with two parts—one was his state grant program and one was my High Hopes. . . . I would say we made a deal. But my staff gets on me when I say that, so I'll call it an accommodation.

If you think of my life in Philadelphia and his life in Vermont, and him being around a long time and me a newcomer—and here we are affecting the lives of millions of kids, just walking around the Capitol together. . . . In the long run, policy analysts and politicians usually come out in the same place, but they go about it in very different ways.

Conference: We got it, the whole thing—except for the name. My entire concept is in the bill, just the way we wanted it—except that it's called Gear Up. That's the only difference.

Aftermath: I always saw High Hopes / Gear Up as my first major legislative victory. And success builds on success. [Republican subcommittee chairman Frank] Riggs has agreed to give me a hearing on my school finance equity bill. So that's next. Success may be years away. But I believe you build currency for your ideas. . . . I'm also having a ball . . . taking advantage of situations that turn up—like [Dick] Armey's auto insurance bill—where my amendment cuts rates in Philadelphia by 40 percent. . . . I want to get the basics of my agenda introduced—the equity bill, investment in cities, auto insurance. I want to get each one laid out and work on them. Then we'll be able to see how good a legislator I really am.

Once again, he ended on a familiar note of personal and policy challenge.

Interested constituents would not be surprised to learn that their Representative's first policy success involved public education. He had been steeped in education and education policy. As he detailed earlier, he had labored in this policy area since his days in the Pennsylvania legislature. For years, he had sponsored a weekend-long Graduate Opportunities Conference in the district—to link education to the job world. When he describes his constituency, he highlights its educational institutions. His personal educational experiences had been a defining part of his life. And his talk to the neighborhood group on Dewey Street touched upon the personal emotions behind his policy commitment to education.

His résumé lists numerous awards for his career-long service to education. During the interim between House and Senate passage of High Hopes [June 1998], I accompanied him to one such award ceremony—at the West Philadelphia College Access Center, which administered the federal TRIO program to mentor college-bound students. He was bringing his constituents a $216,000 award from the Department of Education; they were giving him the first Partner in Education Award from the Pennsylvania Association of Schools and College Admission Counselors.

The trading of grant announcements and credit-claiming is a standard form of representational reciprocity. But since the center was also in the business of encouraging, teaching, and guiding low-income high school students, their TRIO program and Fattah's High Hopes program were approaching the same policy problems with the same philosophy. There was, therefore, an especially strong connection between Representative and constituency—something more than a superficial exchange of compliments. Indeed, Fattah had begun his program with the idea that the mentoring part of High Hopes could be handled through the TRIO program—until his White House talks led to much broader, deeper, and longer mentoring commitments.

Speaking to twenty-five people in the Access Center office, he wove the two programs into his talk. "I am pleased to represent a city that helps young people think through their chances and their choice points in life. . . . I designed the legislation because of examples in my district. . . . Latino and African American young people get lots of negative messages, so it is very important that they get positive messages. If we have high expectations for them, they will do better. . . . In Philadelphia it is important to have professionals like yourselves available, people who know about various programs . . . who can help young people find their way through the admissions process. You enhance the life chances of students because of the work of your great organization. Yours is the best program in the country." [36]

Whether or not media attentiveness had been affected by his Washington activity, I cannot say. But all three major Philadelphia television stations came to get interviews. In each interview, he stressed the value of "early intervention." [These interviews did not, incidentally, appear on his schedule.] Afterward, he said, "If you look at my earlier [press] clips, all they mentioned was my organization. Now, all they mention is policy. I'm a mixture of both."

That 1998 exposure was only a warm-up. Two years later, I observed a capstone constituency connection. At a June 12, 2000, event, Representative Fattah brought closure to the basic representational policy cycle—from idea to enactment to implementation. Having developed a policy idea out of his constituency experiences, and having been able to convert that idea into a nationally important Act of Congress, the Representative had returned to his constituency to superintend the implementation of his policy idea in the place where it had begun. He had come back to participate in the ceremony at which the first tangible benefits of his Gear Up program—the actual 21st Century Scholarship Certificates—would be handed out to students from his own neighborhood.

As we drove to the ceremony, Fattah explained that the citywide kick-off for Gear Up had come a month earlier when President Clinton came to Philadelphia to speak on education—at which event the president had, symbolically, given a single student the first certificate. While the congressman did not mention it, the transcript of Clinton's speech included "thanks to my great friend Chaka Fattah . . . for championing this program. . . . in the future we will look back and see this Gear Up program as a profoundly important step in ending inequality and lifting people in America. And, no matter what he said in giving me credit, it was Congressman Fattah's idea. [Applause.] I wouldn't be here if it weren't for him, and he deserves the credit." [Applause.] [37]

Looking forward to the upcoming ceremony, Fattah commented that he would be missing some roll calls in Washington and that one of them was "my second significant piece of legislation, the College Completion Grant Program." [38] "But my local people have told me," he added, "that it's much more important for me to be here than anywhere. We will hand out the certificates to the first group of seventh graders in the Gear Up program. These students are from the heart of my district, from the neighborhood where I grew up, where I went to high school. Some of them are from my old middle school. Both my children went to school there. This is a major event, and it's where I should be." And, as consolation, he added that his bill would go through without a roll call vote. (It did and became law.)

The upcoming ceremony, he said, was the only one he would attend. He added that seven separate "clusters" had been organized in Philadelphia and that the city's $28 million grant was the second largest commitment made under the program. "We had the advantage," he added, "of knowing the history and the content of the legislation. And we had the author. It would have been embarrassing if our proposal had not been a very good one. It was the most scrutinized of all the proposals because it came from my district." [39]

Over three hundred relatives, friends, and supporters had packed a University of Pennsylvania auditorium to watch fifty-two seventh grade students from a "cluster" of four middle schools officially become the first Gear Up class in Pennsylvania. He received warm praise from the educational professionals who preceded him to the podium. Their introductory remarks were different from, and less standardized than, most—because the hyperbole was so directly connected to tangible accomplishment. The opening speaker began,

> Meetings like this, celebrating the first year of Gear Up, are going on all over the country. But the only celebration that has the author of the legislation present at its meeting is the Overbrook Cluster. Chaka Fattah—*he's ours!* We are privileged to have him here. [Applause.] This is living history! No one has done what this man has done. He has helped millions of Americans. . . . I hope all of you will take this opportunity to shake hands with him afterward.

His introducer followed.

> He has spent a lifetime focused on young people. . . . But nothing is more important to Congressman Fattah than education. And one of his greatest successes—in getting it through the Congress, particularly because it was sponsored by a Democrat—is Gear Up. The person who put it together for the whole nation was Chaka Fattah. We owe him a great debt of gratitude. He went to school right here—at Shoemaker Middle School and Overbrook High School. . . . He is living proof of what any student can accomplish with the proper foundation and preparation. . . . I ask you to give him a great round of applause. [Applause.]

The audience—most of whom came to see their children cross the stage—listened respectfully, patiently, and silently when the congressman opened with his favorite personal theme: "Are we going to *challenge* the young people to do their best to work hard and stay in school? You may look in the dictionary and find *success* before *work,* but in real life, children have to work at it." When he hit closer to home, however, they responded enthusiastically with "right" and "yes." "If they can remember the words of every rap song ["Right!"], if they can, like clockwork, know the intricate details of the television schedule ["Right! Yes!"], they can learn the subject matter that will prepare them to go to college." [Loud applause, the first of the speech.]

"We spend billions and billions of dollars to provide for people who are going to do the wrong thing. It's about time in this country that we start to provide some guarantees for young people who are going to do the right thing." [Applause.] He closed with: "Aptitude is very important, but it is not the controlling factor determining where you end up in life. Your attitude is the controlling factor. . . . If you believe it, you can achieve it." With the presentation of awards, and with picture taking afterward, the congressman completed the grand cycle of policy representation—from a constituency-grounded idea to national-scale legislation to constituency benefit and constituency approval.

The prose of the preceding paragraphs conveys an analysis. But it also conveys my personal approval—almost celebratory approval—because that award ceremony seemed to capture so much of what representative democracy is all about. Representative Fattah was playing out a policy-based cycle as fundamental to the process of representation as the more familiar election-based cycle of campaigning-governing-campaigning is to the electoral process. I was observing a celebration that was the analytic equivalent of a reelection-night victory party.

With respect to these emotional and symbolic aspects of the ceremony, however, there was a large gap between my reaction and that of the congressman. He had already made it clear that it was his "local people" that convinced him that he "needed to attend"; he had finally concluded that this was "where I should be"—not "wanted to be"; and he kept measuring his attendance by what he was missing in Washington. He displayed no eagerness or anticipation at the thought of being in his home territory, with his primary constituency, sharing their approval of his legislative accomplishment. Unlike myself, the congressman saw no "grand representational cycle."

When it was over, when I anticipated some expression of personal pleasure, there was none. He came over to me and asked, "Do you have a ride back to the hotel?" I said, "Yes." He turned and walked away, satisfied. I did not see him again for a year. The difference in our reactions to the ceremony, underlined the single-mindedness with which the congressman pursued his goals. He had long since digested his policy accomplishment and put it behind him. He was looking ahead, as always, to the next challenge.[40]

POWER IN THE HOUSE AND EXPERIENTIAL LEARNING

After six years in Congress, Chaka Fattah had amply met two early challenges posed by his job—winning reelection and influencing legislation. With respect to his personal performance and reputation, he had climbed—and quickly, too—to the top of the political hill in Philadelphia. With respect to a third job challenge—achieving a recognizable power base inside the institution—he still had a lot of climbing to do. The same ambition that had driven him up the electoral and the legislative ladders was also driving him up the chamber's own institutional ladder, but at the time of his Gear Up triumph, he had not yet begun to move.

For individual House members, the path to inside power normally runs through positions in the party leadership, or positions on committees, and sometimes through informal member caucuses or coalitions. He had been assigned to two committees: Education, and Work Force and Government Affairs. When we met, well into Fattah's first term, he was already thinking about changing to a more influential committee.

I could stay on the Education Committee and move up. I waged a fight to get on it, even though it was not my first choice, because I wanted a safe harbor. The lion's share of my work has been in education. So I wouldn't be miserable going to work every morning for twelve or fifteen years on the Education Committee, and maybe getting to be chairman. I'd be comfortable there, and I know I would get a lot accomplished. It does important work, even though it has no pizzazz. . . . But I'd like to get on a big, big picture committee—Appropriations, Ways and Means, Rules, Commerce. My preference would be Rules. I've got a lot of interests, and it would give me range.

As for his chances? "Who knows when the train starts and stops. I've done all the things I should do. I've raised money. I've been a key player in the Black Caucus. But there are only a few seats, and seniority is still important. The way things work around here, if you don't get situated where you want to be during your first four years, you stay where you are." I had no idea what, if anything, he was doing to make a change.

Eight months later, in early 1997, circumstances had dictated his path for him. Any plans and prospects he might have developed were altered by the announcement that the congressman from Philadelphia's First District—a sitting member of the Appropriations Committee—would be resigning from Congress soon to take another job. Citing the rationale for a Pennsylvania replacement on that Committee, Fattah seized the opportunity to announce that "I am very interested." And having already talked with "appropriate" people about it, he added that, "No one has dampened my interest." [42] He began to work for membership on the powerful, money-controlling Appropriations Committee. Participation in the decisions of that committee would give him extra leverage in winning funds for his district and an extra measure of influence with his colleagues in the House.

The battle for a top committee position of this sort is not like the battle for legislation. When there is competition, it involves one's own colleagues, not outside interests. Winning a committee assignment is a more exclusively party-oriented and party-dominated process than making a law. Its inside,

deal-making processes are more personal, more idiosyncratic, more compli-
cated, less open, and altogether less predictable than lawmaking. In sum,
these several factors meant that Chaka Fattah's proven legislative prowess
would be of no special help to him in his quest for a seat on the Appropriations Committee.

He had been working toward this new committee goal for over a year
when we first talked about it in the summer of 1998. He was confident that
his preparatory work had paid off. He had won the support of other aspiring
Pennsylvania colleagues, and he had won the support of veteran Pennsylvania Congressman John Murtha who, as a member of the key decision-
making body, would argue his case in the party councils. And Murtha apparently thought that he already "had a deal" with the party leader.[42]

In our summertime conversation, Fattah wavered between the view that
it was a done deal and the view that it wasn't. "Murtha sees it as a tradition,"
he said, "that Pennsylvania had two members on Appropriations, one from
the west [Murtha himself] and one from the east." As for his party relationships, he added, "I've done all the things I'm supposed to do. I've raised
money for the party. I've given speeches for the party. I even went on the
Ethics Committee for the party. Unless something goes very wrong, I have
crossed another boundary. I have passed my first piece of legislation, and I
have gotten on one of the most powerful committees in Congress." A little
later, he entertained a small reservation. "It's as close to being done as anything can be in politics."

In December politics intervened and something did go "very wrong."
The Capitol Hill newspaper *Roll Call* carried the headline, "Democrats Hand
Out Prime Panel Slots: Murtha Storms out of Meeting after Fattah Fails to
Get Appropriations Assignment."[43] For one reason or another, seven House
members—three of them African Americans—had more support than he.
It would be impossible to re-create the inside maneuvering and support patterns. For Fattah, it was an unexpected blow. The press release announcing
his appointment had already been written and was ready to go. "Up to now,"
said a friend afterward, "it's been Appropriations, Appropriations, Appropriations. Now, he's saying 'I could become Chairman of the Education
Committee.' But his heart isn't in it. He's in a funk." He made no public
comment. But a story circulated that in "making up" with John Murtha,
party leader Dick Gephardt had promised the next committee vacancy to
Fattah.[44]

Two years later, when we rehashed the 1998 debacle, the congressman was back in the committee hunt—riding, I assumed, on some reassurance from leader Gephardt. He was circumspect when he recalled the events of 1998.

> We had done everything possible to make sure that we had it. We were 99.95 percent sure we did. But in politics, 99.95 percent is not 100 percent. We thought the big battle was winning the nomination inside the Pennsylvania delegation. People in the delegation did not believe that the eleven Democrats would vote for a black man from Philadelphia in a secret ballot. But they did. We thought that was the critical vote, and we held a premature celebration. We were assured by everybody that it had been decided that Pennsylvania would get a seat to fill the seat we just lost. . . . I had it all lined up. But power is dispersed among so many people in the [Democratic] Party. And in politics, you always depend on other people.

A summertime article in the *Inquirer* captured his institutional career stage by noting that "For more than four years, Fattah . . . has been trying to make friends and push education bills, but in the House he is still on the periphery of power."[45]

The congressman updated his intentions. "In the end, the only thing that mattered [in 1998] was that I didn't get it," he said. He recalled his talk with an influential Steering Committee member. "He said to me, 'You have two choices. You can fight it and lose. Or you can let it go around. It will be better for your future if you go around.' So I had a choice: concede or try again. I'm a big boy. I understood the process. And I had a nice talk with Gephardt the other day. I'm convinced more than ever—99.99 percent—that I will get it." Once more, he rehearsed his options. "I'd be happy on Education. Getting it in the first place was an accomplishment. [But] education programs that get authorized do not always get funded, and Appropriations sets national priorities. It is a superior choice." "Appropriations," he concluded, "is a 'right now' issue for me. Either accomplish it or flush it."

When we next met, Chaka Fattah had achieved his goal. He was a member of the House Committee on Appropriations. But it had not been easy. "After last year," he explained, "everyone expected and agreed that I was in first place next time if another position became available. But several important circumstances intervened." New suitors, with powerful backing, emerged. "I was still in the lead, but I had to worry," he recalled. The Democratic log jam was broken when the Republican majority party leadership reversed its course and agreed to add one more slot to the minority side of the committee. One powerful contender withdrew and two Democrats were chosen.[46] During our subsequent visit to a middle school, every administrator, teacher and school board member with whom he visited congratulated him on the appointment.

When he rehearsed the happy outcome, Fattah treated the saga as a learning experience. While he already knew, from his experience in the Pennsylvania legislature, how to legislate, he said, "I had to learn the politics of the institution." "Take the importance of the Pennsylvania delegation," he continued.

> In Harrisburg, no one ever talked about "the Philadelphia delegation." It doesn't mean a thing. We were individuals. In the House, it's not like that. Right after I was elected, Bill Gray spent two or three hours with me, bringing it home to me how important the Pennsylvania delegation was to my future in the House. I had not understood any of it.
>
> But when John Murtha from western Pennsylvania asked me if I would go speak to the Johnstown NAACP in his district, I went. He said, "I'll send you by plane and pay your hotel." I said, "Forget the plane and the hotel." And I drove myself out there to do it. There may not have been ten people in the Johnstown NAACP, but that wasn't the point. He asked me to do it, and if he asked me to do it, I wanted to do it. I never understood before I got to Congress how important that was.

The congressman's comments to me over the years had made it amply clear just how important it was. But when I asked him, after the fact, "who were the most important people in your success," he unhesitatingly said, "Number one, John Murtha, followed by my fellow Philadelphian Robert Borski, and, third, party leader Dick Gephardt." He elaborated.

> Pennsylvania had three people on the top committees, and all came from the western part of the state. People from the east argued that we deserved any Appropriations seat that came up. Two people from Philadelphia— Tom Foglietta and Bill Gray—had held a seat on the committee before. Murtha, who came from the west, was put in a tough spot because westerners expected him to back their candidate—Mike Doyle, not me. In fact, Doyle thought he had it. . . . It was a very unpleasant situation for Murtha. But he supported me. It was a gut-wrenching fight inside the delegation, and I won by one vote. Murtha's vote was the crucial decision. If I had not gotten the nod from the delegation, my bid would have been stopped cold in the delegation. One reason Murtha was so upset when I

lost it the first time was because he had gone through such personal agony to go out on a limb for me. Then, to go through such shenanigans in the Steering Committee made him angry. But the fact that we lost the first time was a big asset the following time. There was a lot of uneasiness about what had happened, and that's what put me in first place.

Institutional politics, he had learned, was also home politics.

That conclusion was underscored when he named the second most influential contributor to his success—his senior Philadelphia colleague, Bob Borski.

He got up in the delegation meeting and said that he would not run for it; then he yielded to me; then he led my campaign inside the delegation. Where he helped me even more, however, was with Gephardt. He works closely with Gephardt. He managed Gephardt's campaign for majority leader. Gephardt can't get everyone he wants for the best committees, but he can stop anyone he does not want. Borski's campaign helped me with the leadership. And without that help, I would not have gotten the position.

In elaborating on Minority Leader Gephardt's support, Fattah talked about another learning experience inside the institution, once again in contrast to his previous experience. "I had to learn the importance of the staff. In the state legislature, it didn't matter how well you got along with staff. Here, it does. The higher you go in the party leadership, the more important staff become. When the leadership meets to prepare for the Steering Committee meeting, staffers will say, "People don't like that person; we can't have him in that job." And the leaders listen. I had to learn that." He completed his recollections by mentioning other individuals who helped him—one who "bowed out of the race and supported me" and one who helped gather support inside the Steering Committee.

Interestingly, he did not mention the Congressional Black Caucus. So I asked him about their support. "They supported me," he answered. "During the preliminary leadership meeting to prepare for the Steering Committee meeting, Gephardt asked Murtha to call the chairman and the vice chairman of the CBC to make it very clear that I had their support. Each one said 'yes,' and that settled it. There was no caucus vote on it." In view of the top priority that the CBC has historically given to the salting of its members among appropriate committees, the absence of any positive push in this case is noteworthy.

It was just such a concerted intervention by his fellow African American members that put Louis Stokes on the same committee years earlier. In that case, too, committee politics had been local politics. But Stokes's black colleagues aggressively supported him in the face of opposition from his more senior and hometown delegation colleague, Charlie Vanik. In both disputes, race was the central factor. Vanik played the politics of exclusion, whereas Borski played the politics of inclusion. The two very different power-seeking scenarios give us another measure of change in the impact of race on institutional life from the pioneer cohort to the contemporary cohort. The CBC was a central factor in the institutional life of Louis Stokes. It is a peripheral factor in the institutional life of Chaka Fattah. Both learned something from their experiences in gaining Appropriations Committee membership. The experience and the lessons, however, were different.

To close the circle on his accomplishment, I asked, "What if you had not won?" "Education is a major committee and I was moving up. So there was some upside. The only downside was that I would have taken a hit back here. People would say 'Chaka Fattah wanted it, but he couldn't get it.' I would have taken a hit on my reputation back home. I can take that hit. That's not a problem. But if people said 'he wants to pass legislation, but he can't get any passed'—*that* is a hit I could not take. My goal is not to be on Appropriations. My goal is to be a legislator." It was a nice restatement of his personal goal and his policy-centered representational strategy at home.

POLICY, POWER, AND MEDIA CONNECTIONS

As a group of self-starting, self-propelling politicians, contemporary members of Congress have turned increasingly to the media to give them recognition and definition in their negotiations with constituents. At election time, they rely on their ability to raise money to advertise themselves via the paid media. Between elections, they rely on their ability to attract the interest of the free media. Success varies. Electoral efforts carry their own instant measure of success—victory or defeat. Interelection success, however, is measured by a longer term flow of member activity and media response. Over the six years I watched his interaction with the media, Chaka Fattah appears to have been remarkably successful in producing a flow of mutually advantageous media relationships—to the positive benefit of his constituency connections.

What he gave the Philadelphia media was an appealing story line—of personal ambition and political accomplishment. What the media gave him in return was an enlarged persona—in reputation and in visibility. With the national media, Fattah provided articulate commentary, and they, in return, gave him a wider credibility. In practice, the two sets of media relationships, local and national, were mutually reinforcing. By the time Fattah had engineered his Gear Up legislation and his Appropriations Committee membership, he had also become a media success—nothing approaching "late" Barbara Jordan, but far exceeding "early" Louis Stokes.

From our earliest conversations, the congressman was upbeat about his media relations. In Philadelphia that meant the *Inquirer,* whose opinions on public affairs reflected and shaped sentiment among his biracial supporters in the northwest part of the district. In 1996 he ranked his relationship with the *Inquirer* a "ten." Their support for his election and their support for his policies added up to "a charmed life in the media."

In 2000 the *Inquirer* remained his measure of success. "I've had two front-page articles in the *Inquirer* in the last two weeks," he said then. "And I've had two others in the past five years. Four articles is not bad. No one else has even come close to that coverage." As for the *Daily News,* he commented at the same time that, "I don't think the *Daily News* has written one substantive article about me in five years. They are a tabloid." He had apparently adopted the "rule of thumb" of Philadelphia's mayor: "that if a story appeared in the tabloid *Daily News* and did not appear in the *Inquirer,* then it really hadn't appeared at all." [47] As if to verify the distinction, the *Daily News* devoted an entire section to the congressman's wedding in 2001. "His pending nuptials," wrote a reporter, "landed him on the front page of the *Daily News,* something his legislative feats have never done." [48]

As Fattah's comments imply, he monitored his media relationships carefully. He had a full-time press secretary who handled national as well as local publicity. But she spent most of her time in Philadelphia. Each year, she prepared a handsome packet of his press clippings. Each year's packet became noticeably fatter than the preceding one—a crude measure of increasing coverage by all sorts of local newspapers and group publications.

This growth in local coverage maps closely his increased personal activity inside the institution—first his legislative success in education policy making and then his institutional success with his committee membership. From start to finish, the local press credited Gear Up as Fattah's "legislative brainchild" and credited his new committee as the "most powerful committee" in Congress.

In 2000 I asked him, "Have you been able to put your stamp on the district? Has the Bill Gray influence disappeared?" "Yes, I have put my stamp on the district," he replied. And he tied his answer to the combination of legislative activity and media coverage. "I have had a great deal of publicity—more than any other Democratic congressman from Pennsylvania. The president has been in my district twelve times. He came during the campaign to kick off the Gear Up program. He came to my church. He gave me a White House ceremony to start Gear Up. His attention, his visits have given me unusual exposure." As if to punctuate his reply, that very day a front-page *Inquirer* article had given positive, anticipatory coverage to Fattah's upcoming campaign for statewide equity in school financing.[49]

His successful in-House battle for a coveted committee assignment brought similar exposure at home—and similar results. Indeed, the *Daily News* framed their lead article, "Fattah's a Major Player Now," with a Bill Gray comparison: "Life for Fattah is good. At 44, starting his fourth term in Congress, he's arguably poised to become Philadelphia's most powerful pol since Bill Gray."[50] And a columnist detailed, in the same paper, the committee saga with the opinion, "Nobody tracks power like Fattah, who has been elbowing his way to the front of the line since his freshman year on the Hill."[51]

Chaka Fattah has prospered in his radio and television relationships, too—perhaps even more, given their greater audience reach. As compared with the print media, however, electronic media records are hard to come by and success is more difficult to trace. When, however, Philadelphia's newspapers take notice of their congressman's increasing prominence on national television, something important has happened.

Writing in 2001, the *Inquirer's* political reporter wrote that Fattah had "landed spots on the blue chip political talk shows." And he described the local congressman as the "darling of booking agents from Tim Russert's *Meet the Press* to Chris Matthew's *Hardball*. . . . [Fattah] recently had to turn down an invitation to appear on *Larry King Live* because he had already committed to talking to CNN's Wolf Blitzer."[52] His celebrity attracted the attention of the tabloid *Daily News,* whose political analyst wrote of Fattah, "He's getting national, local and congressional attention. . . . [He's] on NBC's "Meet the Press," CNBC's "Hardball," CNN, Fox TV and others."[53] At that point, the Philadelphia congressman had emerged as a steadfast and articulate defender of his outgoing—and embattled—ally in the White House.

When we first met, Chaka Fattah was already in the protectionist stage of his electoral career. But he was very much in the expansionist stage of his broader public career. In his precongressional career he had not been media oriented. When we first met, he was careful to note, "I am not an ambulance chaser looking to get credit for what others have done"; "The publicity I've gotten at home has been earned publicity"—raising money to "save the city," "attacking the Housing Authority"; "The first time I ever had a profile done on me was when I was elected to Congress." By his own admission, he had a lot to learn when he got to Congress. His initial political skills and strengths were in ground-level organization, not in broad-scale communication.

Furthermore, his experience in the state legislature had been no aid to learning. "The media side of Congress was new to me," he explained.

> You could be in Harrisburg forever and no one would even know you were there. You get a lot more attention here. . . . In the state legislature, my policy with the media was "be completely accessible." But in Congress, I have to triage. Should I go on some cable network that doesn't play in Philadelphia? Should I or should I not take two hours of my time to learn what's important to some reporter, whether or not what he writes will ever be read by anyone? Your office gets a lot of media scrutiny, too. People want to compare your office to other offices and measure you this way and that. None of their interest in comparing offices is in my interest. So I don't spend time on it. It's a very different role for me than I had in Harrisburg.

As a state legislator, he had no need to develop a media strategy. In Congress he did. And he was learning.

Without detailed knowledge of the actual choices he made, it would be hard to detail his media strategy. From the pattern of his first year [1995] schedules, however, it is clear that, from the beginning, his media involvements were considerable. Certainly, his attentiveness to the media—and theirs of him—dwarfed anything we learned about the media connections of Louis Stokes.

It is not easy to compartmentalize Fattah's media connections between those at home and those in Washington. Those conducted in Philadelphia would be aimed there, but those conducted in Washington might be aimed at a local or national audience. The total number, however, seems very large—the more so for a freshman member of the House. During 1995 he scheduled twenty-one media "events" during his home visits—twelve on radio, six on television, and three with the print media. Doubtless there were numerous other media contacts in the normal course of his home activities—when cameras or reporters showed up to cover an appearance, event, speech, or whatever.

In Washington, however, his scheduled media events more accurately reflect his actual media connections. In his first year in office, his office schedule called for forty-two media contacts—seventeen for television, seventeen for radio, and six for print media. As best can be divined, a quarter of these events [eleven] were beamed at Philadelphia. Most of the others anticipated a national audience—NPR, McNeil-Lehrer, C-SPAN, CNBC. In addition, his schedules show half-a-dozen press conferences with others [mostly with CBC members], two lunches with national television reporters, and four receptions with media organizations. The evidence puts on display a sharp learning curve and a fast start for the newcomer in making media connections.

The congressman's own assessment was a modest one. He attributed his quick start to the paucity of first-term Democrats and his later television notoriety to his position on the House Government Reform Committee. "Timing had a big impact on attention that came to me," he began.

I got more than my share in 1994 because I was one of a very few newly elected House members on our side, one of fifty—a comer—in *Time*. Then I went stumbling forward onto the Government Affairs Committee [*sic*] which was always in the headlines because they are always chasing scandals. Later, I got a lot of prominence because I was one of the few on that committee who was capable and willing to offer a defense of the president against the attack on his pardons. So I just stumbled onto a committee that put me in the limelight.

He left it unsaid that he welcomed media attention and that he was effective at meeting media expectations.

Back home, his media connections depended basically upon his policy and his institutional strengths. But his local connections were strengthened when national media attention certified his status as a player on the larger stage. Lacking any public opinion polls—which he does not use—the favorable publicity he gets from his media connections has helped to underwrite a solid king-of-the-hill status in Pennsylvania's Second Congressional District.

But those connections are a means for him, not an end. The goal is good public policy. At the end of my visits, his enthusiasm, his ambitions, and his plans remained focused on policy. And his policy passions, as before, involved education. Looking backward, he recalled his March 2000 trip to Africa with the president. "I negotiated with Clinton over dinner in Africa. And I got him to commit to a commission that will protect Gear Up by monitoring its implementation and its performance." Looking ahead, he said,

"My goal is to get on the Appropriations Subcommittee on Education. When I mentioned that to another committee member, he said that he wanted it, too. He has seniority. So I said 'Go right ahead.' 'Easy does it' is my motto. You can't get too self-important around here."

Where his expertise on educational matters is concerned, however, his intention is to use it. And he hopes to use it in dealing with his former committee—on the subject of equalizing school funding across all districts within each state. He is taking aim at the inequitable locally based funding of schools that deeply disadvantages poor, minority school districts. He does not intend to give it up just because he no longer sits on the relevant committee. "I've had no trouble staying involved," he says. "I was the first person to testify before the Education Committee on school equity. . . . I think people credit me with expertise on education—not because I can talk about it, but because I did it. I passed an important piece of legislation. Even though I am no longer on the Education Committee, the members come to me to ask questions. . . . People on the committee think I know something, and I have good relations with both sides."

When I left him, therefore, he was still pursuing a policy-intensive, policy-centered representational strategy. "School equity is the most important thing I will ever do. No one else is trying to move it forward. It's my issue and it's currency is growing. We already have 183 votes. I can build bridges with the Republicans to move it along. A very conservative Democrat said to me, 'I can't be with you now, but if you get 217 votes, I'll be number 218.'" He was already receiving national publicity for his efforts.[54] "If I pass it, it will be the most important piece of legislation passed by anybody at any time—a profound educational reform. The stakes in terms of my career are quite high." And he added, "There are several career ladders in the House. Mine is the legislative leader ladder."

Beyond his near-term policy goal of school equity, he envisions others. "My goal is that when I leave Congress, I will have passed ten or fifteen major pieces of legislation—just as Adam Clayton Powell did." When he was reminded of Powell's power as Chairman of the Education and Labor Committee, Fattah remained undaunted. "I know that. I will do it through the power of my ideas. Ideas are very powerful." And lest anyone think his policy-centered goals are unrealistic, he returns to his signature outlook. "I know people write that I have high expectations. But no one else can describe my expectations. No matter how high they might put them, they cannot put them anywhere near as high as the expectations I set for myself."

CONCLUSION

Chaka Fattah is the fourth African American to represent his Philadelphia district in the U.S. Congress. He is a self-starting, self-propelling, independent-minded career politician with a defining desire to help make good public policy. His community-oriented upbringing and his energetic activism shaped a lifelong interest in the policy needs of his majority-black constituents. First in the neighborhoods, then in the city, then in the state legislature—wherever he worked—his strongest connections with others were overwhelmingly policy connections. As a member of the House of Representatives, too, he has continued to pursue a policy-intensive, policy-centered representational strategy in connecting with his constituents. Other connections, symbolic, organizational, and personal, contribute to his overall representational relationship. But his policy connections dominate.

Electorally and politically, he is strong and safe and free to pursue his policy interests as he wishes. With rare foreign policy exceptions, his roll call votes in the House pose no problems. He connects with his black-majority constituency primarily through his hands-on, results-oriented involvement in the widest range of their group-related concerns. Representation by immersion, I have called it. With each problem he identifies, his goal has been to fashion and implement fresh, yet workable solutions to that problem—most notably public housing and education.

His primary constituents, his hard-core electoral and political supporters are his issue-oriented, community-minded, problem-solving coworkers in the black neighborhoods. His policy interests and his political independence, however, have also won for him a strongly supportive constituency of white, liberal, community activists. And they have given him a reelection support base that is genuinely biracial. As a Representative, he describes himself as "comfortable" in most all corners and with most all types of people in the district. The breadth of his support is reflected in the attention he receives from the city's most influential newspaper.

As a politician with large ambitions, who thrives on personal challenges, it is not surprising that the congressman's most important learning experiences involved his negotiations with other entrenched political players. After establishing his organizational strength outside of the local Democratic Party, he learned the benefits of cooperation and co-optation from the inside. Within Congress, he had to learn how to pursue personal power in a new and complex institutional environment. By his own account, both sets of trial-and-error lessons served him well. His party negotiations increased his citywide influence. His institutional negotiations increased his intra-institutional influence.

Chaka Fattah's representational connections played out most successfully in the case of his Gear Up legislation. Experience confronted him with a crucial problem of his black neighborhoods; he designed a legislative instrument to alleviate that problem; he worked out the institutional support he needed to pass it into law; and he was able to return to the district's minority neighborhoods to deliver, in person, his promissory scholarship certificates to the seventh grade students there. For a policy-oriented Representative, completing the policy cycle—from immersion to idea to enactment to implementation—is the ultimate success story. It has solidified his connections at home; it has helped him to attract national media attention, and it has encouraged him to take up other large policy challenges inside Congress.

Postscript, 1998

REPRESENTATIONAL CHANGE

In January 1998 Representative Louis Stokes announced that he would not seek reelection later that year. His decision to retire prompted my decision to revisit the representational relationships of his early years, and to update them, as a baseline against which to think about his successor. An opportunity had presented itself to tell a story about representational change in one congressional district—a story that might enrich the scholarly exploration of representational behavior among African American House members. And further, if Lou Stokes's representational repertoire had helped us to think about an early cohort of African American members, then perhaps the repertoire of his successor might help us to compare the pioneer cohort with a later one.

When Lou Stokes announced his retirement, it had been twenty-two years since our last conversation and twenty years since I had thought seriously about him. Obviously, the man making that announcement in the late 1990s was older and more experienced than the man I had known in the early 1970s. My comparisons with his successor might be enhanced, it seemed, if I could get a contemporary picture of the retiring congressman near the point of the transition. In April, therefore, two months after Stokes's announcement, I went back to Cleveland. This postscript is built around my half-day updating visit with him there.

In summary, I found a seventy-three-year-old House member who had— since I saw him last—won eleven consecutive elections by huge margins, whose reputation at home had become borderline iconic, and whose representational strategies and connections seemed both familiar and intact. Reactions from his constituents emphasized his constancy, for example, "never forgot where he came from," "never changed his philosophy." [1] Similarly, my later observations validated my earlier ones, and they also sharpened my approach to his successor.

FIRST IMPRESSIONS

The most important fact about the intervening years was Louis Stokes's accumulated record in Congress. His many accomplishments had gold-plated his already solid reputation and stature in Cleveland's black community—and had improved it in parts of the white community, as well.

Inside Congress, his seniority on the Appropriations Committee had carried him to the chairmanship of the Subcommittee on Veterans, HUD, and Independent Agencies, a group that dispensed every year $90 billion in federal money to certain assigned governmental agencies and programs.[2] His abilities had also carried him, at the request of his party's leaders, to several responsible and highly sensitive legislative positions: Chairman of the House Intelligence Committee, member of the Select Committee to Investigate the Iran-Contra Affair, Chairman of the Select Committee to Investigate the Assassination of John F. Kennedy and Martin Luther King Jr., and Chairman of the House Ethics Committee (twice).

Every one of these public positions was a first for a black member of Congress—and a first, too, for the Ohio congressional delegation. On the day of his retirement announcement, the *Plain Dealer* headline read: "Rep. Stokes to Retire: Clevelander Rose from Poverty to Heights of Power."[3]

We met in his new district office in a reception room filled with reminders of his career. There were pictures of Stokes with Bill Clinton, with Lyndon Johnson, and with Nelson Mandela. There were pictures of Stokes at the Cleveland Summer Arts Festival and at the dedication of the Louis Stokes wing of the Cleveland Public Library. There were two framed copies of legislation, each with the president's signature and a pen used for signing—one a voting rights extension bill, by Reagan, the other an appropriations bill, by Clinton. There was a framed complimentary article (1995) from the *Plain Dealer*. His office decor amply conveyed the "heights of power."

But the office, for whatever reason, was cold and uninviting. "His office," I noted,

is not a typical congressman's district office. It's like a doctor's office. You enter the small waiting room about ten feet wide and twenty feet long. At the far end, is a window three feet by three feet with a glass front. The window is raised about four inches, with a little bell-for-service on the sill. It is off-putting, cold and official. Presumably, you ring for service. . . . [I bent down and called "hello" through the four-inch gap.] There are six chairs and a small table, on which are three or four handouts—notice of a Lou Stokes job fair in May, a pamphlet on the disabled and the blind, a sheet telling veterans where to get help, and an art gallery brochure. There's nothing congressional, like a newsletter . . . nor the usual congressional documents. There's one closed door that leads into the bank of offices beyond. But you have to use a buzzer to get through the door. You can't just walk in. You have to be buzzed in [by someone behind the glass window] like a bank vault. . . . A net impression was that the office was *not* [italics in original] the office of a congressman. It was the office of a dignitary. That is, he is more than a congressman. He's there to serve; but he serves from a station that is a bit *above* the people he serves.

In 1994 he had consolidated his downtown and suburban offices into a single office in a different suburb. Why? "Nicer neighborhood, . . . easier to get to for constituents, . . . no congestion, . . . staff likes it better," he explained. But I thought the new office setup perpetuated—if not increased—that dignified, psychological distance he had always kept between himself and his constituents.

We did not discuss his retirement decision. He had undergone a heart operation, but he seemed in good health. Thinking about the beginnings of his political career, however, I would give considerable weight to his reflections, in a Washington interview, after the death of his brother. "As I survey it," he began, "I think about the things that Carl and I did politically, what the two of us have been about. We used to talk every day. We could run things by each other. We could think and strategize on political issues. I guess without him here, it really has taken away a lot of what I enjoy about politics. It's not the same."[4] Two observations: First, the story of his exit from politics is closely related to the story of his entrance into politics. Second, taken together, the two stories—entrance and exit—make sense only if we give great weight to his constituency connections.

CONSTITUENCY CONTEXT AND ELECTORAL CONNECTIONS

His constituent support remained solid. In order to catch up with his eleven elections, I read him my quotation (see p. 19) about his need for a 55 percent black district and his fear of any 1970 redistricting that would include the large white ethnic suburb of Euclid. "They redistricted me twice," he said. "The first time [1982], they gave me one ward in Euclid plus two precincts that I could live with. Because of the out-migration of blacks into

Euclid, those areas were mostly black. The next time [1992], they gave me the rest of Euclid, which was substantially white. But it's not like it used to be. Because of the out-migration from the city, there are a considerable number of blacks throughout Euclid." In 1992 he added, "they changed the [black/white] ratio from 65/35 to 60/40. It became a very different district. I picked up thirteen or fourteen suburban areas." Among those was Shaker Heights, where he now lived and had his new office. Indeed, the newspaper now identified him as "a Shaker Heights Democrat."[5]

The change had not, however, had any appreciable effect on his election margins—except, perhaps, for the 1992 election. In that year, two fresh uncertainties converged. One was the redistricting. The other was the House bank scandal, which eventually cost several incumbents their seats. On the effects of redistricting, he said, "After the redistricting, several white candidates jumped into the race. They thought the time had come for the white community to take back the [now] Eleventh District—what with the larger proportion of whites and the blacks less likely to be registered. There was the mayor of University Heights and a councilman from Euclid and others. When the black community realized I was under attack from the white part of the district, they rallied around me."

On the effects of his egregious 551 bank overdrafts, he said, "We took a poll and we found there was some falloff. I held a press conference right away and explained that it wasn't a bank and that I had never seen a congressional paycheck in my life. I explained that you deposited your paycheck and wrote checks against it. If you went over, they paid it because they knew your next check was coming. That was the system—the way it was done." In the newspapers, he was quoted as saying, "It's embarrassing to be on that list. I apologize to my constituents."[6] "I think people understood," he concluded. "But we dropped into the 70s [chuckle]. Next time we were back in the 80s."[7] That election, he said, was the only one "that you might want to look into." The limits of his support in the black community and of the community's willingness to trust him had been severely tested in that election, and they had been found to be both generous and secure. That which had brought terror, retirement, or defeat to many of his colleagues registered barely a blip in Cleveland.[8]

At home also, the congressman had used his rise to power inside Congress to improve his relationship with the media. He described his negotiations with the *Plain Dealer:* "A new person came in as publisher about ten years ago," he said.

At that time, they only paid attention to me when they could write something negative. We met and I lamented the situation to him. I said that Cleveland was missing out, that we were doing so much for the community, that for them to be completely negative was doing a disservice to the community. He agreed—to a point—that we represented the city and that he would be fair. From that point, I noticed that while they still take pot shots at us when they can, overall, they've done a better job.

When I announced my retirement, they printed it on the front page for two days running. People couldn't believe the praise. It was as if I had died. . . . It took them thirty years to realize what I had done.

He had never depended on their political support. And, as for their influence, he noted once again that "more people in the community read the *Call and Post* than the *Plain Dealer*. And I get a fairer shake there."[9]

Plain Dealer coverage of the congressman was included in Douglas Arnold's sampling of twenty-five newspapers for the years 1993–1994.[10] As compared with the others, the *Plain Dealer* ranked far ahead of the median in numbers of articles that mentioned him, and far above the median in mentions that involved his law-making activities inside of Congress. Indeed, he topped Arnold's sample in the number of times his paper mentioned the "committee" and the "leadership" activities of their House members. The *Plain Dealer* ranked about average in its coverage of his constituency-related activity. Taking both these activities into account, however, Stokes ranked very low in the percentage of articles that carried a negative opinion of him. As newspapers go, therefore, the *Plain Dealer* of 1993–1994 was conveying to its readers a positive image of Louis Stokes as an important member of Congress.

On balance, therefore, while old memories die hard, his midcareer negotiation with the newspaper had apparently been helpful to him. Even so, Clevelanders had to wait almost to the end of his career—till May 1997, eight months before his retirement announcement—to be able to read (in a magazine) a full-length, informative and appreciative profile of their most prominent member of Congress.[11]

POLICY CONNECTIONS

Lou Stokes's representational strategy—to protect the group interests of the black community—was unchanged. In terms of substantive representation, his policy connections with his perceived constituency also remained unchanged. When I asked him whether he had encountered any problems "representing the district," he replied just as he had in the 1970s. "I know what black people want," he said.

> We all want the same things. Once I proved to them that I would stand up and fight for the things we wanted, they had faith in me; they trusted me. I'm the repository of their trust. As far as voting is concerned, I have complete freedom. They support everything I do. Even if there are only eight votes on our side, my constituents know that I'm doing what's right. They don't question me or ask me to explain. I can take the strongest liberal positions and they will support me. Take the anticrime bill. It was outrageous in the way that it affected minorities. There were only twelve of us on one vote. But I can do that without worrying. It's a matter of trust. ["And what is trust?" I asked.] It's them saying, "We have a very tough time in this world. We need someone to stand up and fight for us. And you're the guy."

The idea that there was, in the black community, a thoroughly recognizable, widely shared set of group interests—interests that any black Representative would work to promote and protect—that idea is the centerpiece of his comments. "Standing up and fighting" for those interests was still the policy foundation of his representational strategy. The idea of a broader black constituency, beyond his district, remained, too. "Black people have the same problems everywhere," he asserted. "When I talk about AIDS and the exchange of needles, I'm talking about people everywhere, not just Cleveland."

SYMBOLIC CONNECTIONS: ROLE MODEL

Our first event—as in 1970—was a visit to a center of black culture. The small and struggling Museum of African American Culture had taken over the bottom floor of an old building on a back street in an out-of-the-way part of the city. The congressman had never visited it before, and his driver had difficulty finding it. The curator's greeting was worth a thousand words in conveying his exalted place in the black community. "A friend of mine," she began, "said that when she went to see you, it was like a pilgrimage. When I think of all that Carl Stokes and Louis Stokes have done for our people, today is *my* pilgrimage." Her sentiment, buttressed by an appreciation of his longevity, bordered on reverence.

She gave him a guided tour of the museum's artifacts, records and exhibits from life in Africa to the modern inventions of African Americans. And she talked of her work conveying that history to schoolchildren. When they paused at a replica of the infamous door in Senegal through which free blacks passed on their way to slavery, he spoke movingly of his visit, as a congressman, to that very place. Afterward, he made two comments. About the museum he said, "It's a shame that a museum like this has to be struggling." He was impressed, but suggested no help. About the curator's reaction to him, he said, "She has no idea what I do." Reverential constituent support like hers was group-related, not job-related. For her, more than ever, he was the symbol of group aspiration and accomplishment.

From the beginning of his career, this symbolic aspect of his representational strategy was unusually strong. He promoted and protected the interests of the black community partly by presenting himself to them as their stand-in, fighting their fight for inclusion. His personal "firsts" were also firsts for the black community. If anything, those symbolic connections were stronger than ever as a result of his three decades of accomplishment. In the 1970s we had driven up and down Fairhill Avenue; in 1998 we drove the same broad artery—now renamed Stokes Boulevard. "Legendary" and "revered" were commonly put before his name in the media.

His symbolic prominence was most striking during the second major event of my visit. At a flag-raising ceremony in front of "my old Central High School," now Central Middle School, he presented himself as someone whose life had set an example for his district's young people. On one side of the entrance walk, a choir of twenty-five dressed-up middle school children [one of them white] stood in a line. On the other side were fifty parents and siblings. The choir sang, and several dignitaries spoke from the platform on the front steps. Then, their congressman spoke to the students directly and in a strong voice.

I remember [pointing to his left] when I used to walk to school from my home down there in the [Outhwaite Homes] projects. I came down this street to school, every day, for three years. I had to leave school every day at two o'clock to go downtown to a shoeshine parlor to help my mother, who was on welfare. Then after a while, I got a job in an Army/Navy store. So I left school every day at two o'clock.

This school was very special to me. When I graduated from Central High School, I went into the service. And when I came back, I applied for admission to Western Reserve College. They looked at my transcript and they rejected me. They said my transcript showed that I might not be able to make it. I went to see my old principal at Central, P. M. Watson, and I showed him my transcript and he said, "That's an outrage. You graduated from Central and there's no reason you can't make it." He called the college and he made them take me into that school. Because he didn't believe that "I might not be able to make it," because he believed in me, I was able to become what I am. That is what Central means to me. . . .

Carl Stokes and Louis Stokes stood right where you are standing today. You are just as good as Carl Stokes and Louis Stokes. If Carl Stokes could become mayor . . . and if Louis Stokes could walk down that street from the projects and become a congressman, you can be whatever you want to be. You are as good as—probably better than—Carl Stokes and Louis Stokes. You are special, and you can be anything you want to be.

He had presented himself (along with his brother) as a role model for black youngsters. However the students may have been affected, the enthusiasm of the parents (as they conveyed it to me) indicated that an inspirational, motivational—and totally nonpolicy—representational connection had been made. As in the museum, so too at the school. I thought that his symbolic connections were stronger at the end of his career—and because of his career—than they had been at the beginning.

ORGANIZATIONAL CONNECTIONS: PARTY AND PROTECTION

In the 1970s the most troublesome of his trial-and-error representational negotiations had centered around the relationship between the organized black community and the white-dominated Democratic Party. Over time, the community's political organization—the Twenty-first Congressional District Caucus—had become, more narrowly, the guarantor of his own political independence. He had constantly readjusted his relationship with those black politicians who had once been his compatriots, but who had hitched their careers to the Democratic Party. When I inquired into the state of his long-running negotiations between the Caucus and the party, he spoke of learning and of change.

His concern, however, was a constant. He remained, to the end, as he had always been, deeply involved in local politics. "For survival purposes," he recounted, "I couldn't stay out of local politics. Remember, I had people back here who wanted to take my place. If I had ignored the local scene, they would have become so strong that they would have been a threat to me. By staying involved, I was able to keep my place for thirty years."

"Staying involved," it turned out, had meant changing his organizational lifeline from the Caucus to yet another political organization.

It was all my doing. I didn't have time to be here and to keep up with the infusion of younger people and keep it viable. The executive director got older, and the Caucus was losing its power. The Caucus had become *me*, period. Somehow or other, I had to pull the elected officials back together. It could only be done on a peer basis and only by me. So, I founded an additional political organization in addition to the Caucus. BEDCO is the acronym—Black Elected Democrats of Cleveland. It has the school board, state representatives, state Senate—twenty-two of them. They aren't from the suburbs unless some of their territory happens to include a bit of the city. It supplemented the Caucus in terms of political activity. The Caucus has some semipolitical activity. It still has a grassroots membership. It still has the Labor Day picnic—which is the biggest thing in town. It had a party for disadvantaged children recently with seven thousand people. But BEDCO is now the potent organization.

He was retracing some old lessons of self-protection. In one form or another, Lou Stokes had been in the protectionist stage of his political career from the day I met him. And that was his outlook to the end.

The new protective arrangement, however, retained the same power instabilities as the original one. It seemed destined to produce a learning and negotiating problem for his successor. Cleveland's popular African American mayor, describing himself as "mayor of all the people," declined to join the new, all-black group. The congressman was at pains to allay any sense of rivalry. "It was not a problem for me. I was happy to have everyone else. . . . I can't think of any threat to my leadership—not in the Caucus or in BEDCO." The mayor's reaction made Stokes's "godfather" status amply clear. "The one or two times we've had a falling out," the mayor said, "I've had sense enough to know I had to pay homage." [12] The congressman concluded, "The media still refers to me as the most powerful black politician in Ohio." That assessment was doubtless definitive for his own career. But it hardly settled all organizational problems for his successor.

MINORITY CONNECTIONS

In the intervening years, Lou Stokes's connections with the white community had, by his account, improved. Still, they remained distant and nonessential to his survival. At the elite level, his leadership status in the black community gave him bargaining power with the white Democratic Party leaders. "When John Coyne [mayor of Brooklyn] wanted to become county chairman, he forged an alliance with me. In exchange for my support, he agreed to give me some of the things I had been working so long for—a spot on the Elections Board, jobs at the board, a black jury commissioner. And with my support, he became [party] chairman."

At the nonelite level, too, he said, his congressional achievements had won him added support among white voters. "I have made more and more inroads into acceptance in the white community. They have begun to understand, and to speak out vocally, that I give them service. They have comprehended that no matter how I vote, I bring money into the district. When they see that I've brought money into their part of the district, I get acceptance plus voting support." His electoral performance provides some evidence. In his five largest white-majority suburbs (Euclid, Shaker Heights, South Euclid, Bedford, University Heights) his percentage of the vote increased from 40 percent in 1992 to 60 percent in 1996.[13]

When it comes to policy, however, his relationship to his black and white constituents was unchanged. For example, "On abortion, I can take the most extreme position and my [black] constituents won't say a thing. I know that there are black people in the churches who disagree with me on late-term abortion. But they don't criticize me, because they know that I'm helping them on everything else. From the white community, I get complaints on the subject. But that doesn't bother me. I tried a town meeting there, and I told them like it is, straight out. After it had gone on for a while, it got kooky. Finally I said, 'You've had your town meeting. That's it.'" It was a trial-and-error effort at negotiation, but it did not work for him and he discontinued it. "I still come home three out of every four weeks . . . to beat the district," he said. It was the black community that he was "beating" when he was there, not the white community.

INSTITUTIONAL CAREER

"Looking back over your thirty years in Congress," I asked him, "what has given you the most satisfaction?" In *second* place, he said, is "all the money I brought into the district." "Did anyone tote it up?" I asked. "In the press they did. But not all of it. It's unbelievable." That achievement, of course, came by virtue of his committee assignment and his presence on the Subcommittee on HUD, Veterans, and Independent Offices. In 1992 he had become its chairperson. When I asked him about housing development in the run-down Hough district, he said, "There are some beautiful homes in Hough that weren't there in 1970. The district is much better off than it was then. . . . The money and [housing] programs I've worked on have helped tremendously. People have taken advantage of them." The frustration he had expressed early on had long since disappeared.

Since the Republicans had taken over Congress, he said, life inside the Appropriations Committee had become more partisan. But, he said, "I've established rapport with the guys. I still get a lot—most of what I want. . . . It would be worse if I were not a senior person, and I've also been chairman of a subcommittee. If I were still chairman, however, I'd get more." [14] Any regrets about your choice of committee? "Nooo way! It's the only committee to be on. All the rest is window dressing."

In the 1970s his founding activity in the Congressional Black Caucus had rivaled—or dominated—his other institutional responsibilities. But a quarter-century later, his committee work and his party work had put the CBC in the shade. Asked about Caucus accomplishments, he summarized that "It grew and prospered and established itself as a force to be reckoned with in Congress. . . . [In 1995 Speaker Newt] Gingrich got rid of thirteen white caucuses in order to get rid of one black caucus. He was out to get us. We are going along just as we always have." But CBC perspectives had changed. "I've noticed," he added, "that the new members have a different set of interests—peanuts and tobacco, stuff I know nothing about. I never studied farm issues." A new generation of African Americans—some of whom admired Stokes as a mentor [15]—had joined the group.

In *first* place among his congressional satisfactions, he said, was the opportunity to set "historic precedents." "I participated in a number of historic moments. I was chairman of the committee that investigated the assassination of two great Americans—John Kennedy and Martin Luther King Jr. I'm the only person now alive who questioned James Earl Ray in public. I was the first black man to be chairman of the Intelligence Committee. [16] I was the first black man to chair the Ethics Committee. I did it once, and I must have done a good job, because I was called back to do it a second time."

"Why were you chosen for these jobs?" "First, because of my background in the law—in constitutional law—which was especially important in the case of the Assassination Committee. And, secondly, because people knew I wasn't afraid to stand up and tell it like I saw it." "Any time," he told another interviewer, "I'm in an atmosphere where I can interrogate people the way I used to be able to do in the courtroom, that, to me, is great fulfillment." [17] He was, from the beginning, more lawyer than politician. But the combination underpinned his success when, as a pioneer cohort African American congressman, he had the opportunity to apply his talent at historic moments to set historic precedents.

Visitors to his Washington office later in his career were greeted by a twelve-square-foot color picture of Lou Stokes's most treasured "historic moment." The picture showed Marine Colonel Oliver North, in full dress uniform, being sworn in to testify in defense of his actions in the Iran-Contra scandal. As a member of the Select Committee, Stokes would respond movingly to North's patriotism-laced defense of his diversion of money to aid the Nicaraguan Contras.

In part:

> Colonel, as I sit here this morning looking at you in your uniform, I cannot help but remember that I wore the uniform of this country in World War II in a segregated Army. I wore it as proudly as you do, even though our government required black and white soldiers, in the same Army, to live, sleep, eat and travel separate and apart while fighting, and in some cases dying, for our country. . . . while I admire your love for America, I hope that you will never forget that others, too, love America just as much as you. And when they disagree with you and our government on aid to the Contras, they will die for America just as quickly as you will.[18]

This public statement was for him, and for his self-placement in history, the equivalent of Barbara Jordan's public statement on impeachment that insured her place in history. Both had reached beyond their local constituencies. She had spoken for a national black and white constituency; he had spoken for a national black constituency.

His long and successful political career, marked as it was by his representational firsts—in substance and in symbol, in strategy and in connections—leads me to a follow-up question: What sort of House member would succeed him, and what kind of representational career would that person develop and display—in Cleveland and in Washington?

CHAPTER 6
. . . .
STEPHANIE TUBBS JONES
2000 – 2002

SUCCESSION

In November 1998 Stephanie Tubbs Jones was elected to Congress from Ohio's Eleventh Congressional District. I visited with her in Cleveland in January and April 2000 and in October 2001. This chapter examines her representational relationships as they appeared in these early years of her tenure. Its main focus will, of course, be on her perceptions and her activities. But, given all that I have already written about Louis Stokes, comparisons between Tubbs Jones and her predecessor can hardly be avoided. Nor would we wish to avoid them. Indeed, the decision to include her in this book was prompted by the opportunity it provided to entertain the subject of congressional succession.

From the outset, the succession context was inescapable. During my first visit, at the entrance to the Unified Technologies Center at Cleveland's Cuyahoga Community College, I was greeted by a huge picture of Congressman Louis Stokes, flanked by two large display cases filled with his awards and other memorabilia. "He is everywhere," said the congresswoman. "But this is his special place. He did so much to help them." Later, as we drove to her next engagement, she commented, "The street we're on now is Stokes Boulevard. It used to be Fairhill. There's also a Stokes wing on the library, a Stokes wing on the art gallery, a Stokes building at Cuyahoga Community College, a Stokes wing at University Hospital." (And, she might have added, "a bridge, a public transit station, a school auditorium, and a Head Start Center."[1]) "He's everywhere," she repeated. "His friend [Representative] Bill Clay says, 'Why don't you just rename Cleveland 'Stokes City!' Then I won't have to come here all the time to speak at dedications.'" Like the successor herself, I could not have avoided the succession influence if I had tried.

In this chapter, I propose to compare Stephanie Tubbs Jones's representational relationships to those of Lou Stokes, to explain their similarities and differences, together with their continuities and changes—if not in measurable magnitudes, at least in observable tendencies. We might expect, for example, that shared characteristics, such as ethnic heritage, political party, and geographical constituency, would point toward representational similarities and continuities. So, too, would the influence of the predecessor on the successor—directly by persuasion or indirectly by emulation. Other characteristics—preferences, careers, and contexts—would allow for representational differences and change. And the sheer passage of time—thirty years in this case—might have that same effect, too.

Comparisons of this sort between predecessor and successor will help, also, to better explain the relevance of this book's main variables—goals, context, and learning. But the main task of chapter 6 is to examine the representational patterns of Stephanie Tubbs Jones.

PRECONGRESSIONAL CAREER

When I met Stephanie Tubbs Jones in January 2000, she was just starting the second year of her first term in the House of Representatives. She was at the same point in her congressional career as Lou Stokes had been when I first met him. She was forty-nine years old. Her career milestones were these: born and raised in Cleveland; educated in the Cleveland city schools; graduated from Case Western Reserve University in 1971 and from its School of Law in 1974; elected to Cleveland Municipal Court 1981; appointed to Cuyahoga County Court of Common Pleas in 1983, to which she was subsequently elected in 1984 and reelected in 1988; appointed as Cuyahoga County Prosecutor (i.e., district attorney) in 1991, to which position she was elected in 1992 and reelected in 1996; elected to Congress in 1998.

As an African American woman, her precongressional career was studded with political "firsts." She had been the first black woman to be elected (and elected while pregnant) to the County Court of Common Pleas. She had been the first black person, woman or man, to be elected as county prosecutor. Now, in 2000, she was the first black woman to be elected to Congress from the state of Ohio. And, marking a change since the time of Barbara Jordan, she had become "congresswoman."

Stephanie Tubbs Jones and her two sisters grew up in a working-class family. "I am a regular person," she says. "I don't try to make myself out to be more than I am. My dad was a skycap for United Airlines, and my mom was a factory worker at American Greetings." "I came from a working family, hard-working folk. . . . I didn't come up with a silver spoon in my mouth." She had a conventional middle-class upbringing. Throughout her lifetime, her parents owned their own home. "We spent a lot of time with the girls," says her mother, "vacations, trips to the library and church." Stephanie took music lessons. "I never wanted for a thing," she told a church group. "I used to wear gorgeous dresses and coats, because that was my mother's thing . . . you had to be dressed." Her father's equivalent interest is golf. "He was," she says, "one of the first black golfers."[2]

The family did not know poverty, but they knew discrimination. "My mother has a two-year teaching degree from Alabama State, came here, couldn't get a chance to teach, worked in a factory or wherever she could get work. . . . My father retired after thirty-eight years of carrying bags for United Airlines," she recalls, "because, at the age of sixty-four, he could not stand one more person calling him 'boy.'" She did not have the political role model guidance of Lou Stokes's politician-brother, or of Chaka Fattah's community-leader parents. But, like Stokes and Fattah, she pushed hard to get an education. And she did so by taking advantage of an antidiscrimination opportunity that had been unavailable to her parents. "I am an affirmative action person," she told one group. "I would not be standing before you if it were not for affirmative action. I couldn't have gone to college without affirmative action." Like Stokes and Fattah, it was her educational career that made possible her career in politics.

When I asked, "*How* did you get into politics?" she answered, "In college, I was active in the Afro-American Society, and eventually I became its president. In law school, I was active in the Black American Law Students Association [now Black Law Students Association (BLSA)], and I became its president. Later, three of us got together to help elect a municipal court judge. We were so successful that when the next vacancy opened up, we decided one of us ought to run for municipal court judge. And somehow I became the one." In a field of five, "several of whom had better political names than I," she won. She was a political "natural." At the age of thirty-one, she had launched herself into a political career. She was twenty-two years younger than Lou Stokes had been when he entered politics.

When I asked, however, "*Why* did you get into politics in the first place?" her first reply was "I've always had trouble answering that question." One of her postelection answers, in 1998, displayed that difficulty. "I just believe it was meant for me," she said, "it is part of what was in the plan for me."[3] At first blush, therefore, there is no easily articulated and dominating motivation—nothing to match Barbara Jordan's oft-stated desire to become an inside player or Chaka Fattah's oft-stated desire to shape public policy.

Beneath the surface, however, there existed a strong desire to help others. Circumstances and opportunities grew that basic desire into a career-long political motivation to engage in public service.

From her earliest days, she had been an activist. Reporters discovered that she had been "prominent and active in Collinwood High School activities."[4] And she described herself as "active there [at Collinwood] in the National Council of Christians and Jews."[5] "All my life," she says, "I had wanted to help others, and I had been active in helping others. I was a Girl Scout. I have been a member of my church all my life, and we always had food banks and clothing drives. I was always interested in service. In my day, the college watchword was *relevant.* I was an undergraduate sociology major. How could I be relevant with that degree? With a law degree, I thought I could bring about relevant change in the world." A law school friend of hers told me that "it was clear from the time we met that Stephanie would be some kind of activist."

After law school, she joined "the largest black women's organization in the United States," the Delta Sigma Theta Sorority. And she did so because it is determinedly and proudly a "public service organization." Its history is one of self-conscious and deliberate change—from a social club to an organization whose goal, as historian Paula Giddings described it, is to give young black women "equity through education, employment, and empowerment."[6] It actively supports young black women in coping with problems of parenting, shelter, nutrition, and academics. "I wanted to join in college," says Tubbs Jones, "but we didn't have a chapter. The reason I joined later was because they were a service organization. That is what attracted me. . . . It got started when twenty-two women broke off from another sorority because that one was not service oriented." More than once during my visits, the importance of her Delta Sigma Theta connection to her political life became apparent—accenting not only her macro-level taste for public service involvements, but also her micro-level taste for enduring personal relationships.

After law school, she entered the public sector, doing law enforcement work in the equal employment opportunity field—first for a regional sewer district, then for the county prosecutor, and finally for the Federal Equal Employment Opportunity Commission in Cleveland. She did not, however, focus her public service activism on elective office. "In the beginning, I had no idea about running for public office," she says. "I remember one year when I came home from college, a friend of mine—whom I had known since kindergarten—pointed at me and said, 'There's the next Shirley Chisholm.' I'll never forget that. Others saw it in me; but I did not."

Not, that is, until an opportunity presented itself—in the form of the municipal judgeship vacancy. When opportunity came, she grabbed it, and her victory put her on the elective public-service ladder. From that point on, her engagement would be in elective public service. Once on that career ladder, she displayed as much progressive ambition in climbing that ladder as if she had wanted it all her life. From that point on, her career-long climb depended on seizing other opportunities when they "opened up." In her words, "God closes some doors and he opens others."[7]

She fought three consecutive elections to climb the judicial office ladder from municipal court to common pleas court. At which point, she reached for the next rung—election to the Ohio Supreme Court. But she lost a statewide campaign for that office. Whereupon another opportunity presented itself, and she resumed her law enforcement climb with two elections as Cuyahoga County Prosecutor (i.e., district attorney). By all accounts, she hoped next for a 1993 appointment to one of three vacancies on the United States District Court. But all three appointments went to other Clevelanders. Leaders of the black community, including Louis Stokes, angrily protested her exclusion.[8] "I am interested in the job, "she said afterward, "and I thank everyone who supported me." It was further reported that "she said she would be interested if another vacancy opened up."[9] "I would have ended my career as a federal judge if the opportunity had opened up," she said. "But another attractive opportunity—a seat in Congress—opened up first."

Again, it was a move up from a smaller to a larger set of responsibilities, and a move to a new office category. The switch from a law enforcement to a legislative office is not an uncommon one in American politics.[10] And she swung easily and naturally onto the legislative office ladder. Calling it "the opportunity of a lifetime," she rationalized that "It made sense to me: I had interpreted the law as a municipal and county judge; I had enforced the law as a prosecutor, and I wanted to make the law."[11]

Her career path, therefore, reveals her early attraction to public service and her later attraction to elective office. It was a career shaped more by circumstances and opportunities than by the desire for a particular office or kind of office. Indeed, "opportunity" is the common thread in all her career discussions. In that respect, she differed from Jordan and Fattah, both of whom pointed early toward legislative elective office—and both of whom knew precisely what they wanted to achieve in that office.

Stephanie Tubbs Jones does, however, share some precongressional career commonalities with Chaka Fattah—commonalities that help to differentiate both of them from Lou Stokes and may help to divide their contemporary cohort from his pioneer cohort. Stokes, for example, came to Congress out of the civil rights movement; both Tubbs Jones and Fattah came to Congress out of local politics. Stokes did not have any precongressional political career; both Tubbs Jones and Fattah had lengthy ones. Stokes had to confront the question of his qualifications; the other two had long since been vetted by their constituents. Stokes was the first African American to represent his district in Congress; neither Fattah nor Tubbs Jones had that distinction. Both Fattah and Tubbs Jones had to labor, early in their careers, in the shadow of an accomplished and esteemed congressional predecessor. In these several ways, they seem to belong to a different congressional cohort than the one in which Lou Stokes was so prominent a member.

ELECTORAL CONNECTIONS AND THE SUCCESSION

On the day that Lou Stokes announced his retirement, speculation began about his likely successor. In Cleveland's *Plain Dealer,* County Prosecutor Stephanie Tubbs Jones was designated as one of two "early front-runners." [12] And the next day, the paper's political columnist described her as the only "clear front-runner." "The right to succeed a legend in Congress," he wrote, "is pretty much Jones' for the asking." With respect to the related question of a Stokes endorsement, he reported that the congressman "had no plans to take a position in the campaign to choose his successor." [13]

She was the front-runner because of her previous success. While her representational strategies may not have been as well formed in the beginning as those with prior legislative experience—Jordan and Fattah—she had run successfully six times for election in Cleveland. She knew how to win, and she had developed a winning set of relationships with a broad range of constituents. Two of her previous campaigns, in particular, were responsible for her front-runner status.

The first was her losing 1990 statewide campaign, as a Democrat against a Republican, for the Ohio State Supreme Court. A political unknown beyond greater Cleveland, she conducted a vigorous race. "I told them, 'I'm not running as a token. If I'm in it, I'm in it to win.' I campaigned in forty counties." She did better than anyone expected, losing by only 3 percentage points. So much so, that twelve years later, in 2002, people referred to it in urging her to run for governor.[14] At the time, it was important because "The [supreme court] race set me up for the race for prosecutor," and the prosecutor race became her pivotal precongressional campaign.

The campaign for Cuyahoga County Prosecutor emerged suddenly. It took place *inside* the Democratic Party. The veteran Democratic incumbent suddenly resigned—between elections—thus opening up an instant vacancy. According to plan, his son quickly announced as a candidate to succeed his father, and the son launched an inside campaign to capture the decisive Democratic Party nomination. Everyone else was caught by surprise. Party rules provided for nomination by a public vote of the 1,600 members of the Cuyahoga County Democratic Committee—within thirty days. "The Corrigan family," Tubbs Jones recalled, "thought that the office was an Irish fiefdom that could be handed down from generation to generation. They put pressure on people and even threatened. . . . People in the black community started calling me and asking me to run, because of my statewide campaign for the supreme court. They said, 'We don't want a dynasty.'"

"I decided to run on January 4, with the vote scheduled for January 18. I ran a ten-day campaign." It was a classic grassroots, person-to-person campaign during which "she phoned so many precinct committee members in a week that she developed a callous on her ear." [15]

"The vote was a public vote, no secret ballot," she continued.

> It was like a convention. The party leader . . . stepped up and supported me. That was very important to me. But most important were my African American supporters. They turned out for the vote—every one of them. Only 1,052 committee people showed up and voted. And I won by 30 votes [541-511]. The Corrigan people couldn't believe it. They were so surprised, they counted the ballots three times. It was a celebration! The newspaper headline read "Jones Topples Old Guard." The word was passed around at choir rehearsals. People watching football saw it on the trailers where they give special weather warnings.

The story beneath the headline stated that "a coalition of east- and westsiders created a new force in county politics." [16] The framed article hangs on the wall of her Cleveland office. Her victory is still recalled as "a stunning upset." [17]

When the public election was held in November, she won with 72 percent of the vote. [18] Reelection followed, and the prosecutor's office became her congressional launching pad.

One month after Stokes's retirement announcement, Tubbs Jones declared for his seat. Subsequently, two other well-qualified African Americans—a state senator and a prominent minister (plus two minor white candidates)—entered the race. In making her announcement, Tubbs Jones emphasized continuity. Her general theme, she said, would be "a new face for an old struggle." Her priorities would "include senior citizens and children." With respect to the overriding succession question, "How do you propose to fill Lou Stokes shoes?" she promised to continue his legacy "not by filling his shoes, but by standing on his shoulders."[19] She hoped for his endorsement.

The problem of Lou Stokes's endorsement of a successor was a subject of my 1998 visit with him. We talked a month before the primary, and a few days after he had attended an AFL-CIO Washington fundraiser for Tubbs Jones.[20] I asked him about his endorsement strategy. "I had mixed feelings about that," he answered.

> It was my intention to endorse Stephanie Tubbs Jones as my successor because I thought she was the best qualified for the job. The other two candidates came to me and asked me not to endorse anyone—that if I did that, it would be all over for them. I agreed not to. Two conditions existed. I knew each of them had a following of some kind. I also knew Stephanie could beat either of them. So why alienate people in either of their camps when I'm leaving Congress? She doesn't need me. I'd only be frosting on the cake—and I'd leave with that alienation. Also, I listened and gave consideration to the merit of their argument. Each one would say, "If it hadn't been for Lou Stokes, I'd have won." I didn't want Stephanie to go to Congress with that hanging over her. And I would have given credence to their explanation. On the other hand, if I gave them their shot, they'll know she beat them.

He was more philosophical than regretful about his recent attendance at the D.C. fundraiser. "In order to help those guys [the national AFL-CIO], I'm taking a beating. By trying not to endorse her, I got a whipping." And he insisted that his presence at the event "was not an endorsement." Needless to say, two candidates were unhappy. Tubbs Jones, who got a tacit blessing, commented tactfully, "I'm very thankful for his attendance [and] I respect his decision not to endorse."[21]

"Of course, I wanted Lou Stokes's support," she said later, "and everybody knew he was supporting me. There was a *Plain Dealer* cartoon that showed Lou sitting with his fishing pole, and sticking out of his back pocket was a paper which said, 'Stephanie Tubbs Jones is OK.'" She had been remarkably careful about that personal relationship. "While Lou Stokes was a congressman," she said, "I never spoke one word to anyone about running for Congress. I never mentioned the subject. I knew Lou respected loyalty, and I knew that if I ever did run for Congress, I wanted to run with his support."

"I watched over the years," she said later, "and I saw that anyone who suggested running for Congress got cut off at the knees." He was king of the hill and she knew it.

Congressman Stokes was certainly right when he said Tubbs Jones did not need his electoral help. The county prosecutor won her congressional primary overwhelmingly. She won 51 percent of the vote—more than doubling the vote of her two African American opponents, who received 22 percent each. She carried Cleveland and all but one (Shaker Heights) of her twenty (whole and partial) suburban communities.[22] "I didn't expect the margin," she said of her primary victory, "but I love it." Her explanation? "My seventeen years of running for public office in the district."[23] That seems right. She had won because of her own well-established political persona, her own wealth of political experience and her own record of pathbreaking firsts.

One of the indispensable organizational components of Lou Stokes's campaigns—the black ministers—was a nonfactor for Tubbs Jones. As she described it, "The ministers were split, because there was a minister in the race. Many of them supported him. But some ministers thought he should not be in politics, and they supported me. The campaign did take place in the churches, but the campaign was fought far away from the churches. Most of the campaign had nothing to do with the ministers. They cancelled each other out and had no effect." She was not Lou Stokes's protégé, and she had in no way depended on him for her victory. In November she won 80 percent of the vote and carried all twenty suburban areas.

On election night, Stokes came to her victory party to place his imprimatur on her victory. "I came by here," he said, "as somebody who held this seat for thirty years. I'm proud tonight to turn it over to Stephanie Tubbs Jones."[24] In her postelection letter to supporters, she sounded a lot like her predecessor. "I thank you for the *trust* you have placed in me. . . . I want to make you *proud*." Constituent trust and constituent pride were bedrock connections for both of them.

PERSONAL GOALS AND REPRESENTATIONAL STRATEGY

In generalizing about Stephanie Tubbs Jones's representational relationships, her actual performance in previous elective offices is not as helpful as it was with Barbara Jordan and Chaka Fattah. Both of them started early and worked single-mindedly to run for, and to serve in, a legislative office. Goals and strategies displayed at the state legislative level provided them—and us—with guidelines in identifying their goals and strategies at the national legislative level. Tubbs Jones's less-focused and less-comparable precongressional career requires that new guidelines be developed in thinking about her national-level goals and strategies. Two sets of guidelines have been most helpful—my travel experience and her 1998 campaign success. Both point toward the primacy of personal connections in her constituency relationships.

My own strong impression of her preference for personal relationships developed out of an experience that was doubly indelible because it came early and because it contrasted so sharply with that of her predecessor. During my first visit, she took me to see some of the personal landmarks of her life. Apparently, she had decided that if I were to understand her as a politician, it would be helpful if I knew something about her as a person. Her impulse turned out to be diagnostic for my assessments of her representational strategy.

"I've lived in just three houses in my life," she said as we traced them from Ostend Avenue to Rutland Avenue to Wade Park. "The house where I spent my childhood," turned out to be a side-by-side duplex. "My father and a friend from work bought this house together," she said. "And his family lived on the other side." I noticed several boarded-up houses nearby. When she was thirteen, the family moved to a street of small, well-kept, wood-frame homes—where her parents still live. "My mother is the enforcement officer of this neighborhood, making sure the grass is cut and the trash picked up—she and three other women." Stephanie, her husband, and their high school age son lived on a broad avenue of large homes. We stopped to talk in her circular driveway. "At one time, this was one of the fanciest streets in the city," she said, "the buffer between the university and the black neighborhoods." Then she drove around the corner to show me the building "where I took music lessons."

She acted as tour guide as we drove around her Glenville neighborhood. Driving up the main street, East 105th: "When I was a child, this was the grand shopping avenue. Now, it's all churches and church parking lots." In the midst of some boarded-up storefronts: "There's Mr. Cloud's flower shop. It's a third-generation business." Passing by a Rite Aid store: "By the time I became a teenager, there was not a single drugstore in the black area. We had to go downtown or to the suburbs to buy our prescription drugs." Stopping in front of the Bethany Baptist Church: "I was baptized in this church and have been a member all my life. We just put on that new extension." Along the way, she spoke warmly of her Glenville political mentor, longtime ward leader, city councilman, and eventually president of the

Cleveland City Council, George Forbes—a sometime ally of, and a some-time irritant to, Lou Stokes. "I have known him for many, many years. I grew up in his ward. He helped me in my career. We have been friends." "Could I say that you were his protégé?" "Yes, you could, absolutely." [25]

Finally, she drove me to see "my school" (Case Western Reserve University) and its impressive medical facility, the Cleveland Clinic—"the largest employer in my district." Public events at the university had created a traffic jam. She pulled alongside a police officer who was diverting traffic. "I'm Stephanie Jones." "I know who you are. We are watching traffic on your street." "Thank you very much." "They are traveling 45 miles per hour on your street." "It's too fast. I thank you." "You can drive straight through."

At the next intersection, another police officer was in the middle of the street directing the flow. As we approached, she rolled down her window, waved and hollered at him, "Are you trying to get run over?" He smiled and waved as we went by. "When I became prosecutor," she said as we continued on, "I met and talked with as many of the policemen as I could. I wanted to get to know them and for them to know me. I also wanted them to know if they did their job, I would prosecute their cases, but that if they did not do their job, I would not prosecute their cases." "I'm sure some of them," she added, "would rather have seen me in jail." Her encounters with the two (white) traffic cops ended our two-hour tour—a sequence that was, in every respect, unlike anything I ever did or could imagine doing with her predecessor.

As we traversed her Glenville neighborhood in her SUV, she commented, "I'm doing something now that Lou Stokes would never do, driving myself around. He always had a driver. But I still ride public transportation—which I often did when I was prosecutor." (I rode in the front seat with her and, usually, in the backseat with Stokes.) As a positive link to her predecessor, she insisted we go to lunch at "Lou Stokes's favorite restaurant." It was a place I would never have learned about from him. Altogether, the "tour" had a very helpful "this is your life" snapshot quality. It gave me a good sense for her ingrained attachments to the black community. But it was her personal touch that was distinctive and diagnostic.

In the 1970s Lou Stokes never mentioned, nor gave me a glimpse of, his personal life, and I did not expect him, or any other House member, to do so. But that is precisely the point. Stephanie Tubbs Jones places a great value on personal relationships—much greater than the others in this book. During our first day, she had said, "You like to be called Dick, don't you—not Professor. Once I learned to pronounce your name, it was easy, but before that, I had to call you Professor." As we finished lunch the last day, she said, "I'd say we've had a good first visit, wouldn't you?"

Her tour had two research results. First, I no longer needed anyone else to tell me how effective she is at person-to-person relations. When I am told that her personality—outgoing, down to earth, and approachable—is a major source of her political strength, my experience tells me to believe it. Second, and more important for this book, her attentiveness to personal relationships, as I had experienced it, predisposed me to think of that behavior as basic to *all* her representational relationships and, thus, to her overall representational strategy. That conclusion was buttressed, too, by the reports and explanations of her 1998 campaign success.

The essential point was made in chapter 3, that a useful first approach to any politician's representational strategy is to study one or two of his or her election campaigns. Representation is a process, I argued, and election campaigns are an essential part of that process.[26] In Tubbs Jones's case, accounts of her winning 1998 primary election campaign served to reinforce the strong impressions I gathered during our first "tour" together.

That primary campaign, against her two African American opponents was, by all accounts, a person-intensive campaign, grounded in her personal rapport with voters. Her campaign brochure carried the theme "Experience You Can Trust," with a paragraph each devoted to education, child care, safety, affirmative action, social security, and health care. But she did not need to elaborate these policy positions at great length. They were the sorts of policies—involving the protection of black interests—that Lou Stokes had always worked for. All required an active government. They were not controversial within the black community, and they were general enough to obviate harsh attacks from without. They did not differentiate her from her opponents. She did not conduct an issue-oriented campaign. She emphasized constituent trust in her as a person more than she emphasized policy connections. Postprimary reports emphasized, accordingly, that she "came across as a trusted friend," that she "enjoys a great deal of trust in the district."[27]

"My assumption, from the beginning," the congresswoman recalled, "was that I would win. I went around and campaigned. But I knew they couldn't beat me. I had three campaign slogans: 'You know me, you know me, you know me.' Wherever I campaigned, I said I want to leave you with three thoughts: 'You know me, you know me, you know me.' And you know me because I have lived and worked in this community. I talk so ordinary people can understand what I'm saying. *I'm a people person.*" She is not a media person. "I'm not on TV all the time," she says. "People know me because I've run so many times and because I'm around so much."

Published accounts of the campaign also focus on her person-to-person prowess. She was invariably described as "popular"—"a very popular Democrat," "a popular vote getter."[28] As a campaigner, the *Plain Dealer*'s political reporter wrote, Tubbs Jones "seems to know every person in the city, . . . has a ubiquitous and gregarious presence," and "fills [a room] with her personality." Observers often described her as "ebullient."[29] "I speak to everybody," she told one. "The dilemma people have running against me is that I campaign all the time."[30] Accompanying her to her son's high school football game two years later—watching her scream "deeefense," schlep hot dogs, holler at friends, visit with cheerleaders, jump several rows to introduce herself to her son's newest girlfriend—I experienced something of the warmth and energy of her campaign activity. And something of the difference from her predecessor, too.

Her campaign rules of thumb stress personal behavior and personal relationships. "I never campaign on race, and I never get personal. I want to campaign in such a way that when it's over, I can go up to my opponent, shake hands, and give a hug." "You know that smile I always have." "Don't do negative campaigning." "Never burn your bridges." "When a political fight gets to the personal level, get out. If you get involved at that point, you will never recover. And you've got to recover."

Among African American campaigners, their persistent worry centers on black voter turnout. The prescribed remedy is assumed to be personal campaigning and the use of person-to-person techniques such as "phone banks, neighborhood canvassing, and radio ads targeted to urban audiences."[31] Those were precisely Tubbs Jones's inclinations and her strengths. They were underscored by her frequent assertion that "I am not a publicity hound. When I was prosecutor, I let the prosecutor's office get the credit." Or, "I do not use the media to generate publicity." After the primary, the *Plain Dealer* reporter concluded that "In the end [her] endearing personality and immense popularity carried the day. . . . [She] was not just sloganeering when she reminded voters that 'you know me.'"[32] In short, her campaign was relied heavily on her person-centered strategy and her personal appeal. My experience on her personal "tour" and her campaign style combine to underscore her dominating preference for personal relationships in dealing with others.

Based, therefore, on evidence from her career, from her election, and from personal observation, I shall describe Stephanie Tubbs Jones's dominant personal goal as *personal engagement in public service.* I shall describe her dominant strategy as a *person-intensive representational strategy.* Her negotiations with her constituents begin with and are grounded in her person-to-person skills and her enduring networks of personal relationships.

CONSTITUENCY CONTEXT

The actual development of her representational relationships, of course, has depended heavily on the constituency context and her perceptions thereof. The geographical constituency Stephanie Tubbs Jones inherited from Lou Stokes is, as it always had been, a majority-black district. And its black voters are solidly Democratic.[33] It is still located on the east side of the city, together with (all, or parts of) what she called "twenty inner-ring suburbs, the oldest suburbs." "With the exception of Shaker Heights, which has some of the wealthiest people in Cleveland, all my suburbs are *working-class* suburbs."

By 1998, as noted in chapter 5, the district had become less black and more suburban than it had been when Stokes took over in 1968. Taken together, those changes gave the district a slightly improved economic profile. That change had been supported somewhat by a downtown renaissance in the 1990s that had replaced the city's "Mistake on the Lake" reputation of the 1970s, to its "Comeback City" reputation of the 1990s.[34] At the margins, therefore, the new congresswoman would develop her representational pattern in a more diversified economic context than the one in which Stokes had developed his pattern.

At the district's core, and concentrated in the city, however, there remained a very large residue of poverty and a very needy African American population. Cleveland remained among the nations most "highly segregated" cities.[35] Nearly one-third of its black citizens lived below the poverty line.[36] Its median household income was second lowest among Ohio's nineteen districts. The "development of downtown," wrote one observer in 1992, "has done little or nothing to cure the real intractable problems that plague the poor neighborhoods of Cleveland: an effective unemployment rate of 50 percent among black males and a high school dropout rate of more than 50 percent."[37]

In 2000, local analysts found that the booming economy had improved the job picture. But they also found that Cleveland had fallen behind comparable cities in its ability to change from old industry to new industry and, thus, to profit from the new prosperity. "Though more people are working in Greater Cleveland today than 30 years ago," said one study, "job growth has lagged far behind that in other [top fifty] cities. . . . Overall, Greater Cleveland does not appear to be well positioned for the rapidly changing national economy."[38] In 2000, two analysts found that, in terms of its "mediocre educational standing," "the region is at a troubling disadvantage." Once more, they noted that "the metro area made a heralded comeback . . . built with office towers and sports arenas, not graduation gowns and research labs."[39] A year later, a lengthy *Wall Street Journal* article, despite some optimism, was headlined "Cleveland, A Center of the U.S. Slowdown."[40] My second visit was punctuated by the prospective layoff of one thousand steel workers and by Congresswoman Tubbs Jones's efforts—within the antitrade Congressional Steel Caucus—to help.[41]

Where the production of skill jobs and education for such jobs lags, the missed opportunities and the hardships hit the black population especially hard. The new House member understood this reality, as any African American Representative from Cleveland surely would. Accordingly, in her campaign, Tubbs Jones had placed "education for the young" at the top of her "three themes"—the other two being "social security for the old" and "health care for all."[42]

With respect to some other aspects of her constituency context, her perceptions were different from those of her predecessor—and different, therefore, from those that had guided his representational activity thirty years earlier. When I asked Tubbs Jones whether she felt as if she was a "second-generation African American House member," she replied, "Yes I do, very much so. Lou Stokes had a predominantly black district. My district is not predominantly black. The largest group is black, but it's not predominantly black. It is 52 percent black and 48 percent white." If that was her perception, then it seems quite likely that her relationships would be different, too.

As a matter of statistics, Tubbs Jones's perception was curiously at odds with the 1990 census figures. They showed her district to be 60 percent black. An easy answer to the discrepancy is simply that black/white proportions had, indeed, changed since the previous census, and her view was more up-to-date. Or perhaps she was referring to actual voter proportions. Or perhaps her calculations anticipated the upcoming redistricting, taking into account local speculation that the upcoming redistricting would, in fact, produce a district that would be split 50-50, black and white.

More interesting, however, as an explanation for the discrepancy between statistics and perception, is the notion that she had developed her own working perception of her constituency. That perception was the product of her own extensive precongressional campaign experience—all of which—citywide, countywide, and statewide—had been in majority-white constituencies. That is, she perceived her constituency to be less black than it was, and, therefore, she treated it politically as if it was less black than the statistics said it was.

"One advantage I have over Lou Stokes," she said, "was that I ran [as prosecutor] in all of Cuyahoga County, where blacks make up only 24 percent of the population. He ran in a Cleveland district where blacks made up nearly 75 percent. He had a very different ratio of tenure to base." Unlike Stokes, that is, Tubbs Jones expressed no need for an assured "65 percent or at least 55 percent" black district. Indeed, her experience taught her a very different lesson: that she could run well as a black politician in white territory.

During her statewide supreme court contest, she recalled, some white county chairmen advised her to disguise her race in unfamiliar areas. She outspokenly refused.[43] Reporters following her in that campaign described an "easy, friendly campaign style that slices across racial lines."[44] Speaking of possible post-2000 redistricting, she said, "I don't care how they redraw the district. Push me east or west and I'm still going to get elected."[45] In her race for prosecutor, she recalled, "I ran well on the west [i.e., white] side, and I could win even if a lot of my [congressional] district were on the west side. It would be harder, but I could do it. That's why I don't worry about redistricting. The Republicans say to me, 'You draw the lines of your district and you can have it.' But I don't trust them. I don't care what they do, I will win no matter how they draw the district or where they put me." As redistricting drew near, however, she put it more positively. "I think they'll give me what I want because they don't want to get involved in a civil rights violation." Her perception of her district is certainly affected by the hard facts of boundary lines, but it is powerfully shaped, too, by her own experience, by her self-confidence, and by what she calls her "comfort level" in white areas.

Her perception is also grounded in a contextual reality—a gradual change in black politics and race relations. According to local observers, the city's era of confrontation between blacks and whites—so dominant in the 1960s and 1970s—has slowly given way to an era of increasing accommodation. Lou Stokes began his congressional career in the shadow of the Hough riots and the murderous Glenville shootout between black nationalists and white police. Stephanie Tubbs Jones—who could banter one-on-one with white police officers—began hers in a time of increasing accommodation. In this respect, more than any other, the story of the Stokes–Tubbs Jones succession is a thirty-year story, not just a 1998 story. In the familiar "from protest to politics" scenario of Robert C. Smith, the context had changed from "lingering protest" in the Stokes era to "mostly politics" in the Tubbs Jones era.

Local politicians and chroniclers of Cleveland politics have said that changing racial moods and changing governing styles were symbolized by the 1989 election of an African American mayor, "who won largely on the backing of white voters."[46] Mayor Michael White was described as "a racial healer," "who sees racial harmony as a key to the city's future." He won national attention as "the most successful of any big city executive in building a biracial alliance in seemingly hostile terrain."[47] "Twenty years ago," said White in 1992, "it was an in-your-face kind of politics," and "racial politics was so much easier to define."[48] In 1992, 77 percent of Cleveland's whites and 73 percent of the city's blacks agreed that the Mayor had improved race relations.[49] The mayor was serving his third term when Tubbs Jones was elected to Congress. They shared similar experiences and similar perceptions of black–white possibilities.

As prosecutor, Stephanie Tubbs Jones actively promoted a changed racial climate, speaking throughout the county on the importance of interracial conversation and the strengths of a multicultural society.[50] "I kept going and going and finally I was like one of the crowd. . . . People say I'm able to go places and get votes, and people don't think about the color of my skin."[51] When the *Plain Dealer* columnist pronounced her the heir-apparent to Stokes, he emphasized "her rock solid base in the black community and her enormous crossover appeal in a district in which close to half of those who vote are white."[52]

When I asked her, twice, to identify the people who would "fight, bleed, and die for you," she gave two answers—neither of which were racial. "They are people who have been voting for me for a long time—black and white working-class people." And "They are the people I went to kindergarten with, the people I went to elementary school with, the people I went to high school with, the people I went to college with, all the people who have touched my life, my mother and father and their friends and every person on a jury or a grand jury when I was prosecutor." "There are people," she says, "who have been with me as long as I have been in politics. I can call on them at any time, and they will come work for me."

"I see myself as an evolution of . . . George Forbes [her own ward leader in Glenville] and Congressman Stokes," she says. "I took their experience and expanded upon it, but I'm also expected to be more. If I hadn't stepped out [to seek support outside the black community], I couldn't have won countywide. Now, there's nowhere in Cuyahoga County I go where I won't get a warm reception."[53] In that spirit of personal outreach, she fashioned her representational strategy. Looking forward to her new job in Congress, she told a reporter, "I will push minority issues, . . . but I'm still a leader *outside the African American community too*" (my emphasis).[54] It was a very different perspective on constituency context and constituency expectations than that of Lou Stokes. That difference accounted for the biggest difference from her predecessor.

As a fighter for inclusion in a context of separation and struggle, Lou Stokes saw himself as the embodiment and the protector of the whole black community. He saw himself as its leader, its organizer, its spokesman. He "helped raise black self-esteem and pride."[55] He rallied the black community around him and moved the group forward as a group toward equality, self-respect, and self-confidence. He did this primarily by expanding black political power. Born of a common separateness and common aspirations, the black community was the most obvious entity for Stokes's attention. A strategy of representation that centered on promoting and protecting black group interests was, in 1970, a natural one. In a context in which his white, hometown Democratic colleague would work to deny him power inside Congress, Stokes's strategy at home would naturally become confrontational.

Stephanie Tubbs Jones came to political maturity in a different context. She had deliberately cultivated broader relationships within every constituency she ever encountered or contemplated. She internalized and pursued the group interests of the black community. She was deeply embedded in the black community and in the black experience. But, in a changed context, she did not make "the black community" the measure of all things—except, as I shall discuss, during the mayoralty contest in 2001. Most of the time, however, she was the self-confident beneficiary of Lou Stokes's groundbreaking leadership, and, as such, she was free to contemplate a more inclusive community constituency for herself than he could.

It was, therefore, natural for her to pursue a more inclusive representational strategy. I have called it a dominantly person-centered strategy, a strategy of personal involvement that begins with outreach to other individuals.

Its emphasis is on her own participatory involvement with others, on a person-to-person basis—a degree of engagement very different from the personal aloofness of the "revered" and "legendary" community leader Stokes. It also involved her personal efforts to encourage a wide variety of others to engage in common efforts to build better lives for large numbers of needy people—black and white. Lou Stokes stood apart—both as an individual and as a representative of the black community. Stephanie Tubbs Jones immersed herself in the racial mix—personally and as a representative. The changed historical context made possible that change in strategy.

Her representational strategy, however, had its costs. During their campaign debates, she recalled, one of her opponents had taunted pointedly, "What have you ever done for black people?" To this specific question she had answered, "When I became prosecutor, there were five black support staff. When I left, there were sixty. When I began, there were ten black prosecutors; I hired—at one time or another—fifty." Her record was clear; but the implication rankled.

In 1999 the *Plain Dealer* politics writer described the changed context as the passing of the city's "golden era of black leadership." "Once," he began, "when black Cleveland's pillars of power spoke, white Cleveland listened. But as the era of Carl and Louis Stokes, George Forbes and Arnold Pinkney came to an end, no politician, activist or group has emerged to fill the black leadership void. . . . today, the community that boasted the area's most cohesive and productive political machine of the last thirty years seems leaderless and lethargic. . . . Many of the new and emerging black leaders, who approach black issues differently from their predecessors, are often criticized in the community for not being 'black enough.'" [56]

Because the Stokes–Tubbs Jones succession made her such a visible "new and emerging black leader," those who bemoaned the changing landscape could be expected to make her a target. The author of the article did exactly that: "In the past, a challenge like the Ku Klux Klan's downtown rally during the summer [of 1999] would have been met head-on by Lou Stokes," he wrote. But "Stokes' hand-picked successor . . . made no public statements about the white supremacist group marching in her hometown." [57]

To that invidious comparison, the congresswoman answered publicly,

I'm not of the opinion that I have to be heard on every issue. I think I am heard on issues that people expect me to be heard on. . . . sometimes people think that because you represent a larger constituency base that it may be more difficult to advocate issues that affect the black community. I don't have that problem.[58]

Later, she rehearsed the newspaper story.

The reporter said there was criticism that I had failed to speak out on any issue of great importance to the black community—like the presence of the KKK in Cleveland. The mayor had cordoned off a big area so that they wouldn't get hurt. There was a lot of talk about it. I knew they had a right to free speech and that the KKK used to be a big issue in the South but that they were not important now. I had just gotten to Washington and I was learning my job. I thought I could do a lot more good for my constituents learning the job than by coming back and making statements about the unimportant little group. But the reporter said that I was not "speaking out" as a leader should do. That tells you something about my relations with the *Plain Dealer*.

These questions about her "blackness" and her "leadership"—and the implication that the answer was "not enough of either"—are questions that come with the territory. They come to anyone who follows a leader who, like Stokes, had shaped and defined an era in the city and in the congressional district.

In 2000, she seemed philosophical about it. "People think that because Lou Stokes was so involved at home, I should be too. But I think I have to learn my job in Washington. People say to me, 'You've got big shoes to fill.' I tell them, 'I'm not trying to fill Lou's shoes. I want to stand on his shoulders to help finish the things he began.' I'm not Lou Stokes. I don't want to be Lou Stokes. I am me." It would remain a dilemma until such time as she had put her own stamp on the district.

The media context in which the new congresswoman worked had both similarities and differences from that of her predecessor. Here, the similarities (e.g., "my relations with the *Plain Dealer*") seemed to outweigh the differences. For my purposes, the relevant local media is the print media, and the relevant newspaper was, and still is, the *Plain Dealer*. During Stokes's early tenure, the weekly black newspaper, *Call and Post,* was his most supportive voice. That paper's support was his lifeline until, late in his term, the *Plain Dealer* began to acknowledge his influence in Washington. By 1998, however, the *Call and Post* editor, a powerful community leader, had passed away, and the newspaper had been sold to outside interests. It gave no comparable sustenance to Stephanie Tubbs Jones.

She was left to face the same unhelpful citywide newspaper that Stokes had dealt with thirty years before. For most members of Congress, their first political race is the most trying and most crucial one of their careers. For black members, who seldom face opposition afterward, it is very much a matter of political life or death. For both Stokes and Tubbs Jones, therefore, the make-or-break election was their first Democratic primary. In both those elections, thirty years apart, the *Plain Dealer* gave its editorial support to another candidate. And in both cases, the newspaper's chosen candidate was swamped at the polls. On both occasions, that is, the *Plain Dealer* actively opposed the overwhelming choice of the black citizens of Cleveland. Small wonder that anti–*Plain Dealer* commentary from politically active black citizens was a constant refrain during all of my visits to Cleveland.

Although the newspaper had given Stephanie Tubbs Jones its "enthusiastic" endorsement for her reelection as county prosecutor in 1996,[59] they concluded two years later that she had "demonstrated considerable and, we think, decisive weaknesses." They acknowledged her "wide support in the community," and her "winning personality," but they expressed doubts about her "ability to take to Congress the thorough study, independence and leadership her constituents deserve."[60]

Basing their decision on their editorial board interviews, board members expressed their preference for her minister opponent as "the most passionate proponent of a traditional liberal agenda," "the most eloquent speaker," "the most commanding presence," the one "most likely to get his colleagues' attention [on the floor of the House] with the power of oratory," and "the smartest candidate in the race."[61] These are the bonds that tend to link political aspirants and editorial boards. As for the bonds that tend to link representatives and their constituents, however, board members seemed dismissive. "You can see right away why she is one of Cuyahoga's most popular politicians," wrote one board member about Tubbs Jones. "She smiles more than her opponents. She engages more with her audience. She connects more."[62] The board dismissed "engaging" and "connecting" activities as electoral or vote-getting talents, and they predicated their endorsement, instead, on the candidate's interview performance in discussing "issues."

The reaction of the newly elected congresswoman to this media treatment was bafflement. "I've always had a decent press until I ran last year," she said. "During the campaign, the *Plain Dealer* kept talking up [the minister], saying how intelligent and bright he was. They called me a people person, but they never called me bright or intelligent. They covered me going to events; but they said I didn't know the issues. My constituents began calling me, asking, 'What's going on here?' Then the *Plain Dealer* endorsed him. And my constituents asked, 'What's the deal?' They couldn't believe it. I couldn't either." "I'm intelligent, and I don't have to use big words," she added. It was a person-to-person theme to which she returned often. "I don't talk down to people. They know I have an important job, but they want me to deal with them on their level. And I do."

Shortly after this comment, she gave a television interview, after which she thanked the cameraman, gave him a hug, and turned to me laughing, "You see, I do have some friends in the media." Not, however, in the editorial boardroom. From an outside observer's viewpoint, the people in the *Plain Dealer* boardroom operated with a myopic view of representation. They did not understand the degree to which the very activities of "engaging" and "connecting" foster constituent trust—without which good representation is impossible. Or perhaps they were overwhelmingly out of touch with the thoughts and preferences of a large proportion of their fellow citizens.

PERSONAL CONNECTIONS

Stephanie Tubbs Jones's winning 1998 primary campaign put on display her exceptional person-to-person political skills. I expected those same skills to be equally prominent and equally important in her postcampaign activities. With differing degrees of prominence and relevance, that is exactly what I observed as she connected with various groups of constituents during my visits. The personal seemed to be a basic building block for all her negotiations at home—always a necessary ingredient, sometimes a sufficient one. It makes sense, therefore, to begin analyzing the congresswoman's constituency activity where I left her campaign—with the personal side of her connections at home.

An overall numerical appraisal of her appointment schedules for the year 2000 makes it amply clear that Tubbs Jones spends a great deal of time in her district. Granted that uncertainty and imprecision inevitably turns any translation of a schedule into an approximation of actual performance, her personal presence at home remains impressive. In 2000, she made the seventy-five minute flight from Washington to Cleveland fifty times and spent 161 "event days" at home. On those event days, she scheduled 382 separate "personal connections" with her constituents—averaging almost two and a half events per day.

The largest number of scheduled events—110—can be catalogued as "community" events. One-third of them were ceremonies honoring an individual or group at which the congresswoman had some officially designated role to play—as master of ceremonies, presenter of awards, or introducer of others. The bulk of the others were supportive, participatory appearances at the fullest range of public and private organizational functions and activities.

In second place numerically were her seventy partisan political events. These election-year events ranged from fundraisers for local candidates to functions related to state and national politics. They included regular meetings of her inherited—now her own—organizations, the Eleventh District Caucus and the Black Elected Democrats of Cuyahoga County. Even without the election-year stimulus, her active engagement in Democratic Party politics is noteworthy.

Third most common were what might be generalized as "meetings." These included one-on-one meetings with constituents in the district office and policy-related face-to-face meetings of all sorts with small groups. Not more than a dozen or so of these sixty-six "meetings" fit the common picture of one constituent talking about a personal difficulty one-on-one with the House member. Such "casework" meetings were bundled into two or three of her home visits. The great bulk of the meetings involved issues of particular concern to groups—civic or private. A most distinctive ingredient in these meetings was her unique willingness to meet with many such groups at *their* place of business, a practice reflecting a person-intensive representational strategy.

Ranked fourth in terms of numbers, but higher in terms of importance, were the forty-five events denoted on the schedule as "keynote speaker" or "speaker." In fifth place were her twenty-two media events—mostly radio interviews, a few television appearances. Scattered event counts were also produced for interviews with print media, school visits, plant tours, church visits, and staff meetings. For Tubbs Jones, as for all members of Congress, personal connections at home come in many varieties.

Among the varieties of personal contact, none could be called purely personal. That is, nearly every variety of personal contact with constituents bears some relationship—however tenuous or invisible—to a matter of public policy. It is helpful, therefore, when emphasizing personal connections, to recognize the entangling policy connections. It is always a matter of proportions. In this book, with its nonrandom sets of observations, all of my distinctions have to be couched in the language of rough proportions—using words like *dominance,* for example. In Tubbs Jones's case, the personal component of her home activity is dominant—and the more so when compared with the contrasting behavior of Louis Stokes and Chaka Fattah.

With respect to the contrast with Fattah, a difference in their Web sites in 2001 is instructive.[63] His Web site contained only a single picture. He is speaking at the podium during the White House ceremony launching Gear Up, with President Clinton sitting in the background. He is presenting himself as a policy-making Representative. Her Web site has a gallery of nine photos. In each one, she is featured talking or meeting with others—with constituents or with House colleagues. Some of the pictures convey policy connections: civil rights, the steel trade, prescription drugs. Others convey personal connections: with House colleagues, with the vice president, with schoolchildren, with a reporter, with African American constituency leaders. But almost all of them convey—in pictures and descriptions—a personal interaction with others. She is presenting herself as a personally engaged Representative. The two Web sites reflect the different emphases in their representational strategies.

A PERSONAL / POLICY MIX

It is true for all House members that any dominance of personal or policy connections is a matter of proportions. In calibrating the personal / policy proportions of various House member–constituency connections, therefore, it is helpful to make a distinction between "soft" and "hard" policy connections. Policy-related talks to constituency organizations, typically followed by a question-and-answer period, together with media interviews, are prototypical soft policy connections. Roll call votes in Congress are prototypical hard policy connections. Soft connections have no immediate, direct, or traceable connection to legislation; hard connections are concrete and irrevocable, with measurable effects. In between, there are gradations. A meeting with constituents to explore interest, exchange information, or canvass preferences in a defined area of public policy might, for example, fall somewhere in the middle.

The point of a heuristic distinction between soft and hard is this: in soft policy connections with constituents, there is much more room for the play of personal connections. Although the hard policy connections of two House members—their roll call votes, for example—may be identical, their soft policy connections at home may be quite different. Stephanie Tubbs Jones's personal connections at home revealed various proportions of this personal / policy mix.

THE LIBRARY APPEARANCE

An event at which the personal ingredient was nearly total and the policy component nearly zero was her "stop by" appearance at "A Commemorative Program in Honor of Dr. Martin Luther King Jr." on King's birthday, held at the Cleveland Public Library. On her schedule, it was labeled "tentative" and scored as a "community" event. She had no part to play in the program. But she had been the first African American woman on the Library's Board of Trustees, and she wanted to express her continuing support by showing up at the end of a busy day. The program was two-thirds over when we arrived. Someone spied her standing in the wings. The main speaker [a local, white, television celebrity] stopped in midspeech to acknowledge her presence. And she was greeted by what I noted as "a huge, heart-warming, spontaneous, appreciative cheer" from a racially mixed audience of about three hundred people. She waved, and we stood in the wings till the program ended.

When it was over, she spent nearly an hour greeting people, hugging people, signing autographs, having her picture taken, swapping sentiments on current events, and entertaining a couple of personal requests. "How many of the people here do you guess you know personally?" I asked. "One in three, maybe two in three, because I served on the Board of Trustees." For her, therefore, it was old home week among fellow supporters of the library. For me, however, it seemed like the continuation of her election campaign—a perfect illustration of her "you know me, you know me, you know me" citywide appeal. Support for the library may give the event a very soft policy connection, but it was probably as close to a purely personal connection—and a purely personal constituent response—as one gets in an organized setting.

THE YOUTH VIOLENCE CONFERENCE

On the first day of my visit, I observed a very different mix of personal and policy activity. In this case, Tubbs Jones had organized a conference to address and to publicize a particular policy problem—youth violence. The meeting exemplified a soft policy connection because there was a large personal contribution to its organization, its spirit, and its success. I catalogued it, also, as a "community" event—one in which she had a specific role to play as organizer.

In their belated general election endorsement in 1998, the *Plain Dealer* had reminded Tubbs Jones that "Her longstanding service to and popularity within the district should help her carry out her campaign pledge: to use her congressional post as a bully pulpit to engage community groups and individuals in addressing problems such as *youth violence* [italics added], for which federally funded programs cannot be the sole solution."[64] It was a campaign promise she had already begun to keep when I arrived.

During her first year in office, she had brought two students from the district to a Washington conference on youth violence run by the House Democrats.[65] Now, in her second year, she had organized her own conference on youth violence—Reclaiming Our Youth. It was held in her district, and it was the second such conference in her short tenure.[66] Because her personal contribution was so large, and because it was my first glimpse, her connective behavior at the conference had a major impact on my overall assessments of her representational strategy. Like the personal "tour" that I would take two days later, the conference turned out to be diagnostic for my study, so I shall treat it at some length.

On a Saturday morning, about one hundred high school students had come to one of the district's middle schools to listen and to hold group discussions on youth violence. The congresswoman and I introduced ourselves in the lobby and went directly to the school cafeteria, where fifty or sixty students were having doughnuts and soft drinks. It took me five minutes to recognize how very different Stephanie Tubbs Jones's person-to-person representational connections were going to be from those of Louis Stokes. She was clearly more attuned to her district's young people than he, and her personal approach to them foretold a more down-to-earth relationship with her constituents.

She plunged in, shaking hands with students and their school counselors, making personal connections with some, hugging a lot of them, keeping a photographer busy snapping pictures with others. Several times, she broke off to come over to tell me about connections she had just made. "We went to elementary school together." "Those are the kids from Collinwood, my high school." She brought a tall young woman over to meet me. "This is Janet Braxton, assistant coach of the Rockers [Cleveland's women's basketball team]. I'm a big women's sports fan, and I was google-eyed when I met her. A group of us—about seventy-five—got together and bought some tickets for every game. If we can't use them, we give them away." Braxton, along with two members of the Cleveland Browns football team and one member of the Cleveland Crunch soccer team, had come to participate in the group sessions. The 105 students came from twenty-five high schools, seventeen public and eight private. There were slightly more girls than boys, and about 80 percent were black. Like a mother hen, she soon herded the group out of the cafeteria and into the auditorium, shouting,

"Let's go everybody. . . . Are we ready? . . . Here we go!" The degree of her informal personal engagement was unusual.

Opening the conference, she reminded everyone of the schedule and of the three questions they were to tackle in their discussion groups. The idea was that at the end of the morning, each group would report their answers to the whole. Their questions were: "What are the five most important problems kids face? What are the best methods for dealing with them? What theme song would you suggest to carry your message?" Each group session was led by an adult expert—a professor, a public defender, a social worker.

During her introductory remarks, she told a story: "In the House of Representatives," she said,

> We had a "bring-your-daughter-to-work day." I was in one group where the mothers were talking "mom talk," and the girls were nodding off. So I jumped in and asked them, "How many of you have a boyfriend?" They perked up and raised their hands. Then I said, "How many of them are scrubs?" They all put up their hands and started laughing and talking. The mothers had no idea what was going on. So I asked them, "Do you know what a scrub is?" No one knew. So I said, "You ought to have a sixteen-year-old boy like I do; I learned it from talking to my son. [Later, she told me that *scrub* comes from a rap song and refers to "a boy who takes everything from a girl and gives her nothing in return."]

Her story brought cheers from her audience.

The informality continued when she introduced the main speaker, an expert on gang violence. "I could read you all his awards and his vita, but I'll just say this about David. He's been through a lot. He knows the street. And he's my buddy." All in all, it was a good example of her personal outreach in the service of policy.

At the close of the conference, she told the group, "I want to try and meet with you and some of your friends three or four times a year." Then pictures were taken. As described in my notes:

> Her directing of the end-of-the-conference picture taking was a great performance. She did it all herself—first getting all one hundred plus to have a group picture taken at the front of the auditorium and, then, having her picture taken with each school delegation—twenty-five separate ones. She did it by hollering continuously, calling out the name of each school, gathering them on stage with her in the middle. Sometimes, the kids mugged, hugged her, put their heads on her shoulders. She hugged most

of them, especially the girls. In between group photos, she would do a little dance step or sing along when a kid grabbed the mike and started singing a hymn. It was an informal performance—a cross between movie director, tour guide, and mother hen. A happy atmosphere. I go into this detail because it was striking as a *total contrast* [italics in original] to Louis Stokes."

Impressively, the students stayed until 1:30 p.m.

After the cleanup, the congresswoman took the whole staff, a couple of other workers, plus the two students who had gone to Washington, plus her teenage son, for a "thank-you" pizza lunch. Everyone was pleased, and there was a lot of laughing and joking. When she retold the scrub story, a boy–girl discussion followed and several abortive efforts were made to sing the relevant rap song. Their collective success had produced relaxation. Her son's date that evening, with the girl who won a citywide contest for two tickets to a basketball game, was the subject of much joking.

"I want to bring the young people back into politics," she said when we parted. "There's a disconnect between young people and their government. Today I was working with the eighteen-year-olds. Next I want to bring back the nineteen- to twenty-five-year-olds." Her goal was to instill in young people her own commitment to community service.

The next day, the conference was featured, with two full-color pictures, in a story on page one of the *Plain Dealer's* second section. And on page two there was a black-and-white picture.[67] Tubbs Jones, the story said, wanted to create a youth advisory council "to build in them a desire to want to be engaged in the process." The congresswoman, however, did not appear in any of the three pictures. Given the newspaper's direct editorial admonishment to keep her promises on youth violence, the decision not to picture her at all seemed further evidence of media coolness. Credited or not, there could be little doubt about her personal commitments in the area of youth violence, nor about her continuing ground-level connections with young people.

Writ large, the policy problems Tubbs Jones addresses at home are no different from those Lou Stokes addressed throughout his tenure. But the youth violence conference involved a level of engagement and a representational strategy different from his. His goal was to protect the group interests of his black constituency, and his frame of reference was the black community. He tended to connect at that broad level. Tubbs Jones's personal goal is civic engagement, and her frame of reference is more grassroots-oriented than "the black community." Her youth violence conference and her personal involvement in it reflect a more relaxed, more nuanced, more ground-level connection with constituents. At that level, too, whites are included. By her example, everyone is encouraged to contribute and to serve. Her very personal message may well have had a greater impact on her constituents than a purely policy message would have.

THE SYNAGOGUE TALK

On the day of her youth conference, the congresswoman made another constituency connection—one in which the personal/policy proportions of her involvement tilted slightly more toward policy. Still, however, the personal connection remained noteworthy. After the participants in her youth conference had broken into groups, she had skipped out to another part of Shaker Heights. "I was asked to speak at the largest and most influential synagogue in my district," she explained, "and you don't pass up a chance to talk to them. So I'll bob and weave—go there for a while and come back." On her schedule, the event was marked "keynote speaker." Driving over, she commented, "They are strong supporters. Lou Stokes worked very hard to cultivate this group. I have wonderful relations with the Jewish community." Shaker Heights was (perhaps because one opponent lived there) the only part of her district that did not support her in her crucial primary. She, too, was working hard to connect.

She carried a prepared text on the subject of religion and politics. It focused on the common principles motivating both Martin Luther King and Judaism and on common historical experiences of discrimination. While the text surely carried a connective policy message, her distinctly personal improvisations were more noteworthy. Her first gesture was to lean over the pulpit, look out over the congregation and say hello to half-a-dozen people, by name. She began to speak, then spotted a little girl, stopped, and said, "Hi hon. I didn't see you before. How are you?"

After a few minutes "on message," she left the text entirely to discuss public policies of great interest to the overwhelming majority of her Park Synagogue constituents—public money for private schools, tax support for "faith-based institutions," and restrictions on abortion. Without drawing any partisan distinctions, she declared her strong opposition to all three.

Then, after an unsuccessful effort to return to her text ("I was nervous. I don't know why. I never get nervous."), she abandoned it in favor of a reliable policy connection with the congregation. "I want to take two minutes to change the subject and tell you something I did that was one of the most exciting experiences of my first year in Congress. I took a trip to Israel." She gave a bit of a travelogue—"they worked us hard, from seven in the morning to seven at night, we had meetings with Prime Minister Barak and Mr. Arafat." And she concluded, "It was exciting to me as a Christian woman to put my foot in the Sea of Galilee and put my hand in the river Jordan." (It would not be the last time I watched her abandon her text and "get personal" when she felt she was losing her audience.) In a question period, one person thanked her for her newsletter. That was all. We left and the Sabbath service continued. Several people followed her to talk with her outside.

She had connected on policy grounds with a group of supporters. It was still a soft connection—promissory but not cast in stone—and allowing plenty of room for the play of her personal strengths. Her policy connections had been intertwined with her personal connections, and she had made use of the invitation on both dimensions. Driving back to her youth conference, she repeated a familiar theme. "I knew 50 percent of those people. Don't forget, I had run several times in this area before I ran for Congress." And later that day, "Nothing is very formal with me. The most formal I ever get was this morning at the synagogue." (If true, that may account for some nervousness.) For me, since I was most struck by her informality, her comment was one more measure of her preference for personal connections.

POLICY CONNECTIONS AND EXPERIENTIAL LEARNING

POLICY VOTING

In making her hard policy connections with her constituents—her roll call votes—Stephanie Tubbs Jones had little to learn. In Washington her voting record on matters of public policy mirrors and underlines the strongly liberal pattern of Lou Stokes and Chaka Fattah.

In the Poole-Rosenthal ideological rankings for her first term—the 106th Congress, 1999–2000—only thirty-two of her House colleagues had a more liberal voting record than Tubbs Jones. Among House members of the CBC, sixteen ranked more liberal than she and eighteen ranked less liberal than she. Indeed, Tubbs Jones and Chaka Fattah had nearly identical liberalism scores. Only two Democrats separated them from one another in the rankings of House members. According to this hard measure of her hard policy decisions, her very liberal voting record reflects her consistently strong support for government help on behalf of her needy, working-class constituents.

As I expected, the voting records of Stokes, Fattah, and Tubbs Jones track closely with one another and with the voting records of their fellow African Americans from northern urban centers. For them, the core socioeconomic agenda—to alleviate poverty, unemployment, and discrimination and to promote health care, housing, and education—is dominant, settled, and noncontroversial. For them, the consequential votes in these public policy areas are rarely problematical. In Tubbs Jones's words, quoted earlier, "Sometimes people think that because you represent a larger constituency base, it may be more difficult to advocate issues that affect the black community. I don't have that problem."[68]

"My constituents do not beat on me about my votes," she generalizes. "I'm very fortunate in that respect. They don't ask me how I voted. I'm comfortable voting for what I believe in. I'm confident that when I vote, I naturally vote the way they want me to vote because I have lived with them so long and because I am around them all the time." So positive were these reflections that she was moved to joke, "Who knows, I might not even have to campaign at all." To which she quickly added, "But, of course, I'd be crazy not to."

Like Stokes and Fattah, she has difficulty recalling "a tough vote." During my first visit, she managed to dredge up two troublesome votes. Both involved omnibus appropriations bills requiring, therefore, balanced and easily defensible judgments. For example, "I voted for the omnibus appropriations bill, even though most of the Ohio Democrats did not, because of all the money that was in there for my hospitals—the Cleveland Clinic and University Hospital. They convinced me that they could not hold their ground without the money. . . . The Cleveland Clinic is the biggest employer in my district. . . . There was a lot I did not like about that bill. Only two members of our delegation voted for it." Those who cared enough to parse that complex vote would find it hard to disagree. If that was her most troublesome vote, she would seem to have nothing to worry about. On the China trade vote that was so troublesome for Fattah, she had "no trouble at all—I have no trouble on any trade vote."

During my last visit, in the aftermath of September 11, she talked about some recent votes before a liberal, all-white audience of about 125 peace activists at Cleveland State University. "My black constituents are smart, but they are not demanding," she noted afterward. "They want me to work hard, not to disappoint them, and to make them proud." "Some of my white constituents," she said, "are more likely to write or call." The Cleveland Peace Action Conference, convened originally to mount a campaign against President George W. Bush's proposed missile defense system, exemplified those white constituents who were "more likely to write or call" and to be concerned about specific issues and votes.

Her review and explanation of her recent voting record drew rousing, sympathetic applause at several points. Her opinion of the so-called Star Wars missile defense program: "Nothing that happened on September 11 would have been prevented by a missile defense." Her vote against the airline "bailout": "My father was a sky cap for the airlines for thirty-five years. They were making $2.00 an hour, and they had no sick pay. When one of them was sick, the other ten would pass the hat. . . . There was everything for the airlines and nothing for the workers, nothing for those who had lost their jobs." Her vote against the antiterrorism bill: "I'm a patriot. I wear red, white, and blue. I have my red, white, and blue scarf. But I worry that in the name of patriotism we are going to lose all those liberties that we have worked so hard to establish and which make us the country people want to come to."

The vote to authorize the president to prosecute the war against terrorism: "I bring you greetings from my dearest friend, Barbara Lee" (the only member of the U.S. Congress to vote against the legislation). Tubbs Jones's vote on that issue: "Bush already has the power. I thought about it for a long time and finally decided that, in the name of unity in the country, I would stand up." This drew only isolated clapping—no applause. But she received a warm standing ovation at the end. Privately, she returned to the vote. "I almost decided to vote 'no,' but I didn't. That was a hard vote—maybe my hardest vote. All the rest of my votes since September 11 have been easy votes—no trouble at all." Looking back on her speech, she said, "I like to give speeches like that on the issues. Pump up the crowd and then leave. I used to think I had to stay. Now I know that it's expected that I'm busy with other things to do." And she added, "These people will be with me no matter what."

That evening, she spoke to a large biracial dinner gathering to celebrate the accomplishments of the district's largest community development corporation. There, too, she began by explaining her recent policy votes—in opposition to the antiterrorism and airline bailout legislation. Like her morning talk, her explanation was cast in terms of "Please do not believe that I was not touched by September 11 and that I am not a patriot, because I am, but . . . " we cannot sacrifice our liberties and we cannot forget our workers. Her explanations of both votes were much more detailed than in the morning, and they drew little response. On antiterrorism, she discussed her experience as prosecutor and the various dangers of wiretapping. Given "the responsibility of being prosecutor . . . you have to understand the power that you are invested with. And I opposed John Ashcroft for attorney general, so I don't have to say any more." [Laughter.] On the airlines, she engaged in a similarly lengthy discussion of the various provisions in the bill, concluding, "That's a problem for me when there was no money provided for the workers in the workplace at all." And she concluded that "right now, we are operating in what seems to be a bipartisan vein. But behind the scenes many of us continue to fight. . . . And I've tried to be heard in Washington on your behalf."

Unlike the peace activists at the morning event, this group, whose concerns were neighborhood development, remained quietly attentive. Only when she pushed the Ashcroft button did she get a response. Sensing their sobriety, she began riffling through several sheets of her prepared text. "My staff has written a great speech," she said, "but I'm going to skip over this stuff. Don't tell my staff what I've done." She concluded with a couple of stories in praise of their work. "All of them are for me," she said afterward, "but they are not as interested in what I am doing as the morning group. When I talked about my votes, I lost them. That's why I didn't read my speech. I said to myself, 'The hell with it. I'll just stop now, and they'll give me credit for getting them home by nine o'clock.' "

Both groups certainly approved of her policy votes. But her connection with the morning group exemplified a hard, vote-based policy connection, while her connection with the evening group exemplified a softer, overall policy connection. For certain, a larger proportion of the neighborhood group knew her personally and resided in her district than was the case with the peace group. Personal connections, therefore, bulked larger in the neighborhood group than in the peace group. On the surface, at least, her explanation of her policy votes dominated both speeches. But she connected best with one group by talking about her policy voting, and she connected best with the other group simply by showing up—and by talking about whatever she wished.

POLICY LEARNING

A very small portion of the policy agenda confronting Congress bears directly on the work of a county prosecutor. With no legislative experience whatever, the first-term House member from Cleveland had a lot to learn—and the policy component of her personal/policy mix grew steadily. My introduction to these changing proportions was a luncheon with a dozen of Cleveland's most influential bankers. She and they had come together to discuss policy concerns over which she, because of her membership on the House Banking and Financial Services Committee, had direct decision-making authority. Most striking to me was the clear evidence that the sophomore House member—two years into her legislative career—was gradually learning, through experience, how to do her new job.

Around the table, in a private dining room high atop a bank building overlooking the city, were ten men and six women. Eight were black; seven were white. All three top executives of the city's largest banks were white men. Four of the five black women were the congresswoman's Delta Sigma Theta sorority sisters. Her good humor and approachability was much in evidence. She greeted each one warmly as they came in and hugged several of them. When she began to talk, she turned to the men on either side. "You'd better move away a little because when I get going, I'm likely to hit you." When the man on her left started to move his chair, she said to him, "You don't have to worry. My right arm is a lot stronger than my left." Whereupon the man on her right shrank and ducked. Everyone laughed.

The mood was good. None of that was surprising to me. What was new to me was the extent of her policy knowledge and the development of her policy priorities. The knowledge base had come from the learning process inside the committee, knowledge that she said had increased "tenfold" in her first years.[69] The bankers wanted the get-together because they understood her influential committee position and because she was becoming outspoken in making distinctions among good and bad practices in the home mortgage lending business.

In late 2000, in a speech to the Ohio Credit Union Convention, she had attacked "predatory" money lenders. "Predatory lending is wrong. Predatory lenders drain equity from consumers in a variety of ways, including excessive loan fees, costly and unnecessary insurance policies, large balloon payments, high interest rates, and frequent refinancing . . . systematically target[ing] low-income and minority families."[70] She had obviously been doing her homework.

She was being noticed, too, by some natural allies. In early 2001 she had been introduced by the president of Fannie Mae—a major, government-sponsored mortgage lending institution—as "a true hero of home ownership." "On no less than six separate occasions last year," he told a Fannie Mae audience, [she] stood up, knocked down every missile heading our way. . . . Her presence alone said, 'Don't mess with Fannie Mae. Don't mess with my constituents. And don't you dare mess with the American dream.' . . . She is a hero to the mayors, the housing advocates and all of us who know the difference that decent affordable housing makes."[71] In the face of banking industry attacks, Fannie Mae had worked especially hard to cultivate the support of African American House members.[72] A couple of months later, the chairman of the National Credit Union Administration had given a speech in Cleveland saying, "Thank you Congresswoman Tubbs Jones . . . for taking such an active and strong role in Congress in seeking ways to combat the financial piranha we have come to call predatory lending."[73]

The Cleveland bankers had taken notice. The local bankers wanted to make sure that they were not included in these broadsides and wanted to assure her that they, in their own self-interest, certainly wanted to drive out what she had called "unscrupulous money lenders preying on unsuspecting home buyers." They wanted to protect their bona fides against all competitors in providing mortgage money to minorities. Their overriding concern was their competition; they were interested in regulations to prevent predatory lending and protect their interests, and they wanted to hear her views.

Interest group and Representative had a constructive exchange. Everyone spoke. The bankers told their stories of unscrupulous mortgage bankers and illegitimate subprime lenders who preyed on low-income people. She expressed her worries about predatory lending—primarily from the perspective of the consumer rather than from the perspective of the bankers. She placed her highest value on home ownership for everyone who could possibly afford it: "I want people to be empowered, and home ownership is the key to empowerment." She stressed education to produce informed consumers: "The poorest person, who might be illiterate, understands money. Instinctively, people understand money—if you tell it to them honestly." She did not automatically credit all bankers with high-mindedness in dealing with low-income consumers.

After forty-five minutes of back and forth, she suggested items, culled from the conversation, that she could look into on their behalf. Then she said, "I have my assignments. Now, what are you going to do?" "My vision," she told them at the end, "is wealth-building. For every person, and for most people, a house is their greatest asset. We must protect that asset. From where I'm coming from, education—some sort of cooperative educational effort, *led by the bankers*, is the answer. . . . This is a long-term problem; but we've got to mount a community effort to work on it." The man who led the meeting acknowledged the challenge. He added, "We have been impressed by the breadth and depth of your understanding of our subjects."

Driving to a television interview, she concluded, "I agree with them on some things, and I disagree with them on some things. But we have a good relationship. We understand each other. That was a good meeting." And when at the television interview she was asked, "What issues are you working on?" she answered, "I'm working on issues like what it means to have credit, about mortgage money, predatory lending, where people are preying on communities in order to get them to enter into mortgage agreements. I'm working with bankers. They have been very supportive in getting education out on these matters, teaching children the value of money, to understand credit so they can buy a home." Having held her own, as far as I could tell, in fast company, she was displaying increased confidence in talking about her policy involvements. As a result, her constituency connections were likely to have an increasingly large policy component.

Later that evening, in her talk to a public administration class at Cleveland State University, she articulated her policy priorities again. "My belief is that the way we equalize our community is that we have economic justice, that we have wealth-building, that we have economic empowerment, that we have economic development. For working-class people, the main asset they have is a home. . . . Wealth-building is the great equalizer. It's the only equalizer. . . . If there's anything I want to remember when I leave Congress it is that I helped people learn how to create wealth and that we have economic development."

Taken together, the banker's luncheon, the television interview, and the class lecture were indicative of a set of policy connections I had not heard during my first visit fifteen months before. She readily acknowledged the change. It rested, she said, on an earlier learning experience: "When I first went to Congress, I thought we were going to do great things. The 434 others and I were going to work together to do great things for the country. It didn't happen. I learned from that experience that in order to survive, I have to set a parallel agenda for myself. We have just finished a two-day staff retreat to talk about that agenda. I have also learned that the office is a bully pulpit." She was learning about the necessity and the opportunity for "speaking out" on matters of public policy.

When I asked her whether, in the light of the Stokes legacy, she felt she had been able to "put your stamp on the district," she answered, "Yes I have. In the beginning, I had some trouble because people said I wasn't doing what Lou Stokes would have done. And I said, 'I don't want to walk in his shoes. They are too big for me. I want to stand on his shoulders. But I am not going to be Lou Stokes.' I have spoken out on housing, on predatory lending, on financial institutions, and I've done a lot of work with kids." "Last week," she added, "we had a youth conference on The Biz of Show Biz—on what it means to run a business, all about money and credit, the whole nine yards."

Several times in the course of this second visit, she used the words "speaking out" to convey the idea that her constituency connections had changed.

"Now," she said, "I want to be known more than I have been for my involvement in the struggle for affirmative action, for equal access, for helping people build wealth. In college, I was always an affirmative action person, speaking out. . . . So I've come full circle. No, full circle is not the way to describe it. It's a development. I want to be known, now, for being involved and for speaking out." She was comfortable doing just that. "I think this is the job I should have had from the beginning," she said. "I remember some of my friends saying, 'You don't want to be a municipal judge. A judge can't speak out, and you should be speaking out.'"

The person now "speaking out" on policy and talking about it was a former prosecutor in the process of learning by experience to be a legislator. Her luncheon with the bankers, she said, was the result of a learning process. "One of the things I didn't understand when I went to Congress," she explained, "was how much people wanted to meet me. When I was prosecutor, a few people might have wanted to meet me, but now everyone does. I've begun to realize that because they do want to meet me, I can bring groups together—like the bankers at lunch today—and we can talk to each other and get things done."

Four months later, a *Plain Dealer* profile featured her tough questioning of the secretary of Housing and Urban Affairs in her committee. "Welcome to the new congressional face of Stephanie Tubbs Jones," wrote the local observer. "Using charm in some settings and toughness in others [she] increasingly is trying to establish herself as a vocal and vigorous champion of the poor."[74] Noting once more "the burden of following a congressman who . . . was able to direct huge amounts of money to Cleveland," favorable comments were elicited from constituency leaders for her work on community development and on minority business. Her success in this latter area drew extravagant praise. "She crushed the issue," said one business leader, "with day-to-day, call-to-call, office-to-office, brass knuckle–type retail politics." The reporter summarized, "If there is a hallmark to Tubbs Jones's style, it is precisely that relish for personal contact." Another local leader entered the caveat that "This is not Lou Stokes. She has a certain amount of things she has to learn." On the evidence, she was learning—how to put her personal negotiating skills to work in the service of the policy needs of her constituents.

In estimating the relevance of her personal negotiating abilities in working for the poor, we should not neglect her personal familiarity with the problems she deals with. On the way from one engagement to another during my last visit, she took me to see the Hough neighborhood—scene of race riots in the 1960s—an area described to me in the 1970s as "dying." "We've got some time, so I'm going to turn off her and show you what's happened in Hough, where the riots started. I want you to see the redevelopment that's transformed the neighborhood." It was my personal tour number 2. We drove up and down streets with nice new single-family homes, with well-kept lawns and flowers. "There are a couple of streets I especially want you to see." And she searched till she found "the house with the indoor swimming pool."

At one intersection, she stopped to show me "the exact spot where the shooting started. There's the little corner park with the memorial commemorating the event." It was a large stone pillar with "Hough" in large letters running down the side, with a nicely tiled and flowered area around it. As we drove up and down, she described the financing arrangements for each cluster. She stopped twice to yell at friends she spied walking along the street.

After a lot of show and tell, she declared, "There's one piece missing from this picture—business. . . . You cannot have successful redevelopment without business. The Clinton administration helped with the housing through federal–state partnerships. Now we need partnerships devoted to business. . . . Integration actually hurt business. Before integration, people had to shop in the neighborhood and black business thrived. When integration came and black people could shop everywhere, black business suffered." Louis Stokes had brought a lot of the money into that neighborhood. In 1998 he had pointed off in the distance and told me, in answer to my question, that much of Hough had been restored. But Stephanie Tubbs Jones drove me around the area and explained it, with a combination of enthusiasm and immersion, plus hometown pride—showing a visitor "*my* city." Again, this strong sense of personal commitment underpins her policy involvements and her policy learning.

SYMBOLIC CONNECTIONS

MARTIN LUTHER KING JR.'S BIRTHDAY

For African Americans, one of the most cherished symbols, of struggle and of hope, is civil rights leader Dr. Martin Luther King Jr. His inspirational teachings, his life of leadership, and his martyrdom have combined to make him a guiding influence in people's lives, both individually and collectively. His powerful symbolic presence in the national community was insured when his birthday became a national holiday. In black communities—and in white communities, too—King's birthday is spent in public gatherings to celebrate his life and to draw, from his life and from his teachings, lessons to live by.

While it is true that whites as well as blacks draw inspiration from the life and the words of Dr. King, the impetus and the sustenance has come from the black community. While he may speak *to* the white community, he speaks *for* the black community. He is a child of the black community, and his life experience is the experience of black people. His battles and aspirations are theirs—direct and not derivative. In January 2000 the congresswoman spoke at two commemorative gatherings—both of which were designated on her schedule as "keynote speaker."

By her participation on that symbolic day, Tubbs Jones made both personal and symbolic connections with her constituents. With the words of Dr. King as the connecting link, she wove inspirational talks around the general theme of service to others. Her embrace of his symbolic strengths came all the easier because so much of his teaching embodied her own personal goals as a Representative.

At Cuyahoga Community College she was the featured speaker at an early-morning kickoff for "A Community-Wide Day of Service" by students from several Cleveland colleges. Seventeen community service organizations—under the rubric of the Cleveland Area National Service Coalition—were sponsoring a day of volunteer work at twenty-one separate "service sites" throughout the city: homeless shelters, soup kitchens, senior centers, rehabilitation units. Their chosen charge was one by Coretta Scott King: "The greatest birthday gift my husband could receive is if people of all racial and ethnic backgrounds celebrate the holiday by performing individual acts of kindness through service to others." The congresswoman spoke in praise of public service.

The standing-room-only crowd of students numbered more than three hundred, a few more than half of whom were black. The Cleveland Coalition, she began, embodied "two ideals central to . . . Dr. King, community and service. . . . Community," she said, "is a sense of caring and belonging. It is a willingness to share your gifts and talents with those less fortunate and helping to bind the ties of brotherhood and sisterhood. . . . We must concern ourselves with the plight and struggle of our brothers and sisters, white, black, brown, or red, who may not be as fortunate." With respect to service, Tubbs Jones said, "Dr. King had a dream. It was rooted in the American spirit of service. Today, he would want us to strive continuously to be change agents in solving the problems that plague our society . . . homelessness, unemployment, violence, and man's inhumanity to man. . . . We must continue to address injustice, whether it is homelessness, drugs, teenage pregnancy, high school drop outs, or violence." She talked policy, but in these very general terms. Her connections were insufficiently concrete to be considered as policy connections. Her exhortations, as a leader, to do better and to serve others were akin to the inspirational and symbolic role-model presentations of Chaka Fattah and Louis Stokes.

Her presentational style and her rapport reminded me of her high school conference. She began by telling the students how pleased she was "to come and hang out with you." At least twice, she stopped after reading a pertinent quotation and asked the group to repeat it a couple of times with her in unison. With increasing enthusiasm, the group repeated Dr. King's instruction that "Everybody can be great because anybody can serve." Later, she led the audience in repetitions of "You only need a heart full of grace and a soul generated by love." Her obvious comfort level in connecting with young people was, once again, impressive. And once again, too, her involvement seemed more personal and more in sync than anything I had seen from her predecessor.

Later that morning she spoke at the Community of Faith Church. Her talk was even more personal than the previous one. The context was largely responsible for the difference. The church was at the corner of her mother's street, and it was a neighborhood, storefront church.

The one-story, cinder-block Community of Faith Church had originally been a bar. It had no windows, only several blocks of thick, translucent glass to bring in light. It was one room, about seventy-five by thirty feet, with six lengthwise rows of wooden-backed benches with an aisle in the middle. Up front was a raised podium with a large, rough-hewn wooden cross. An altar stood off to one side. At one end, near the door, was a tiny office for the part-time minister and a stairway leading to a usable basement. About forty black parishioners were in attendance—some middle-aged but mostly elderly, a few children, slightly more women than men. They were dressed in as spare a manner as the furnishings.

"The room," I noted, "is about as drab as one could imagine. But the spirit is warm and alive, and participation is total and heartfelt." Several times, for example, the entire congregation stood up and held hands—during the opening prayer, during the singing of "We Shall Overcome," during the minister's blessing of a half-dozen children at the altar, and during the singing of the Negro National Anthem. Once, we shook hands with everyone nearby and exchanged "God bless you." During the benediction, we stood while the minister prayed, in part: "Lord, protect our congresswoman. Put angels to the left of her, angels to the right of her, angels beneath her, angels over her, angels all around her." After her talk and the question period ended, the pastor reminded everyone to bring their used clothing to the church to help the less fortunate. Her mother invited me to "join us for refreshments." Several people came over to hug me on their way out. It was an emotional experience. It gave this outsider a tiny, fleeting glimpse into the importance of "the black church" in helping to knit, nurture, and activate the black community.[75]

The congresswoman's theme—love, family, and service—matched the personal intimacy inside the building: "I am blessed with a wonderful mom, and I am glad to have her here." "On Dr. King's birthday, we should direct our attention to love," she began. And she said, in part:

> Dr. King said that without love, nothing is possible. He believed that love conquered all. . . . Love is key to our coexistence today. And I am talking about family. . . . Why, you may ask, is love so important? Today in our society, families are in crisis. Statistics bear out this truth. Over three thousand children and teens a day see their parents' marriages end in divorce. A growing number of fathers forsake their families. Tonight, 40 percent of the kids in America will go to bed in a home without a father. Too many kids turn to television, music, and their peers for guidance and direction. More and more children are sexually active. Rates of substance abuse among children and teens are skyrocketing. Thirty-eight percent of all eighth graders have experimented with drugs, and teen violence is on the rise. Between 1988 and 1992, the arrest of juvenile homicide offenders climbed 93 percent. In addition, each day an estimated 270,000 guns are carried to school. . . . Those statistics are devastating. [Each sentence was followed by murmurs of agreement, "Yes, yes."]
>
> Love is a cornerstone of every family. It is through love that we can reconnect with our families, and particularly with our children. The reality is that when there is no love in the home, there will be no love in the community. . . . I'm a huggy, a feeling person, you know, and I remember when I was county prosecutor, people would say to me, "I never hugged a prosecutor before! Are you sure you're a prosecutor?" [Laughter.] I tell my son everyday, "Mervin, I love you." Even when I'm angry, I say,

"Mervin, I love you." When Mervin was a little boy, I'd call him my love boy. And we'd sing, "I love you a bushel and a peck, a bushel and a peck and a hug around the neck."

The same concern for young people that motivated her conference on youth violence infused her talk in church. It struck uniquely, I thought, not only her personal chords, but a woman's chords as well.

"On this holiday," she continued,

What I want to impart to all of you is that we must embrace our love for a much larger family. If you have love in your home, you need to spread that love out to your neighbors, at your place of employment, in your schools, and in your community. We need to love a family larger than those who eat dinner with us. . . . On our street, Ostend Avenue, everybody knew what was going on. On Rutland Avenue, everybody knew what was going on. And it wasn't being nosey, it was about being community and being family.

She urged her listeners to set a community-minded, service-oriented example for their children. "If your children don't see you giving, they won't know what it is to give. If they don't see you in service, they won't know what it is to be in service. If they don't see you in church, they won't know what it is to go to church. If they don't see you being kind, they won't be kind." Communicate with your children, spend time with your children, she said, with examples from her own family.

Then, back to her favorite theme of service to others. "We can have community if we continue on the path of Dr. King's dream. We can have community if we look out for our neighbors, our grandparents, our children, and ourselves—if we come together for a common purpose. Our community is us. . . . Dr. King had a dream. It was rooted in the spirit of love. He would want us to try continuously to be change agents in solving problems that plague our society."

Her talk was unlike anything I heard during my research travels. At bottom, the community problems she confronted were the same ones that concerned the three others. But her approach to those problems was more personal in its focus, warmer in its tone, more family- and child-centered in its substance. And, like her previous talk, this one was altogether related to and expressive of her dominant personal goal of service to others and community involvement. It echoed her oft-stated aspiration to be—in the spirit of Dr. King—a "change agent" in society.

INAUGURATION CEREMONY

Symbolic and personal connections were intertwined when Tubbs Jones attended the inauguration of the first female mayor of a district suburb. The ceremony, in a 98 percent black town of twenty thousand people, was rich in African American symbolism. Her presence connected her to that symbolism. At the same time, it put the spotlight on a special set of the congresswoman's personal connections—connections that, once again, emphasized public service.

The Warrensville Heights Civic and Senior Center was standing-room only for the overflow, 98 percent black, Sunday afternoon crowd. I had attended church services with several staff members that morning. The praise-the-Lord atmosphere of the two events was very similar—church choirs, loud singing, and rhythmic clapping.[76] At various points, two church groups—the Cuyahoga Faith Center Praise Team and the Ecumenical Disciples—sang two hymns each—the latter group ending with a rousing "Battle Hymn of the Republic." The ceremony closed with the crowd of over four hundred standing and singing all three verses of the Negro National Anthem, "Lift Every Voice and Sing." Emotionally, liturgically, and symbolically, it was clearly an African American ceremony.

On the business side of the event, Stephanie Tubbs Jones's role was to administer the oath of office to the new mayor—who was to Tubbs Jones a very special woman. "Marcia Fudge is my oldest friend," she explained. "We didn't go through high school together; but we met in high school. I was Collinwood; she was Shaker [Heights]. She was my chief assistant when I was Judge of the Common Pleas Court. She was the budget and finance officer in the prosecutor's office. Since I have been in Congress, she has been my chief of staff. And she's the president of my sorority. In Washington and in Cleveland, she staffs me. But when we go to the Delta Sigma Theta convention, I staff her." The importance of Tubbs Jones's sorority connections was reflected in the unusual prominence accorded to Delta Sigma Theta throughout the inauguration ceremony.

The dignitaries on the platform included local officials of Delta Sigma Theta and seven of its directors, national and regional. Each one of the seven directors was recognized individually from the podium. Each of them came forward with a gift for the new mayor and praised her as a sorority sister. One director of a black male fraternity came forward to present a gift and heap praise on the sorority. Each time one of the seven directors came to the microphone, those women in the audience who were members of Delta Sigma Theta were asked to stand while the presentation was made. At their seats, at various places in the room, about thirty-five women stood, dressed in identical red and white suits. The importance of this connection for college-educated black women was manifest. This "largest black women's organization in the United States," with 200,000 members, is explicitly a public service organization. (It was also Barbara Jordan's sorority, though she never mentioned it.) Its members include many contemporary public servants, and several sorority sisters in the House have eased Tubbs Jones's entrance into congressional life. Their visible presence in Cleveland had both symbolic and personal overtones.

In policy matters, Tubbs Jones often spoke for and to a broad biracial constituency, but in symbolic matters, she spoke for and to an African American constituency. And symbolic connections are vitally important to any minority, to the maintenance of their group identity, to the pursuit of their group interests, and to their pursuit of inclusion and equality. A white member of Congress can easily make policy connections with black constituents, but only a black member of Congress can make symbolic connections with black constituents. That is the idea implicit in minority-group emphasis on descriptive representation. Symbolic connections, again, are descriptive representation in action. On Martin Luther King Day and at the mayor's inauguration, the celebration of black leadership—spiritual and political—united black citizens through the reminders and the rituals of their common heritage. The congresswoman's words and presence at those unifying, symbolic events reinforced and deepened her ties to her primary constituents.

ORGANIZATIONAL CONNECTIONS

THE LEGACY

For Lou Stokes, organizational problems consumed the greatest amount of his time and energy when he was at home in Cleveland. For both partisan and personal reasons he, along with his brother, created and nurtured an empowering political organization—the Twenty-first Congressional District Caucus—which rallied the black community of Democrats, Republicans, and ministers against the county Democratic Party. Soon, the Caucus became his personal political base. Later, when the group seemed to lose its clout, he created the Black Elected Democrats of Cleveland Organization (BEDCO) to shore up both black political strength and his own personal strength. His was an unending up-and-down organizational battle at home. When we spoke in 1998, he was feuding with the chairman of the Cuyahoga County Democratic Party because, said Stokes, "He thinks it's to his advantage to go against Lou Stokes."

The inevitable question arises as to whether and to what degree his successor would inherit, confront, or be burdened by the same organizational problems as he. The answer is twofold. At the beginning of the succession, Tubbs Jones did face organizational problems, but they were not the same as his. She had never participated in his conflicts with the Democratic Party. Indeed, the current party chairman, with whom Stokes was at odds, had been Tubbs Jones's crucial supporter in her crucial intraparty battle to gain the party's interim appointment as county prosecutor. And he had led the county Democratic Party in endorsing her in her pivotal 1998 congressional primary.[77] Further, if any Cleveland power broker was her political protector within the party, it was not her predecessor in Congress, but rather Councilman George Forbes, an uncertain ally of Stokes.

Tubbs Jones's initial problem was not that she had inherited Lou Stokes's problems—certainly not his problems with the Democratic Party. Her problem was whether and under what conditions she would, or would not, inherit the leadership of his organizations. Her succession to his office had been settled by law, but her succession to his organizational base would be settled by politics.

It was here, on organizational matters rather than on electoral matters, that the early help of her predecessor was critical. She did not need votes from Stokes; she did need his organizational support. And it was here that she received it. On organizational matters Lou Stokes's strong support decisively underwrote a smooth transition. As she put it, "Once he came aboard, he came shooting both barrels."

"When we talked after the election," she recalled,

I told him that I wanted to be able to appoint my own executive director of the Caucus. He said that was fine and that he would tell Mrs. Chatman. She had been executive director for twenty-five years. So I made my choice and I took her with me to my first Caucus meeting. I assumed Lou had told Mrs. Chatman, but, to my horror, when we got there, I found that he had not told her she was through. When I went over to her to say hello and introduce her to her successor, she said, "There must be some mistake. I am still the executive director." So I went over to Lou and said,

"Mrs. Chatman has not been told of our arrangement." He said he'd talk with her. So he went over to her and told her she was being replaced. Just like that!

She shook her head without comment. Then she drew the relevant lesson for her succession. *"He was passing the mantle to me."*

With Lou Stokes's help, she had become the undisputed leader of the Caucus. Indeed, after twenty-eight years of presiding over its traditional Labor Day picnic, he deliberately stayed away from Tubbs Jones's inaugural 1999 leadership effort. She called the picnic "a tradition I had to continue," but she added, "everything can use a facelift."[78]

The *Plain Dealer* headline read "New Face, New Feeling at Democrats' Annual Picnic."[79] Among the changes: a new name, "The Eleventh District Caucus for the Millennium"; bimonthly instead of many monthly meetings; a shorter picnic; and the appearance, at the picnic, of officeholders snubbed by Stokes in the past. Most important, perhaps, was Tubbs Jones's signature attentiveness to young people and to their engagement in public life. "I'd like to start the process," she said, "of bringing in [to the Caucus] younger people who haven't been politically active, but want to be politically active. Stokes left a rich tradition, and I hope to put my footprint on it."[80]

There were inevitable bumps. "I'm running into the woman thing," she said at one point, alluding to backbiting from members of the "in crowd." She told the story of an ambitious Caucus member who pushed for influence in one key policy area. "He used to come to all the Caucus meetings and raised questions about the policy—to show that he knew the subject. He asked me if he could be the spokesman for the Caucus on these issues. I told him that I would not let him do that. I said that if I wanted to say something about that policy subject, I'd say it myself. He has not taken it well." While her normal connective mode is personal warmth, she is icily clinical when it comes to her political survival. She assessed several potential primary opponents in 2000: "He's not serious"; "He couldn't win"; "He won't risk it"; "He has reached the limit of his ability."

In dealing with BEDCO, however, Tubbs Jones needed to fight for herself, because Lou Stokes's control over his second organizational creation was less secure than with the Caucus. Tellingly, BEDCO had not endorsed anyone in her 1998 congressional primary race.[81] As she tells the story,

After my election, I let everyone know that I was going to go to Washington, and for the first six months, I was not going to get involved in local politics—I was going to learn my job. I like to prioritize, and I thought that was the best use of my time. I learned that one of the men who thought of himself as a leader of BEDCO had called a meeting—without notifying me. I called him and asked him, "Why did you do this without so much as calling me?" He said, "Why should I call you? It was Lou Stokes's organization." So I got on the phone and got the meeting quashed. The group had been started by Lou after my election as prosecutor. When Lou retired, the group was split. Lou and the party chairman had been fighting like cats and dogs—a terrible fight. One of Lou's opponents had done the calling. I came home. We had a meeting. And I was elected chairman of BEDCO.

From this account, too, she drew a relevant conclusion: "I found it impossible to stay out of local politics." That comment was a prelude to her ever-increasing involvements.

THE BOND ISSUE

When I returned fifteen months later, I found her deeply immersed in a local political initiative, Proposition 14. Given her lifelong local involvement, it seemed natural. She had become the co-chair of a citywide campaign for a $380 million bond issue for school repairs. The vote was one month away. As it turned out, she was also in the process of writing a local success story unmatched by her predecessor.

She greeted me with the story of her private dinner meeting the night before at which she tried to persuade the president of the Cleveland NAACP, her old mentor George Forbes, to change that organization's decision to fight the proposal.

Wherever we went that day, she pitched the proposal. During her television interview, she said, "I'm a Cleveland public school graduate, and I want the children in my district to have the same kind of education. I am the co-chair of the education bond issue for public schools to be voted on May 8, and I hope everyone will get out and support it." Where appropriate—at a dinner of urban politics students at Cleveland State—she distributed the colorful, picture-filled, provote flyer: "Vote for Issue 14, Safe Schools for Cleveland's Children." Privately, she emphasized her admiration for the superintendent of schools, who was carrying the heaviest burden of public advocacy. They kept in touch by cell phone during the day.

As the newspaper told the story, the mayor had decided not to get involved, and in his absence, Tubbs Jones "has become the most prominent politician pushing the bond issue."[82] The NAACP did change its position, and she was widely credited with having been the key African American persuader.

The congresswoman's local involvement is of particular interest because it contrasts sharply with the behavior, and the success, of her predecessor in a similar situation six years earlier. At stake in the fall of 1994 was a vote on a tax increase to add $43 million to the Cleveland school budget.[83] In view of Lou Stokes's opposition to a previous (failed) effort, his support was deemed critical to a 1994 victory. One month before the vote, however, the congressman remained undecided. Without him, his fellow black officials in BEDCO would not endorse the increase. The supporters of the proposal were described as "scrambling to persuade Rep. Louis Stokes to bless their levy try" because they were "counting on Stokes' support to help boost . . . the turnout of black voters on the East side."[84]

When he finally did produce his "long-sought-after present," by endorsing the school tax proposal—and by bringing his organization, BEDCO, with him—the school superintendent exuded confidence. BEDCO's decision, he said, "means everything." And Stokes's personal decision, he said, "means more than everything. . . . We can't reach everybody. . . . But if they see a name they recognize who supports it, they'll vote for us. Congressman Stokes is very tough. He put us through a test and we passed it."[85]

There was a sharp contrast in the connection patterns of Stokes and Tubbs Jones. Lou Stokes did not lead. He waited to be persuaded. From above the fray, he granted his support. Given his status, it was assumed that his support would make a difference. It did not. The 1994 tax proposal failed, with 45 percent of the vote.[86] Later, he recalled, "I relied on the [teacher's] union. And they had no money." Stephanie Tubbs Jones, on the other hand, did lead. Enthusiastic from the outset, she worked wholeheartedly to persuade others. No one predicted that her support would make a difference, but it did. The 2001 bond issue won, with 60 percent of the vote, and it was the level of voter turnout in the black community—which made up 70 percent of the district—that carried the day.[87]

The two House members made different personal choices. Lou Stokes's choice suggests the limits of reputation as a source of influence in the constituency. Stephanie Tubbs Jones's choice suggests the possibilities of personal activism as a source of influence in the constituency. As part of the succession story, the contrast in choices and outcomes suggests this: that once the incumbent had convincingly passed his organizational "mantle" to his successor, she could, and she would, navigate the constituency according to her personal compass.

THE MAYORALTY RACE

Three weeks after her school board victory, a *Plain Dealer* poll of likely Cleveland voters stunningly certified her personal success.[88] In a hypothetical contest with the city's three-term black mayor, Stephanie Tubbs Jones led by 51 percent to 28 percent—a 23-point margin described as "phenomenal" by the poll's director. Among black voters her margin was 37 points, 61 percent to 24 percent. Among white voters, her margin was 11 points, 43 percent to 32 percent. For the mayor, faced with a fourth-term decision, the poll was not encouraging. Two other mayoral possibilities—both white—polled almost neck and neck with the incumbent. "If she wants the job," said the poll director of Tubbs Jones, "she's the 800-pound gorilla in the race." Asked to explain these results, a local political scientist pointed to her personal appeal. "What makes her so appealing," he said, "is her lovability, her warmth, her openness. It's all those things associated with personality." The poll and the assessment confirmed everything I had seen and heard and read concerning the dominance of her person-intensive representational strategy.

In the spring of 2001 the incumbent mayor announced his retirement, and "the 800-pound gorilla" faced a major career decision. The mayor's announcement, wrote a reporter, "made Tubbs Jones the city's most prominent black politician," and "her popularity across the city also made her the most formidable potential candidate."[89] Her immediate reaction was to think it over. "I previously said I was not interested in being mayor because I have always been [the mayor's] supporter. But the mayor's announcement changed the whole political landscape."[90] From the middle of May till the first week in July, all other potential candidacies were put on hold for five weeks until she announced her decision. "My place is in the House," she said, "but I won't be far from home."[91] Five months later, when I went back to Cleveland, she was again totally engaged—this time in trying to elect another African American to the position.

Retracing her own decision not to run, she explained,

So many people asked me to run that I had to think about it. Their argument was that we had a black mayor and we had to have a black candidate in the race to protect the black community. The experience of other cities has been that when a black mayor is followed by a nonblack mayor, the black community receives a much lower level of service than before. But when I thought about it, I realized that while I might not be able to do as much for the city directly, I could have a much broader impact in meeting the city's needs if I stayed in Congress.

On my committees . . . I was well positioned to have an impact on housing, small business, and the local economy. Because of the importance of seniority, I was building a foundation for greater influence. On my committees, I was building a foundation to move to an even more influential committee. I realized, too, that being a judge and a prosecutor gave me an exposure that few of the newer colleagues ever had and I could be of value in that way. And I realized that I liked being in Congress. I like the personal relationships. I like the kind of people there. . . .

My family was against it. They are used to the arrangement—four days home, three days away. My son will be away at college next year. My mother, who always told me to "go, go, go" told me to "stay where you are." Also, a lot of people want to be mayor for the ego and the publicity. They want to be in the limelight and do not want to share it. I have a big ego, but I don't need to take credit for everything. So the publicity part of the job was of no interest to me.

Having made that decision, she faced another decision: whether or not to get involved. "In the beginning," she said, "I didn't know whether I wanted to get involved or not. But I knew that the black community could not give up without a fight. People wanted a credible black candidate. They had a black mayor for eight years, and they worried about what would happen to the protections they had won." Her decision-making context had become explicitly "the black community." Several African American candidates appeared and solicited her support. She decided to back one of them—Raymond Pierce, born and raised in Cleveland, without any previous political experience, but with a record of public service in the Clinton administration's Department of Justice. At home, he was unknown.

She recruited the most experienced campaign manager in the black community—indeed, the very person who had managed Lou Stokes's crucial primary victory in 1968.[92] And he, better than anyone, was positioned to describe the importance of the Tubbs Jones endorsement. "Four black candidates were in the race," he explained. "And it was clear that whoever Stephanie endorsed would be the [black] candidate. The nomination had been hers for the asking. Only she could bring to a candidate—I don't want to say the Tubbs Jones organization—but the Tubbs Jones *force*. When she put her force behind Pierce, he became the black candidate." To which the congresswoman commented, "I'm deeply involved in local politics. I have to be. My white colleagues have a choice; I don't." It was a quintessential Lou Stokes strategic assessment.

Three days after her endorsement, the *Plain Dealer*'s top political analyst described its impact. "In one of the most stunning political developments in the city's long history, Raymond Pierce went from a political nobody to very much a somebody—literally overnight. When a candidate barely registers in the polls one day, then is championed by Rep. Stephanie Tubbs Jones and a posse of influential black ministers the next, people take notice."[93] Three weeks later, a *Plain Dealer* poll found him at 17 percent, bunched with three white candidates, whose support registered at 22 percent, 19 percent, and 16 percent.[94]

The *Plain Dealer* declared its support for the (white) front-runner in an editorial that devoted twenty-nine build-up lines (twenty-five positive, four negative) to its candidate and four dismissive lines (two favorable, two unfavorable) to Pierce.[95] A week later, the primary result showed the front-runner with 30 percent of the vote and Pierce at 29 percent, with the other poll leaders at 19 and 16 percent.[96] The unknown, underexposed, and underfunded nobody was in the November mayoralty runoff. And, wrote the analysts, "The key to his campaign was the endorsement from Tubbs Jones which turned him from a no-name to an instant contender."[97] It was the "Tubbs Jones endorsement which instantly made Pierce a strong contender," and "gave him instant credibility."[98] His unexpected victory at the polls was, for her, a landmark victory in the black community.

In October I asked her once again, "Have you been able to put your stamp on the district, and how would you know?" She began with the primary.

> I think the primary did it. The nomination victory of Raymond Pierce has done it—that plus our big victory on Proposition 14 [the school bond issue]. If Pierce had lost badly, that would have hurt me. But because his second place was such a surprise and because he was recognized as "my candidate," I've done it. The result was as good for me as it was for him. The primary was of huge importance—huge importance.

> In fact, Lou Stokes and I have talked about it. How do you galvanize the community and bring them along so that they work together? When I succeeded Lou, people just watched to see what I would do. They made me earn my spurs. No one gave me anything. I had to prove something to them. I have worked and worked and worked at it. Sometimes, it hasn't worked out. I think the primary victory, following after Proposition 14,

showed people that I could do it, that I can bring people along. No black politician would endorse Pierce until I did. If he had flopped in the primary, I would have been in trouble. It showed I could deliver. A defeat in the general election will not matter. I have proven myself. I'll be fine.

While she would never put it this way, her self-appraisal—"No black politician would [move] until I did"—echoed Lou Stokes's self-appraisal at the height of his leadership influence. Step-by-step, cautiously and gradually, she had finally taken his place. The outcome of the mayoralty primary was, for her, the equivalent of Chaka Fattah's Gear Up legislative outcome. In each case, an individual accomplishment enabled a successor to establish a secure individual reputation in the district—one that was independent of a prominent predecessor. In keeping with their differing representational strategies, one move depended more on personal-oriented relationships, the other more on policy-oriented relationships. But the succession was certifiable in both cases.

The Cleveland congresswoman did not rest on that accomplishment. At multiracial and all-black events during my visit—a community development dinner and a black police officers' banquet—she shepherded Pierce, prodded him, and introduced him to everyone, individually and collectively: "I want you to meet *my* candidate for mayor." And it is important to note the distinctively personal basis of her support. In the primary and in the general election, Tubbs Jones did not have the organizational support of the Eleventh District Caucus, or of BEDCO, or of the Democratic Party, or of the AFL-CIO, or of the teacher's union. Hers was not an organizational accomplishment—though she did have the support of the majority of the city's black ministers and scattered smaller unions.[99] Pierce was outspent three-to-one by the front-runner. Her accomplishment was, indeed, a dominantly personal one—very much in keeping with the orientation of her representational relationships in general. She could not, however, save him from a 54-46 percent loss in November.[100]

In summary, Stephanie Tubbs Jones's organizational connections have fluctuated from securing old ones bequeathed to her by her predecessor and building new ones. The ones she inherited were exclusively inward looking, devoted to identifying, reflecting, and strengthening the black community. The ones she built were sometimes inward looking but often outward looking.

Lou Stokes was constrained by being first—and in an unfriendly context—to organize in ways that would instill pride inside the community and a new power on behalf of the community. His successor was less tightly tied to such internal tasks and freer to do a good deal of organizing across racial lines—in getting herself elected and in pursuing citywide policy changes, as in the school bond issue. On the other hand, there were conditions under which she, like him, would focus on organizational connections within and for the black community.

In the mayoralty race, she took the lead in organizing to protect the group interests of her fellow African Americans. As an observable by-product, her language during this endeavor became thicker with references to "the black community" than it had before. For purposes of city politics, she had adopted Lou Stokes's group-interest goal and Lou Stokes's inward-looking black-community-centered perspectives. Her congressional-level politics tends toward biracial politics, but her city-level politics tends toward black politics. Changing circumstances alter the degree to which her organizational connections are expansionist or protectionist.

There are, I conclude, times when the black community wants or needs or will accept organization and leadership. Insofar as House members are positioned or equipped to provide that leadership, it can only come from African American House members. White members of Congress could not do it. In this respect, organizational connections are a lot like symbolic connections. To the degree that either type of connection is of special importance to African Americans, only African American House members can connect. However well-intentioned they may be, white Representatives cannot take the lead in performing those representational tasks. Such constraints do not apply, however, to policy or personal connections. That distinction might usefully inform such perennial black–white puzzles as majority–minority districting.

INSTITUTIONAL CAREER AND EXPERIENTIAL LEARNING

Newly elected members of Congress divide their earliest days between looking forward to their new job in Washington and looking backward to the familiar home factors that got them there. Mostly, they look forward. When asked, five days after her election, about her early plans, Stephanie Tubbs Jones emphasized learning and opportunity. "I think I'll be able to adjust. In life, you have to learn to be fluid. You have to be willing to see what else is on the horizon for you." And she added, "I'll be concentrating on learning Washington, Congress, and my position, as well as constituent services. I'm not naive enough to think I will go there and immediately pass a piece of legislation. What you do is, you go there, learn the process and get involved. Then you have opportunities." With respect to Lou Stokes, she added, "I will do whatever I can to return whatever funds I can to the district, but I don't anticipate I'll be able to do what he did." [101] She would learn; she would get involved; she would, as always, capitalize on opportunities. And, like Chaka Fattah, she would confront comparisons with a predecessor.

From the time she ran for Congress, Tubbs Jones had been in the advanced, protectionist stage of her electoral career. From the time she entered Congress, however, she was in the early expansionist phase of her *institutional career*. She had had a long electoral life, and she knew almost everything about personal relationships. But she knew almost nothing about legislative relationships. Her situation was in sharpest contrast to Chaka Fattah, who had come to the House with twelve years of legislative experience.

She had a lot to learn, and, given her energy level, she wasted no time in gaining traction. Two weeks after election day, she had succeeded in getting herself selected as the representative of the newly-elected Democrats on the party's Steering Committee—the group that controls the committee assignments of House Democrats. She did it by applying the same person-to-person skills she displayed in her campaigns. "Before I left Cleveland," she said, "I thought about getting involved in leadership. So I sent letters to my class and ran a campaign like you run a campaign." [102] Her desire to become engaged in the person-to-person work inside the institution was all of a piece with her goals and strategies at home. Early observers described her as "a first-class schmoozer" with "formidable people skills." [103] On the Steering Committee, she would be in close working contact with party leaders, and she could bargain on-the-spot for her committee assignments, free from the local internecine warfare Lou Stokes had to surmount.

Her requests to be appointed either to Rules or to Ways and Means—two of the most sought-after House committees—were untutored and unrealistic. [104] Accordingly, they went unrealized. She was assigned to the Banking and Financial Services Committee and to the Small Business Committee—from which, as I have shown, she launched her campaign at home on behalf of low-income home buyers. She did not, however, abandon her two first choices. But neither did she settle quickly on a clear preference. When we first met, it was Rules. "I want to get on Rules. People say it has drawbacks, but that's the committee I want. Everything goes through you." Similarly, she told an interviewer that, "My ultimate goal is to go on Rules." [105] A year later, however, her choice had changed to Ways and Means. "I want to be on Ways and Means," she said. "I have told everyone that." After two terms, she was still learning to match her preferences to her opportunities. When she announced her decision not to run for mayor, she declared that the primary goal of her institutional career was to become the first African American woman to sit on the powerful Ways and Means Committee.[106] She has held to that ever since.

In the meantime, she had to make the transition from prosecutor to legislator. "Before I came here," she said, "I had 300 employees. I could say, 'This is what I want to happen.' I can't do that here, and that is the worst part of the job, although I'm adjusting."[107] It was helpful that she carried her home-based emphasis on personal politics into the new setting. In an early interview, for example, she showed a sensitivity to her position in a partisan minority and her proven talent for building alliances. "When you are in the minority," she said, "you have to find other means to accomplish what you have to accomplish . . . to 'work your show,' and you do that through making alliances with other persons. I have been used to doing that all my life."[108]

Her first legislative success was one such "alliance." She signed on with a Republican colleague, Deborah Pryce from Ohio, as the original cosponsors of a small bill that they pushed, with bipartisan support, onto the statute books. It increased the funding for preventing child abuse—"an important issue for me in light of my experience as County Prosecutor and Judge. As the Cuyahoga County Prosecutor, I created a child abuse prevention unit within my office."[109] The bill provided $10 million, collected from fines and forfeited assets, to be used to fund state and local advocacy centers and to train child care providers. During the debate, her contribution was acknowledged on the House floor. The bill was signed into law in March 2000.[110]

From that experience, she said, "I learned that I can work outside my committee to pass legislation on any subject I want, so long as I can get someone on the right committee to introduce it." When asked at the time what legacy she would like to leave, she said, "What I want to be able to say when I leave the U.S. Congress is . . . that I forged relationships, that I built bridges, and I made coalitions."[111] Her "little bill" gave her a confidence-building start.

During her first term, she tended her relationship with her predecessor with care—to the end that his comments and media comments would speak favorably about it. "He's my friend; he's my colleague; he's my mentor," she told one interviewer. "I worked in his campaign for Congress the first time he ran in 1968, as a high schooler."[112] Describing their relationship as "close," she told a reporter in July that she spoke with him every week.[113] He reciprocated. "I get good reports on her in the [Cleveland] community. . . .

People have to be patient with her and give her time to develop her way of representing the district." [114] At year's end, he said, "To her credit, she has stayed in touch and been a delight to work with." [115]

In the *Plain Dealer,* her report card suggested comparisons by invoking "the shadow" of her predecessor. She was said to have "kept a low public profile" while "emerging from the shadow of Rep. Louis Stokes." [116] Or, while "adjusting to the vagaries of Capitol Hill," she "has spent her first year in office working in the shadow of the legend she replaced." [117] Early reports were favorable, but probationary. She expressed confidence that "Over time, I have been able to make my mark in the positions I have held and people will give me the opportunity to grow into this position." [118]

When we met near the end of her first term, she seemed almost at home in her new career. "I think now," she said, "that I should have been a legislator from the beginning. I'm glad, however, that I have the knowledge of the law and the experience I got as a judge and prosecutor. It has made it much easier to do what I do in Congress. It gives me more authority when I speak and when I make an argument." Her judgment had already gained some support from an informal survey of Congress watchers in January 2000. The Capitol Hill newspaper, *Roll Call,* named forty prospective "next generation of Hill leaders"—ten from each party and each chamber. Tubbs Jones was named as one of the ten most "up and coming" House Democrats— between the sixth and the tenth ranked.[119] "Maybe," they wrote, "an active style, smarts, popularity and a safe district will add up to a future leadership role in the [Congressional Black] Caucus. Or maybe not."

The use of Congressional Black Caucus (CBC) leadership prospects as the media's standard for handicapping institutional success for African American House members has all the earmarks of racial profiling. When newcomer Chaka Fattah was named by *Time* magazine as one of the nation's fifty most promising young citizens, they, too, concluded with the benediction that he "will someday lead the Congressional Black Caucus." [120] It was the same career destination that *Roll Call* had established for newcomer Stephanie Tubbs Jones.

Congressman Fattah certainly participated in the life of the CBC. But his institutional ambitions and activities were focused elsewhere. Asked later to comment on that *Time* forecast, he dismissed it, saying, "I would never run for chairman of the CBC. It's just not my interest." His personal goals and his representational strategy encompassed a much broader, much fuller, more open-ended legislative and institutional outlook than the one established for him in *Time.* And so, in time, might hers.

Given her less-focused political ambition, however, the extent and direction of Tubbs Jones's new career were less clear and more provisional at the outset than in the case of the policy-driven Fattah. When I asked, directly, whether she preferred a route to internal institutional influence that ran through the CBC or one that followed a wider institutional course, she demurred, "It all depends which opportunity opens up." It was a reply totally in keeping with the opportunistic pattern of her career—from judicial to prosecutorial to legislative office.

Much more than Fattah, she has, in fact, worked within the CBC. Early on she described that relationship: "In a new situation, I just sit back and observe to get the lay of the land. There are some things the Caucus can do and some things it can't do. We meet for lunch every Wednesday. I like those meetings and I look forward to them." A year later, she had become more involved. "I'm the chairman of the Housing Committee," she said. "I have good relations with all the members. I stay out of all their fights and feuds. In the vote for chairman, I did not support [the winner]. But I am naturally friendly toward her, and she has me working already as her sergeant-at-arms, keeping order in the group." As a summary assessment of her CBC involvements, she noted during the mayoralty race, "I believe I have earned the respect of my colleagues in the CBC. I'm having a fundraiser in Washington for Raymond [Pierce] and I have 33 of the 36 members lined up—all who can come."

Her chairmanship of the CBC Housing Committee gives her—not a working committee, but an individual portfolio—one that dovetails nicely with the policy subjects of her House committee and with her future ambitions. "I can get individuals to help," she says, "but my colleagues let me do just about anything I want to do. It gives me a platform to talk about the issues I want to talk about. Those issues are closely related to the issues in Ways and Means. And I have a leadership title that is helpful to me here at home." Indeed it is, since local observers use it as an indicator of institutional growth.[121]

With respect to the surrogate representation of a national African American constituency, her learning curve in this respect was sloping upward as I watched. Five days before I arrived in 2001, a white police officer had shot and killed an unarmed black teenager in Cincinnati—Ohio's second largest city, four hundred miles to the south of Cleveland. Two days later, protest marchers and bottle throwing had begun in the city's black neighborhoods. For two days, the confrontation with the police had intensified into vandalizing and looting on one side, and bean bags, rubber bullets, and tear gas on the other side. On the morning I met with Tubbs Jones, the *Plain Dealer* was reporting sixty-five injuries and sixty-six arrests. Cincinnati's mayor was threatening to call in the National Guard.[122] The raging racial conflict was a front-page lead story in all the national media.

During the day, neither Tubbs Jones nor her staffers with whom I spoke mentioned the subject until, during a prolonged wait in the television studio, she received a call from a colleague in the Congressional Black Caucus. From it, she learned that the former head of the CBC, now president of the NAACP, was on his way to Cincinnati to see what he could do. Her colleague was thinking, too, about going to Cincinnati, and was calling Tubbs Jones as a courtesy to the home-state CBC member. To that point, the idea of "speaking out" on the Cincinnati riots, much less going there, had apparently not occurred to the Cleveland congresswoman. She simply had not thought of it as part of her job. The telephone call triggered a late afternoon flurry of Cincinnati-related, "what-to-do" cell phone conversations—and considerable reflection.

She talked at length about the incident as part of her ongoing learning experience. "I had already learned," she began,

> that because I am the only black member of Congress from Ohio that I can be helpful to people outside my district. Many black people call on me for help because I understand their situation. When I first went to Congress, I didn't realize that people outside my district would look to me for help and that I could be helpful. *Today I realized that I still don't fully understand the scope of my influence.* You have heard about the rioting in Cincinnati? My [CBC] friend called me and wanted to know if I was going down there or if I had spoken out on the situation. It was a courtesy call from someone who was thinking about coming to my state.
>
> You know, it never occurred to me to speak out on that subject or to go down there. Yet I *am* the only black member of Congress from Ohio. I thought, well, my friends are always looking for publicity; I'm not. When I was prosecutor, I was always critical of the politicians who were making trouble by speaking to the press about this or that. Their publicity-seeking was an intrusion. But I'm learning that there may be times when I should speak out on behalf of black people who are in trouble outside my district—that it's not just publicity-seeking.

Her reflection resulted in a personal call to the Cincinnati mayor's office to offer help, and in temporizing replies to MSNBC and to black news organization requests for comments. She asked her staff to call a Democratic Party friend in Cincinnati to find out "what is going on down there."

It was a trial-and-error story of experiential learning—about the recognition and the tending of her symbolic connections with a national African American constituency. The potential of these broad and less tangible connections came much earlier to Lou Stokes, with his national-level civil rights experience, than they did to Stephanie Tubbs Jones, with her county-level experience as local prosecutor.

Quite apart from her African American connections, she has steadily pursued her broader institutional interests. "I'm a party loyalist," she said at the beginning of her second term. "I'm the party whip for the sophomore class. I went on the Ethics Committee [considered—as with Fattah—to be a credit-building personal favor within the party] because the leader asked me. I'm in the leader's face all the time. He knows I'm there, and he knows I want to be on Ways and Means. I've been with him every time except on the selection of the national party chairman. And I told him why." "I know," she says, "that Ways and Means is thought of as a protrade committee. But I think there ought to be some antitrade people on the committee, to reassure the membership that the issue has been massaged internally." The leader, for his part, publicly praises her "political and people sense," and says, "She's very good with people; she's very popular." [123]

Meanwhile, she continued to do what came naturally. "I'm building up personal relationships. Nancy Pelosi and I discovered we had friends in common, and we've become good friends. I was one of her earliest supporters, member of her team, and a whip in her [winning] campaign for the party leadership. She will support me for Ways and Means." Again, "After I was elected, Lou Stokes told me that the one person I had to get to know in the House was John Murtha. As soon as I got there, I went to see him, and I told him that Lou Stokes had said he was the first person I should get to know. He is a wonderful man, knowledgeable and kind, and I love him. I have his support for Ways and Means." From a Republican colleague from Ohio ("When we were both prosecutors and went to conventions together, he used to say I was his date.") comes evidence of cross-party relationships. "Here in Congress, it's all about relationships, and she's a people person. . . . She has friends on both sides of the aisle." [124] *Roll Call's* prescription notwithstanding, she was, when I left her, pursuing a multisided, person-to-person centered, sophomore strategy—waiting, as always, to see "what opportunities turn up."

When she drove me to my hotel for the last time, she asked as usual, "Was that a good trip?" And I said, "Yes it was." "My husband is driving me to Columbus tomorrow," she said, "to a meeting of the state Democratic com-

mittee. I'm looking forward to that. I'm the vice chair of the state committee and a member of the national Democratic committee." Her anticipation
brought back memories of my trip to the Democratic state convention in
Columbus during my last visit with Lou Stokes. He had gone, delivered a
speech to show the flag, endured hostility, and left to describe it as the worst
event of my visit. Twenty-five years had, indeed, made a difference.

CONCLUSION

Stephanie Tubbs Jones's defining personal goal is to be engaged in
service to others. Her service-centered goal took the form that it did—elective public service—because that is where the first community-level opportunity opened up for her. As later opportunities presented themselves, she
climbed the public-office ladder, first in the law-enforcement hierarchy, then
in the U.S. Congress. Taken together, her public-service ambitions and her
public-office opportunities provide guiding themes of her political career.

The opportunity that led her to Congress was the retirement of veteran
Congressman Louis Stokes. And her triumph in the succession contest was
a personal accomplishment. It resulted from her electoral experience, her
record of public service, and her "I'm a people person" appeal. Of particular
importance were her down-to-earth personal qualities of warmth, enthusiasm, and empathy as they sustained old friendships and attracted new voters. Of necessity, she began her new job "in the shadow" of her predecessor.
But she was not indebted to him for her victory. She tended their relationship respectfully and tactfully. But contextual changes allowed her to operate in a more outward-looking biracial world than he. She presents herself
more regularly than he did before racially mixed audiences. Her rock bottom political strength lies in the black community, as demonstrated in her
appointment contest for county prosecutor. But her proven electoral
strength has extended beyond the black community.

Policy representation has been no more of a problem for her than it was
for her predecessor, given the needs and wants of Cleveland's African American community. Her liberal, prolabor voting record has the approval of her
supportive white constituents—both working class and professional.
Should the play of black interests and white interests force her to choose, as
they did in the mayoralty race, the former will surely dominate.

The distinction between hard policy connections, which get registered by
roll call votes in Washington, and soft policy connections, which get registered in face-to-face contact at home, highlights the crucial contribution of

her "people person" strengths to her overall representational success. Even more, personal strengths such as openness and authenticity have helped her to build the symbolic connections that are so critical a part of the representative-constituent relationships within the African American community. Taken together, her personal electoral connections, her soft policy connections and her symbolic connections with her constituents are the defining elements of her person-intensive representational strategy.

Building on the help of her predecessor, who bequeathed to her his Eleventh Congressional District Caucus, the congresswoman has immersed herself in local politics and negotiated her own set of organizational connections. She has been freer from intraparty conflict and personal rivalries than he. And she has used her maneuvering room step-by-step to establish herself, by 2001, as the preeminent black political leader in Cleveland—and in Ohio, as well. She does not yet wield the degree of power in the constituency that Louis Stokes did. But the scope of her power—as reflected in the 2001 mayoralty primary—may well have become as broad as his. In any case, she no longer labors in his shadow at home.

Inside the House of Representatives, where experience counts so heavily, she has a long way to go to match the influence and reputation of her predecessor. As compared with Barbara Jordan and Chaka Fattah, her early adjustment was slowed by her total lack of experience in legislative institutions. Nonetheless, she has been extremely active in negotiating inside personal relationships. And her experiential learning curve has been both steep and steady. Her steadily increasing confidence in "speaking out" on economic empowerment, clearly observable over the course of my visits, predicts continued growth and success.

CHAPTER 7
. . . .
CONCLUSION

REPRESENTATION AND HOME

Going Home is about the activities of members of the United States House of Representatives when they are back home with their constituents. It has two main purposes. The first is to examine, in detail, the various constituency activities of four African American House members. The second is to propose some conceptual guidelines to help in studying in-the-constituency activities. The observational and the conceptual purposes are joined in the pursuit of an overriding purpose—to enhance the study of representation in the American political system.

From the outset, it has been clear that four separate, narrative-style studies of African American House members cannot produce definitive conclusions—not about black politics and not about representation. It is easy to see why. The number of cases is tiny; only one of the four was deliberately chosen for comparative purposes, and taken together, they are in no sense a sample of the African American politicians now in the House of Representatives. Furthermore, the narratives are based on personal observation—the timing, the context, and the content of which were beyond my control as the observer. Political scientists come to a district to participate only when they are allowed to come; they go only where they are allowed to go; they see only what they are allowed to see; and they are told only what each Representative chooses to tell them. Given these research contingencies and uncertainties, comparability is limited and strict comparability is impossible. Outsiders must take what they are given and make the best of it.

"Making the best of it," however, can produce a sense of direction and substantive encouragement. Political science analysis does, after all, depend heavily on observation. And participant observation, despite its limitations, provides rich opportunities to observe. In addition, the narrative form of presentation has considerable exploratory and probative value—particularly in the early stages of inquiry. If nothing else, narratives encourage scholarly attention to the importance of time and sequence and change. Assuming, then, that the narrative reports are reasonably accurate, I shall continue to "make the best of it" by pulling together some concluding comments. My hope is that they, too, might stimulate further inquiry and lead, eventually, to the development of more definitive generalizations. My conclusions must be stated in terms of tendencies; perhaps further research can turn them into probabilities.

Representation is a large, many-sided idea, and it has been a major object of research and reflection among political scientists. The focus in this book is on representation as a process—a continuous process—that links the activities of elected officials to the activities of their constituents. The context is, of course, the United States' system of single-member districts. Heretofore, the most heavily researched activity of our elected representatives has been their votes in Congress, and the most heavily researched activity of the constituents has been their votes at election time. This emphasis on the two sets of voters is certainly the right one, because the linkage between them is the bottom-line relationship in a representative democracy.

The bottom-line relationship, however, begins at home; yet most linkage research has been focused on voting patterns in Washington. From the home perspective, however, there are multiple linkages between House members and their constituents. As an aid to home-centered analysis, I have expressed the multiple linkages as *connections*. I elaborated representational strategies for each Representative by examining five types of connections—electoral, personal, policy, symbolic, and organizational.[1] These categories are based primarily on observation—on what each House member did, and what we talked about, by way of connecting with his or her constituents. Taken together, these categories are designed to capture, and to highlight, the importance and the diversity of home relationships.

Home connections turn out to be diffuse, long-term, and cumulative. They flourish before, after, and in between the casting of votes. They may, of course, be directly and immediately related to House member votes or to constituent votes, but most of them are not. This fact makes home activities hard to conceptualize in the normal cause-and-effect language of political scientists' vote studies. They produce patterns rather than traceable relationships of independent and dependent variables. They are designed to build, reinforce, and maintain House member reputations and constituent support. They convey information, they create perceptions, and they affect the operative leeway of Representatives and the predispositions of constituents. They occur at campaign time and between campaigns. They strive for durability. And they are most easily understood in the sequential, over-time language of negotiations and learning and the winning of trust.

House member activities in their home districts help to shape the decisions of House members in Washington and the decisions of constituents at home. It is impossible to conceive of representational politics in America without them.

The conventional distinction between descriptive and substantive representation—as explained earlier—has not been very useful for examining representational activities at home. Both categories, therefore, have been enlarged to meet the realities of home activity. The effect of a conceptualization that emphasizes several connections—instead of two types of representation—has been to turn this book away from conventional discussions about the compatibilities and tradeoffs between descriptive and substantive representation. In home-centered analyses of dominantly black districts, "descriptive" versus "substantive" dilemmas seem not to occur.

That, at least, is the story of the home connections of four highly successful African American Representatives. In the four cases studied here, the problem of tradeoffs between descriptive and substantive representation, as conventionally identified, did not arise. Five types of connections were identified, and black constituents in each district enjoyed all of them—not to the same degree, but without noteworthy conflict. For other House members in other constituencies, of course, all questions remain open for home-based investigation.[2]

CHANGE AND COHORTS

At the beginning of this book, I offered two broad themes—*change* and *diversity*—as guidelines. Looking back at the text, "diversity" has been a good deal easier to pin down and describe than "change." Nonetheless, political change has been a thematic staple in the literature on black politics, and I deliberately built the idea of change into this project by adding two members from the 1990s to compare with two members previously studied in the 1970s. To aid in the study of change, each pair was folded into a separate group—a 1970s "pioneer cohort" and a 1990s "contemporary cohort" of African American Representatives. The classification is, admittedly, arbitrary, and it may not deserve to survive this book. But it has served a useful heuristic purpose here, by directing our attention to two different periods of time and to the overall subject of political change.

I used the two time periods to compare the representational activities of Louis Stokes in the 1970s with those of Stephanie Tubbs Jones in the 1990s. Here, in the same constituency and at the same point in their respective congressional careers, a change had taken place from the inward-looking, group-interest pattern of Stokes's relationships to the outward-looking, personal-engagement pattern of Tubbs Jones's relationships. There were, of course, some basic continuities—based on his organizational legacy to her, on her desire to keep his goodwill, and on their overlapping support base in the district. But there were differences in careers and context that were the product of a quarter-century of change—in Cleveland and in black politics more generally.

His career began during the civil rights revolution; he was nudged into politics by his brother; he was a neophyte in a harsh political climate; and he worked at home to build, nurture, and lead an organized black community. Her career began as the era of movement politics was ending. She had been elected in several biracial constituencies before coming to Congress. She operated in a more negotiations-oriented home context than he did. In that more fluid context, her personal abilities enabled her to nurture a supportive, reelection constituency that, while anchored in the black community, contained white working-class and liberal supporters as well. The change from Stokes to Tubbs Jones would seem to be a useful example of the widely cited "protest to politics" transition in black politics in the late twentieth century.

There is no reason to expect that these two representational patterns would be typical of their respective cohorts. A parting conjecture, however, might be this: that because Stokes was a "first," and because he was the product of movement politics, and because the racial context in which he worked was duplicated in other northern urban constituencies, *his* representational patterns might be a fruitful guide to further research among other Representatives from northern urban districts within his 1970s cohort. The high percentage of Stokes's fellow "pioneers" among David Canon's defining category of "difference representatives" supports this possibility.[3] If such is the case, the category of "pioneer cohort" may well prove useful to later researchers.

The same prospect is not in store, however, for the larger and more heterogeneous "contemporary cohort." Very little cohort-wide guidance can be expected from Stephanie Tubbs Jones's representational pattern. She and her contemporary colleague, Chaka Fattah, did share common characteristics—their extensive precongressional electoral careers and the constraining legacy of their distinguished predecessors. But neither of these shared descriptors seems promising as a common characteristic of the contemporary cohort, given its large number of southern newcomers. Furthermore, Chaka Fattah's representational relationships may have more in common with those of Barbara Jordan—the single-mindedness of their ambitions and their institutional goals—than they have with those of Tubbs Jones. And to further confound cohort comparisons, Jordan had little in common with her 1970s contemporary Lou Stokes.

When, as in these cases, within-cohort differences are as large as across-cohort differences, the usefulness of the two designated cohorts in capturing change becomes suspect. Thus, the designation of cohorts may have served a rather limited purpose. Nonetheless, its main objective—to underline the importance of change—remains central to the study of representation.

DIVERSITY AND PERSONAL GOALS

As a characteristic of African American politics, "diversity" is easier to spot and to specify than "change." Indeed, this book has been mostly about diversity. Its basic organizing concepts—goals, contexts, and experiential learning—are designed to help me generalize about diversity. So, too, is the typology of constituency connections—electoral, personal, policy, symbolic, and organizational. So, too, is the category of institutional careers. It would serve no good purpose, now, to rehearse the detailed application of these conceptual guidelines to each of the four individuals. I will content myself, therefore, with some general reminders and closing observations.

The discussion of diversity began with an emphasis on the *personal goals* of each individual. Why did each one decide to get into elective politics in the first place? What did he or she want to accomplish? My assumption was that the only way to make sense out of their political activity at home was to gain some understanding of their underlying motivations and ambitions—their personal goals. The further assumption was that it is necessary to specify personal goals in order to talk about representational strategy. Strategy implies making choices. And to understand choices, it is necessary to understand goals.

To these ends, I talked to them, watched them, and read about them in order to settle on that personal goal which—assuming the goal of reelection—gave me the greatest leverage in explaining the greatest proportion of each individual's representational behavior at home. The aim was not to find or to claim a goal that would explain everything—all Representatives have mixed goals and pursue mixed strategies. The aim was to identify a goal that would make the most sense and could carry the heaviest burden in explaining the behavior patterns of each individual. That is why I used such cautionary qualifiers as "intensive" or "dominant" or "oriented" or "driven" when relating an individual's goal to his or her representational strategy. And the qualifiers were meant to be interchangeable. For example, Barbara Jordan's representational strategy and her representational relationships could be described equally well as influence-intensive, or influence-dominant, or influence-oriented, or influence-driven. The intention in all cases is to convey, and to employ, a central tendency in the subsequent analysis.

Thinking about this set of personal goals might raise two questions. First, to what degree, if at all, can the four goals—group-interest intensive (for Stokes), influence intensive (for Jordan), policy intensive (for Fattah), and person intensive (for Tubbs Jones)—be thought of as applying exclusively to African American House members? The answer is: to a very small degree, if at all. Only Lou Stokes's group-interest goal comes close. Although, in his case, it applies to African Americans, it cannot be called a uniquely African American goal. It is, however, a minority-interest goal. Thus, it might come naturally to representatives of other minorities who find themselves in contexts similar to Cleveland's in the 1970s. Except for that possibility, the personal goals identified here apply to all U.S. Representatives and are unrelated to distinctions between blacks and whites.

A second question might be asked about the fortuitous ascription of four different goals to four different Representatives. Might not this match have been driven by an irresistible desire to maximize the diversity of individual goals and, thus, expand the diversity of House member activities at home? That question can best be put to rest by noting that a case of policy-intensive representation and a case of person-intensive representation have already been uncovered and elaborated on in an earlier study.[4] That is to say, some cumulation has already taken place. The hope is that as the number of cases grows, more clumping will be found and exploited in a move toward generalization.

In the process of identifying personal goals, the two best sources of information and direction—other than direct conversation—were the careers and the campaigns of each individual. Careers reveal choices; campaigns reveal connections. Both invite analysis over time. Especially useful were pre-congressional public careers and early congressional campaigns. The idea is that individual motivations and ambitions usually develop early and can be uncovered by investigating a House member's active public life before election to Congress or during an early winning election to that body. By cross-checking back and forth, from on-the-spot observation to written accounts to personal conversation about careers and campaigns, I was able to form judgments about each House member's goals.

Among the precongressional public careers examined here, consider the usefulness of Lou Stokes's early civil rights work, Barbara Jordan's early adjustments to the Texas State Senate, Chaka Fattah's early immersion in neighborhood problems, and Stephanie Tubbs Jones's early countywide electoral activity. Among the early congressional campaigns of the four individuals, consider the usefulness of the Stokes campaign theme of black community power in 1970, the Jordan campaign issue of relative legislative accomplishments in 1970, the Fattah antiorganizational campaign of 1994, and the Tubbs Jones campaign issue of personal trust in 1990. In sum, accumulating and assessing knowledge about careers and campaigns will go a long way toward constructing a dominant goal for each individual.

As important as careers and campaigns are to the study of personal goals, they are equally important as gateways to the idea of representation. Since both activities are developmental and continuous over time, the more we build them into our analyses, the more we buttress the notion of representation as a process. Precongressional careers help to explain early representational choices. Career stages—protectionist and expansionist—are useful markers for later analyses. Election campaigns provide clues to the sort of representational strategy the victorious candidate will pursue at home afterward. In their promises and their execution, campaigns are about connections with constituents. Campaigns are not just about winning. They are also about articulating standards and setting expectations for representational relationships at home.

CONTEXT AND POLICY CONNECTIONS

The diversity of personal goals among the subjects of this book must not be allowed to obscure their commonalities. All are African American. All represent urban areas. All think of their primary constituencies as black and predominantly working class. All are Democrats for whom the Democratic primary is the only election that counts. All share the same liberal policy priorities—improvements in education, employment, housing, health care, and safety. So overwhelming are these needs for so many of their constituents, that these Representatives face few, if any, problematic vote decisions. The three for whom comparable vote scores are available have clustered, always, at the far liberal end of the conservative–liberal voting scale.

Nothing on this list of shared characteristics will come as a surprise. But embedded in that recognizable cluster is a common characteristic that, to this observer of the home context, *was* a surprise. It is their uniformly high-priority preoccupation with education. All four of them worked hard to get an education, and all of them singled out their education as the key to their later accomplishments. Cumulatively, they spent more time talking about education than about any other single subject—and not because their traveling companion was an educator. Publicly and privately, they dwelled upon its relevance to their own careers; they made it the centerpiece of their role-model presentations to constituents, and they harped on it continually as the necessary foundation of African American strength. It provided an important trace element in understanding the context and the stakes of black politics. And it put a distinctive gloss on the "educative" function of elected politicians in a representative democracy.

Because every House member interacts with constituents within a legally and politically created district, the resulting district makeup sets conditions that govern the connection activities of each member. The demographic, socioeconomic, and partisan makeup of each district includes most of what is meant by *context*. Given the long history of the purposeful underrepresentation of African Americans through manipulative boundary drawing, the key feature of all four districtwide contexts was a sufficiently large black population to ensure the election of a black Representative to Congress. Indeed, Jordan, Fattah, and Stokes had a direct hand in the redistricting process that created their respective districts.

All but Jordan worked in a majority-black district, and hers—which she drew for herself—had nearly a black majority. That one contextual wrinkle, however, may well have accounted for the most noteworthy constituency constraint on liberal policy voting to have turned up in the entire study— her oil and gas exception. Otherwise, in contexts dominated by needy black constituents, liberal policy voting in Congress was encouraged. And in that respect, the four House members were nearly interchangeable.

The four studies—especially those concerning Fattah and Tubbs Jones— make it crystal clear that voting in Congress is not the only policy connection between House members and their constituents. Indeed, a vote in Congress is but the tiny tip of a huge iceberg of policy dialogue and policy connections at home. The most cursory inspection of their yearly schedules shows that a sizable proportion of their putative personal connections at home have policy implications.

In the chapter on Tubbs Jones, I make a distinction between "hard" policy connections via a vote in Congress and "soft" policy connections via some activity at home. Further, I gave examples of gradations of soft-to-hard connections. In the lengthy policy process, there are periods of incubation, formulation, testing, revision, and so forth. Depending on their policy priorities inside Congress, members will dip in and out of this policy process when they are at home interacting with constituents—a speech, an appearance, an office meeting, a luncheon. And these connections prosper even though the member's hard policy voting on the House floor may be a long way off. In short, policy connections and policy dialogue will be embedded in many of the other connections pursued by House members at home.

SYMBOLIC AND ORGANIZATIONAL CONNECTIONS

If the narratives of this book are credible, they indicate that the symbolic connections and the organizational connections of African American House members cannot be treated in the same way as their policy connections. The symbolic and organizational connections discovered in these four settings are more central to an analysis of black representation than they would be to an analysis of white representation. Symbolic connections provided an essential link between the four House members and their respective African American constituents. They are a good deal more important in this home-based study than they appear to be in studies of black politics that center on redistricting and minority representation nationally.[5]

Similarly, organizational connections, while not much studied in other representational studies, also provide a special member–constituent linkage in a home-centered study. Both types of connections were necessary and separable ingredients of the representational relationship between the four African American Representatives and their black constituents.

Some constituent expectations are different in the black community from what they would be in the white community. With respect to symbolic connections, the very success of Lou Stokes and Barbara Jordan as the first black person elected to Congress from their city and their state, made them instant leaders with the obligation to "stand for" as well as "act for" their constituents. When they connected back home as individuals, both of these African American Representatives invoked a sense of group identity and a sense of group progress toward inclusion in American political life. Lou Stokes emphasized the pride his black constituents took in his position and in his leadership. He deliberately cast himself as a role model for others to follow in his Central High School talk. Barbara Jordan invoked group pride and the importance of group accomplishment in discussing her exploits and her hopes at Wheatley High School. And she reassured her supporters at Settegast that they were joined in the same struggle.

Without actually saying so, the idea of "linked fates" seemed to be present in these symbolic linkages.[6] That is what their uncommon emphasis on education was all about—that the education of individual citizens would strengthen the claims of the community. Chaka Fattah's talk on Dewey Street used his youthful experiences to inspire a group of mothers and young people who could relate to him as a black man and a role model. In her communitarian talk in the church near her mother's street and by her very presence at the mayor's inauguration, Stephanie Tubbs Jones reminded her fellow African Americans of their heritage and their obligation to one another.

In all four cases, a black political leader met with, talked to, and connected with ordinary black constituents in ways that no white Representative could have duplicated. White Representatives, if they wish, can easily vote the policy preferences of their black constituents. But to the extent that symbolic attachments are important to black constituents, white Representatives cannot make the requisite connections. As noted earlier, the concept of descriptive representation does not begin to tap the amount of active personal engagement involved in these black Representative–black constituency connections at home. *Only* a black Representative could have made these symbolic connections with black reelection constituencies. And Katherine Tate's research tells us that they matter when constituent votes are cast.[7]

With respect to organizational connections with black constituents, the "blacks only" relationship was almost as strong. In each of the four districts, the important organizational connections involved the relationship between individual black members of Congress and the dominant white political organizations in their constituencies. Other organizational links surely occupied the time of the four individuals. Many of them can more easily be thought of as intermittent personal connections with specific and numerous constituent groups. The important and enduring organizational activity for each of the aspiring black Democrats was negotiating satisfactory connections with preexisting local, white Democratic Party organizations. The negotiating process differed in scope and intensity from case to case, but all four confronted serious problems with their partisan-organizational relationships.

In the most confrontational relationship of all, Lou Stokes led a black counterorganization in a frontal electoral attack on the Cuyahoga County Democratic Party. Building and maintaining black political organizations dominated his constituency life. Barbara Jordan negotiated a personal relationship with the potent Harris County Democrats—by successfully demonstrating an ability to win strong black support at the polls. Chaka Fattah recruited and built his own electoral organization and defeated several candidates of the Philadelphia Democratic Party before he negotiated a truce and a partnership with them. Stephanie Tubbs Jones worked out her own connections with the local county Democrats by running successfully in a series of nonconfrontational elections that served to sublimate organizational conflict between blacks and whites. Her support of the losing black candidate in the recent contest for mayor may, however, necessitate some repair work.

In all four cases, these African American office seekers met early resistance from the organized white establishment. All four had to organize and hold black support to overcome the resistance. All four, therefore, had to get involved in local politics, and three out of the four remained active in local politics. In urban settings, it seems likely that black Representatives will feel obligated to stay involved locally to consolidate gains, to nurture a sense of community, and to mobilize black citizens in their long-running fight for inclusion. In the words of one, "I'm deeply involved in local politics. I have to be. My white colleagues have a choice; I don't."

To sum up, whenever institution-building and political-empowerment efforts are highly valued by the black citizenry, only African American politicians can make and keep the requisite organizational connections with their supportive black constituencies. Under those conditions, white politicians can neither lead nor represent.

PERSONAL CONNECTIONS

With respect to personal connections, the best summary reminder is simply that they are an observable element in almost every home connection. They are more obvious in some cases than others—especially so in the Tubbs Jones chapter. But the cultivation of personal connections is a stock in trade of all members.

In order to provide some basis for discussing the more formalized aspects of their personal connections, I examined a year's worth of their appointment schedules. Because of differences in degree of specificity, differences in descriptive indicators, differences in the completeness of entries, and lack of knowledge about which appointments were actually met, comparison across cohorts was impossible and comparison within cohorts was nearly so. Moreover, I was not allowed to observe during one-on-one appointments between constituents and House members.

Nothing in their records, however, conflicts with the idea that, except for extreme or persistent cases, constituency-service help with the problems of individuals is the province of the office staff, not the Representative. And all seemed to have competent, effective home-office staffs.

Most of their scheduled office appointments seemed to have been devoted to the concerns of local groups or locally represented national groups, public and private, involving a myriad of specific but unidentified local or national matters. In these cases, personal service and public policy concerns were intertwined.

Taken one at a time, the four sets of appointment schedules—in conjunction with member comments—do reveal some personal patterning. Lou Stokes's schedule and discussion reveal careful discrimination in judging the relevance of a variety of personal connections. Barbara Jordan's schedule showed that, even though she was in her first term, she already made more speeches outside of her district than any of the others did while I watched them. Chaka Fattah's extraordinary success in attracting media attention was highlighted in his scheduling record. And Stephanie Tubbs Jones's extraordinary attention to local political activities was highlighted in hers. Given some comparability of information, these differences are real and reflect four quite different personal allocations of effort.

NEGOTIATION AND LEARNING

Representational relationships are not imposed by elected politicians on their constituents; nor are they imposed by constituents on the politicians they elect. Representational relationships are *negotiated* relationships, and the negotiations are both complex and gradual. I have illuminated that complexity by exploring several types of connections, and I have honored the gradualness by making observations at several points in time. But the negotiating process, in which each side makes gradual adjustments to the expectations and actions of the other, is hard to trace.

This book examines only the actions and the adjustments of the Representative. There is no evidence—except, perhaps, a successful reelection—from the constituent side of the relationship. From the angle of the elected member, however, I made an effort to identify negotiations and adjustments by focusing on *experiential learning*. Where trial-and-error learning has taken place, goes the rationale, adjustments are probably being made. And where adjustments are being made, some negotiation is probably taking place. The various types of connections were used as a guide to identify, for each House member, important learning experiences.

For Lou Stokes, who had almost no prior political experience, his main, long-run adjustment problems were with his fellow politicians. He had to learn how to cope with the local Democratic Party organization, with his own counterorganizations, and with other local, black politicians who coveted his prerogatives if not his position. Barbara Jordan's most important negotiations came early and centered on the support of the local white liberals who controlled the nominating process. Later, she had to adjust to a more nationally oriented group of white businessmen who dominated her district's largest industry. Chaka Fattah's district-level adjustments centered on his rocky relationship with the local Democratic Party. In order to relate to his constituents, he also had to learn which of his state legislative experiences were helpful and which weren't. Stephanie Tubbs Jones, who came to Congress without any legislative experience, had to learn how to be a legislator— how to set up shop for herself, how to organize to speak out on policy at home, and how to enlarge the scope of her activity in the new job.

INSTITUTIONAL CAREERS AND HOME

If the only impact of a House member's life at home on his or her life inside Congress were registered in the House member's voting records, the study of representational relationships might well end with the analysis of roll calls. But the impact of home activity on House activity is much more complex than that, and the reciprocal impact of "inside" and "outside" activities adds to the complexity. The constituency-to-Congress-to-constituency interactions in Chaka Fattah's educational efforts are a dramatic example. As a way of acknowledging and reporting this complexity for each of the four individuals, I introduced the idea of their inside, *institutional careers* to match the idea of their outside, constituency careers. In each case, I made the argument that a full understanding of a member's home activities could not be gained without a modest glance at that member's institutional activities.

In this book, the story of the four institutional careers is largely the story of their committees. It is the story of how they won committee memberships and how they exploited their committee memberships. Neither part of that story is complete without the other—without, that is, both a constituency perspective and an institutional perspective.

A look backward at their campaigns for committee memberships suggests that the aphorism "all politics is local" might be amended to read "all House committee membership politics is local." Lou Stokes's next-door congressman in Cleveland tried hard to torpedo his bid for a better committee assignment. Chaka Fattah, on the other hand, owed his prized committee assignment to his neighboring Philadelphia congressman. Barbara Jordan's committee request was shepherded to success by a retired politician in Texas! Stephanie Tubbs Jones will need Ohio assistance if she is to reach her strongly preferred committee.

In terms of their institutional accomplishments, all four members concentrated on the work of their respective committees. When they were back home, they talked a good deal about the subject matter of their committees. They were trying to build and maintain their home reputations by using their committee-based experiences. Stokes's late-blooming local reputation depended heavily on his Appropriations Committee activities and upon his public prominence as chairman of the Intelligence and Ethics Committees. Jordan's impeachment-centered reputation depended entirely on her Judiciary Committee membership. The passage of Fattah's Gear Up Program would have been impossible without his membership on the Education and Work Force Committee. Tubbs Jones's dominant emphasis on economic empowerment when she is at home grows directly out of her position on the Financial Services Committee.

In sum, a sizable proportion of each House member's institutional activity is committee activity, and a sizable proportion of committee activity is also home activity. If you want a clue to the behavior of a member back home, watch that member in committee. And if you want a clue to the behavior of a member in committee, watch that member at home. To the extent that institutional politics and constituency politics affect one another, studies of each will be entangled with, and enriched by, studies of the other.

To end where I began, four studies do not constitute convincing evidence of any cause-and-effect propositions. I hope that they have helped to demonstrate that representation is a process, one in which the complexity of activities in the home district is an integral part. I also hope that by focusing on the home activities of African American Representatives, some special characteristics of the representational process will be sharpened for students of black politics. I would hope that all students of American politics might come to think about a distinctive home-centered "representational process" as broadly as they now think about an "electoral process" or a "legislative process." And, should the idea of a home-centered representational process ever become a commonplace analytical category, I would hope that the narrative exploration of representational strategies and connections in this book will have made a useful contribution. The test will come if, as, and when more political scientists find themselves "going home," too.

NOTES

CHAPTER 1

1. For example, Peter Boyer, "The Rise of Kweisi Mfume," *New Yorker,* August 1, 1994; Peter Carlson, "Living with History in the Often Bloody Struggle for Civil Rights, John Lewis Has Been There, Done That," *Washington Post National Weekly Edition,* June 22, 1998. See also note 5 below.

2. For example, David Lublin, *The Paradox of Representation: Racial Gerrymandering and Minority Interests in Congress* (Princeton, N.J.: Princeton University Press, 1997).

3. For example, Robert Singh, *The Congressional Black Caucus: Racial Politics in the U.S. Congress* (Thousand Oaks, Calif.: Sage, 1998).

4. For example, Kenny Whitby, *The Color of Representation* (Ann Arbor: University of Michigan Press, 1997).

5. Carol Swain, *Black Faces, Black Interests* (Cambridge, Mass.: Harvard University Press, 1993); David Canon, *Race, Redistricting, and Representation: The Unintended Consequences of Black Majority Districts* (Chicago: University of Chicago Press, 1999).

6. See, for example, Swain, *Black Faces, Black Interests;* Canon, *Race, Redistricting, and Representation;* Lublin, *Paradox of Representation;* Jane Mansbridge, "Should Blacks Represent Blacks and Women Represent Women? A Contingent 'Yes,'" *Journal of Politics* 61, no. 3 (August 1999); Katherine Tate, "The Political Representation of Blacks in Congress: Does Race Matter?" *Legislative Studies Quarterly* 26, no. 4 (November 2001): 623–38.

7. Herbert Asher and Herbert Weisberg, "Voting Change in Congress: Some Dynamic Perspectives on an Evolutionary Process," *American Journal of Political Science* 38 (1978): 25–44.

8. John Hibbing, *Congressional Careers: Contours of Life in the House of Representatives* (Chapel Hill: University of North Carolina Press, 1991), esp. chap. 8. More generally, I have been helped by Lawrence Rothenberg, *Linking Citizens and Government* (New York: Cambridge University Press, 1992), esp. chap. 2.

9. Richard Fenno, *Home Style: House Members in Their Districts* (Boston: Little Brown, 1978).

10. As portrayed, for example, in the study of the same period by Robert C. Smith, *We Have No Leaders: African Americans in the Post–Civil Rights Era,* (Albany: SUNY Press, 1996).

CHAPTER 2

1. James Q. Wilson, "Two Negro Politicians, an Interpretation," *Midwest Journal of Political Science* 5 (1960): 349–69.

2. Swain, *Black Faces, Black Interests.*

3. Canon, *Race, Redistricting, and Representation.*

4. Tom Brazaitis, "Stokes Era Comes to an End," *Cleveland Plain Dealer,* January 18, 1988. Hereafter, citations to the *Cleveland Plain Dealer* will be abbreviated as *PD.*

5. Ellen Szita, "Louis Stokes," *Ralph Nader Congress Project,* (Washington, D.C.: Grossman, 1972), 2.

6. Carl B. Stokes, *Promises of Power: A Political Autobiography* (New York: Simon & Schuster, 1973), 20.

7. Ibid., 45.

8. Brazaitis, "Stokes Era Comes to an End."

9. Joe Hallett, "Congressman Says He Has No Preferred Successor," *PD,* January 18, 1998.

10. Ibid., 72. Additional insight will be found in Kenneth Weinberg, *Black Victory: Carl Stokes and the Winning of Cleveland* (Chicago: Quadrangle Books, 1968), 36–38, 44–49, 110–13, 205–6, 239–40.

11. Richard Fenno, *Congress at the Grassroots: Representational Change in the South, 1970–1998* (Chapel Hill: University of North Carolina Press), 2000.

12. Fenno, *Home Style.*

13. Michael Dawson, *Behind the Mule: Race and Class in African American Voting* (Princeton, N.J.: Princeton University Press, 1994), 57. See also Katherine Tate, *From Protest to Politics: The New Black Voters in American Elections* (Cambridge, Mass.: Harvard University Press, 1993), and Andrea Simpson, *The Tie That Binds: Identity and Political Attitudes in the Post–Civil Rights Generation* (New York: New York University Press, 1998).

14. Richard Fenno, *Senators on the Campaign Trail: The Politics of Representation* (Norman: University of Oklahoma Press, 1996), 74–80.

15. Carol Poh Miller and Robert Wheeler, *Cleveland: A Concise History, 1796–1996,* 2d ed. (Bloomington: Indiana University Press, 1997), 172, 175.

16. Ibid., 171.

17. Michael Barone, Grant Ujifusa, and Douglas Matthews, "Districts," *Almanac of American Politics, 1974* (Boston: Gambit, 1975), 813, 815, 817, 819.

18. Miller and Wheeler, *Cleveland,* 171.

19. On Hough, see Stokes, Promises of Power, 94. On Glenville (and Hough), see Louis Masotti and Jerome Corsi, *Shoot-out in Cleveland: Black Militants and the Police: July 23, 1968* (New York: Praeger, 1969). See also Estele Zannes, *Checkmate in Cleveland: The Rhetoric of Confrontation during the Stokes Years* (Cleveland: Case Western University Press, 1972).

20. Philip Porter, *Cleveland: Confused City on a Seesaw* (Columbus: Ohio State University Press, 1976), 248; Pranab Chatterjee, *Local Leadership in Black Communities* (Cleveland: Commerce Copy, 1975), 146.

21. Robert C. Smith, "Black Power and the Transformation from Protest to Politics," *Political Science Quarterly,* 96 (1981): 431–43. A full-length study of this transition will be found in his book *We Have No Leaders.*

22. Stokes, *Promises of Power,* 72, 134–35, 267.

23. Zannes, *Checkmate in Cleveland,* 61, 88.

24. Stokes, *Promises of Power,* 135.

25. Ibid., chap. 10.

26. Miller and Wheeler, in their book *Cleveland,* devote three chapters to the period of his tenure but do not once mention him.

27. Stokes, *Promises of Power,* 42.

28. Fenno, chapter 6 in *Home Style.*

29. John Nussbaum, "200 from District 21 Hear Stokes, Jackson in Debate," *PD,* May 4, 1968.

30. Editorial, "In 21st: Jackson and Lucas," *PD,* April 15, 1968.

31. From records of the Cuyahoga County Board of Elections.

32. James Naughton, "Louis Stokes Wins," *PD,* May 8, 1968. See also *PD,* May 9, 1968, 18, for vote totals.

33. Brazaitis, "Stokes Era Comes to an End."

34. Ibid., 54−61.

35. From annual edition of Barone, Ujifusa, and Matthews, *Almanac of American Politics.* By contrast, his average ACA (conservative) score was 9 percent and his average NAB (probusiness) score was 5 percent.

36. The technique is described in Keith Poole and Howard Rosenthal, *Congress: A Political-Economic History of Roll Call Voting* (New York: Oxford University Press, 1997).

37. For an example, see Fenno, chapters 3 and 4 in *Congress at the Grassroots.*

38. Anne Phillips, *The Politics of Presence* (New York: Oxford University Press, 1995).

39. Chatterjee, *Local Leadership in Black Communities,* 145.

40. The case of Rep. Ralph Metcalfe and the Daley machine in Chicago has many similarities. See *National Journal,* October 7, 1972, 1582.

41. Stokes, *Promises of Power,* 267.

42. Lawrence Bobo and Franklin Gilliam, "Race, Sociopolitical Participation, and Black Empowerment," *American Political Science Review* 84 (1990): 378−93.

43. Fenno, *Home Style,* 116−17.

44. William O. Walker, "Sidney Andorn Is Suffering from 21st Districts," *Call and Post,* December 12, 1970.

45. Quoted in Stokes, *Promises of Power,* 243. A formal 1971 statement of the "objectives and purposes" of the caucus will be found in "21st District Caucus Clarifies Its Aims," *Call and Post,* March 6, 1971.

46. For an excellent picture of the changes in the caucus over time, see William E. Nelson Jr., "Cleveland: The Evolution of Black Political Power," in *The New Black Politics,* 2d ed., ed. Michael Preston, Lenneal J. Henderson Jr., and Paul Puryear (New York: Longman, 1987).

47. The results will be found in, Robert McGruder, "21st District Blacks Regain Front Seat of Politics Bus," *PD,* June 10, 1976.

48. Ibid.

49. Mark Winegardner, "The Congressman," *Cleveland Magazine,* May 1997, 63−64.

50. Powell Caesar, "Present Congressmen Win in 3 Races," *PD,* June 12, 1976.

51. See Swain, *Black Faces, Black Interests,* 204.

52. Frederick Harris, introduction to *Something Within: Religion in African American Political Activism* (New York: Oxford University Press, 1999). Harris's much longer first-hand account of a black U.S. Senate candidate in a church meeting with ministers is a pathbreaking model for the kind of interaction described here.

53. Szita, "Louis Stokes," 7.

54. Chatterjee, *Local Leadership in Black Communities,* 144.

55. Quoted in Canon, *Race, Redistricting, and Representation,* 160.

56. Press release, Congressman Louis Stokes, December 1, 1970. See also "Cuyahoga Dems Use Vanik to Whip Stokes into Line," *Call and Post,* December 12, 1970; Robert McGruder and William Barnard, "Stokes Rules Out End to Caucus Party Rift," December 3, 1970, and "Vanik Rejects Post for Representative Stokes," *PD,* December 2, 1976; "Cong. Vanik Shows His True Colors," *Call and Post,* December 12, 1970.

57. Dear Colleagues letter, December 8, 1970. See also Robert Havel, "Want Representative Stokes Appointed, Blacks in Congress Chide Vanik," *PD,* December 10, 1970; "Black Congressmen Back Stokes' Bid for Seat on Appropriations Committee," *Call and Post,* December 12, 1970.

58. "Congressional Report," *Call and Post,* January 2, 1971.

59. "Cuyahoga Dems Use Vanik to Whip Stokes into Line," *Call and Post,* December 12, 1970.

60. "Black Caucus Not for Sale," *Call and Post,* December 26, 1970.

61. Editorial, "Not for Sale," *Call and Post,* December 26, 1970.

62. Charles Lucas, "The Pressure Is On," *Call and Post,* December 12, 1970.

63. Charles Lucas, "A Christmas Present," *Call and Post,* January 2, 1971.

64. "Vanik to Appoint Stokes to Committee," *Call and Post,* January 2, 1971.

65. Szita, "Louis Stokes," 7.

66. Ibid., 1.

67. See Singh, *Congressional Black Caucus;* David Bositis, *The Congressional Black Caucus in the 103rd Congress* (Washington, D.C.: Joint Center for Political and Economic Studies, 1994).

68. William Clay, *Just Permanent Interests* (New York: Amistad Press, 1992), 116–17.

69. Ibid., xii, 71.

70. See for example, Susan J. Carroll, "Representing Women: Congresswomen's Perceptions of Their Representational Roles," in *Women Transforming Congress,* ed. Cindy Rosenthal (Norman: University of Oklahoma Press, in press).

71. Singh, *Congressional Black Caucus,* 78.

72. Marguerite Ross Barnett, "The Congressional Black Caucus," *Proceedings of the Academy of Political Science* 32 (1975): 36, 38.

73. Ibid., 39.

74. Alan Ehrenhalt, "Black Caucus: A Wary Carter Ally," *Congressional Quarterly,* May 21, 1977, 968–69.

75. Barnett, "Congressional Black Caucus," 65.

76. Ehrenhalt, "Black Caucus," 970.

77. Quoted in Singh, *Congressional Black Caucus,* 1.

CHAPTER 3

1. Barbara Jordan and Shelby Hearon, *Barbara Jordan: A Self-Portrait*, Doubleday (New York, 1979); Mary Beth Rogers, *Barbara Jordan: An American Hero* (New York: Bantam, 1998).

2. The terminology is described and used in Canon, *Race, Redistricting, and Representation,* esp. chap. 4.

3. Rogers, *Barbara Jordan,* 20.

4. Molly Ivins, "Barbara Jordan," *Washington Post,* October 22, 1972.

5. Rogers, *Barbara Jordan,* 25–34.

6. Ibid., 78–79.

7. Jordan and Hearon, *Barbara Jordan,* 111.

8. Rogers, *Barbara Jordan,* xii.

9. Ibid., xv.

10. Mary Beth Rogers, "Barbara Jordan Biographer Mary Beth Rogers Speaks at Library," *Among Friends of LBJ,* April 30, 1999,

11. There were actually four contestants, all African American, in the primary. Two, B. T. Bonner and Milton King, were never serious possibilities. She never mentioned either one of them. Each drew 3 percent of the primary vote. They do not figure in my account.

12. Editorial, "Forward Times Refuses to Endorse Either," *Forward Times,* April 22, 1972, 12A.

13. Charlotte Phelan, "State Senator Barbara Jordan Wins Her Battles through the System," *Houston Post,* May 24, 1970.

14. Jordan and Hearon, *Barbara Jordan,* 140.

15. Rogers, *Barbara Jordan,* 123. It was a view she held to the end of her life. James M. Hirsch, "Driving Miss Jordan," *Wall Street Journal,* January 19, 1996.

16. Barbara Jordan, "How I Got There: Staying Power," *Atlantic,* March 1975, 39.

17. Jordan and Hearon, *Barbara Jordan,* 145.

18. Rogers, *Barbara Jordan,* 114.

19. Jordan and Hearon, *Barbara Jordan,* 141.

20. Rogers, *Barbara Jordan,* 115.

21. Phelan, "State Senator Barbara Jordan Wins."

22. Rogers, *Barbara Jordan,* 146.

23. Ibid., 149.

24. Jordan and Hearon, *Barbara Jordan,* 152; Phelan, "State Senator Barbara Jordan Wins."

25. Jordan and Hearon, *Barbara Jordan,* 145.

26. Barone, Ujifusa, and Matthews, *Almanac of American Politics, 1973,* 1003.

27. Robert D. Bullard, *Invisible Houston: The Black Experience in Boom and Bust* (College Station: Texas A&M Press, 1987), 27, 30.

28. Robert Schwab, "Barbara Jordan: Professional Politician," *Austin American Statesman,* as reprinted in *Congressional Record,* daily ed., September 16, 1976, E5041–43.

29. Rogers, *Barbara Jordan,* 157.

30. Jordan and Hearon, *Barbara Jordan,* 155.

31. Bullard, *Invisible Houston,* 10–11. Another description of the neighborhood housing is Chandler Davidson, *Biracial Politics: Conflict and Cooperation in the Metropolitan South* (Baton Rouge: Louisiana State University Press, 1972), 20–21.

32. Bullard, *Invisible Houston,* 121; see also 110–11.

33. Clifton McCleskey, "Houston: Tripartite Politics," in *Urban Politics in the Southwest,* ed. Leonard Gooda II (Tempe: Institute of Public Administration, Arizona State University, 1967), 85.

34. Beth Ann Shelton, Nestor Rodriguez, Joe Feagin, Robert Bullard, and Robert Thomas, *Houston: Growth and Decline in a Sunbelt Boomtown* (Philadelphia: Temple University Press, 1989), 19.

35. "Elect Barbara Jordan," *Houston Chronicle,* April 10, 1972. See also Rogers, *Barbara Jordan,* 163. On their conservatism, see Ben Bagdikian, "Houston's Shackled Press," *Atlantic Monthly,* 218 (August 1966): 87–93.

36. David Mayhew, *Placing Parties in American Politics* (Princeton, N.J.: Princeton University Press, 1986). See also McCleskey, "Houston: Tripartite Politics," 74–76; Rogers, *Barbara Jordan,* 84–86.

37. See Fenno, *Home Style,* 24–27.

38. Jordan and Hearon, *Barbara Jordan,* 112, 115, 116, 143.

39. Davidson, *Biracial Politics,* 58–67.

40. Jordan and Hearon, *Barbara Jordan,* 117, 107.

41. Ibid., 119, 117.

42. Rogers, *Barbara Jordan,* 231. In that race, she defeated State Representative J. C. Whitfield, 18,317 to 10,007.

43. Ibid.

44. Davidson, *Biracial Politics,* 196–99.

45. Jordan and Hearon, *Barbara Jordan,* 132.

46. Phelan, "State Senator Barbara Jordan Wins."

47. Ibid.

48. Rogers, *Barbara Jordan,* 115, 115–16.

49. Ibid., 135.

50. Van Hetherly, "Black Political Symbols Clash in the 18th Congressional Race," *Houston Chronicle,* April 30, 1972.

51. Rogers, *Barbara Jordan,* 84.

52. Canon, *Race, Redistricting, and Representation,* 26–30.

53. Molly Ivins, "Barbara Jordan"; John Pierson, "Barbara Jordan's Star Reaches Dizzy Heights for House Sophomore," *Wall Street Journal,* February 14, 1975; Meg Greenfield, "The New Lone Star of Texas," *Newsweek,* March 3, 1975, 31.

54. Susan Carroll, "Representing Women."

55. Rogers, *Barbara Jordan,* 141.

56. Ibid., 164–65.

57. Joanne Levine, "Impact on Congress," *Christian Science Monitor,* reprinted in *Congressional Record,* daily ed., April 1, 1974, E1972–74.

58. A leading proponent of which was the Reverend Bill Lawson, a member of Graves's steering committee, whose views were featured in Bill Moyers, *Listening to America* (New York: Dell, 1971), 278–88. His prominence is registered in Bullard, *Invisible Houston,* 115–17.

59. Van Hetherly, "Black Political Symbols Clash."

60. A third minor candidate, B. T. Bonner, was included in the debate. His time was filled with complaints that no one took him seriously.

61. "Barbara Jordan Defeats Graves," *Houston Post,* May 7, 1972, 20; "Voter Analysis," May 7, 1972, 19. Curtis Graves received 14 percent, and two minor candidates took 3 percent each.

62. Van Hetherly, "Barbara's Commanding Win: She Was Singing in the Rain," *Houston Chronicle,* May 8, 1972, sec. l, p. 14.

63. Jordan and Hearon, *Barbara Jordan,* 181–82.

64. Rogers, *Barbara Jordan,* 154.

65. Ibid., 188.

66. That decision is discussed in Smith, *We Have No Leaders,* 39–41. The Gary Convention and its importance are discussed in detail, in Smith, *We Have No Leaders,* chap. 2, and in Barnett, "Congressional Black Caucus," 37–38.

67. Jordan and Hearon, *Barbara Jordan,* 178, 179.

68. Rogers, *Barbara Jordan,* 190–91.

69. Ehrenhalt, "Black Caucus," 970.

70. Levine, "Impact on Congress."

71. Rogers, *Barbara Jordan,* 188.

72. Greenfield, "New Lone Star of Texas."

73. Pierson, "Barbara Jordan's Star."

74. Myra McPherson, "Black, Women's Groups Complain as Eloquent Texan Goes Her Own Way," *Washington Post,* October 30, 1977.

75. Pierson, "Barbara Jordan's Star."

76. Jordan and Hearon, 224.

77. Rogers, *Barbara Jordan,* 230.

78. Ibid., chap. 15.

79. Records obtained in personal visit to Washington office, May 1974.

80. Rogers, *Barbara Jordan,* 187.

81. Ibid., 228.

82. Two notable exceptions: Cragg Hines ("A Voice for Justice Dies: Barbara Jordan Lived as a Pioneer and Prophet," *Houston Chronicle,* January 18, 1996): "With a will of iron and a voice of gold, she was one of the few black women to make a name in U.S. politics." Hirsch ("Driving Miss Jordan"): "She had little sympathy for protesters and confrontational tactics. Of Jesse Jackson, she said, 'He'll never run for an office he can win.'"

83. Harris Survey, June 1976, Roper Center, University of Connecticut, Public Opinion Online, no. 0058494.

84. Harris Survey, July 1976, Roper Center, University of Connecticut, Public Opinion Online, no. 0059646.

85. Gallup Poll, December 1976, Roper Center, University of Connecticut, Public Opinion Online, no. 0047218.

86. Rogers, *Barbara Jordan,* 290.

87. Ibid., 297.

CHAPTER 4

1. Bositis, *Congressional Black Caucus in the 103rd Congress,* 5, 47.

2. His generational distinctions were eerily similar to those of his predecessor, Bill Gray, as reported in Swain, *Black Faces, Black Interests,* 51.

3. Richard Champagne and Leroy Rieselbach, "The Evolving Congressional Black Caucus: The Reagan-Bush Years," in *Blacks and the American Political System,* ed. Huey Perry and Wayne Parent (Gainesville: University of Florida Press, 1995). As a reminder, however, that our cohort lines are not hard and fast, they cite Bill Gray as "the chief symbol of the integration of CBC members into the mainstream of House politics" (148). See also Richard Cohen, "A New Breed for Black Caucus," *National Journal,* September 26, 1987.

4. A description can be found in Marc Schogol, "Still Raising Boys to Become Men," *Philadelphia Inquirer,* May 27, 2001.

5. The primary vote: Democratic Party, Lucien Blackwell—39 percent; Consumer Party, Chaka Fattah—28 percent; Independent Party, John White—28 percent. White was the State Secretary of Welfare. He did not run again.

6. Deborah Kalb, "Rep. Chaka Fattah," *The Hill,* October 25, 1995.

7. Fenno, *Congress at the Grassroots.*

8. Kalb, "Rep. Chaka Fattah."

9. Suzanne Oliver, "It's the Costs, Stupid," *Forbes,* October 21, 1996, 252–54.

10. Buzz Bissinger, *A Prayer for the City* (New York: Random House, 1999). The "dying" idea will be found on pp. 23, 32–34, 278, and in the epilogue. See also Blaine Harden, "The Operation Was a Success, But . . . " *Washington Post National Weekly Edition,* March 23, 1998.

11. Barone, Ujifusa, and Matthews, *Almanac of American Politics, 1972,* 683.

12. Ibid.

13. Rhodes Cook, "Actual District Votes Belie Ideal of Bipartisanship," *Congressional Quarterly,* April 12, 1997. In 2000, Al Gore carried the district with 89 percent.

14. Bissinger, *Prayer for the City,* 212.

15. On Germantown, see Jane Eisner, "No Paint Brushes, No Paint," *Brookings Review* (Fall 1997): 39–41. On Chestnut Hill, see Bissinger, *Prayer for the City,* 272.

16. Tim Whitaker, "Heads Up," *Philadelphia Weekly,* January 29, 1997.

17. Rick Rothacker, "Frosh Watch: PA's Rep. Fattah is a Democratic Rising Star," LegiSlate News Service, www.politicsnow.com, June 15, 1996.

18. Helpful treatments of Bill Gray are Swain, *Black Faces, Black Interests,* 59–72; Carla Hill, "How a Philadelphia Preacher Won Converts to His Budget Gospel," *Washington Post National Weekly Edition,* June 10, 1985; David Shribman, "Decision by

House Whip Gray for UNCF Post Creates a Black-Power Vacuum," *Wall Street Journal,* June 20, 1991.

19. Rothacker, "Frosh Watch."

20. Chris Mondics, "In GOP Congress, Fattah Struggles against the Tide," *Philadelphia Inquirer,* February 2, 1998.

21. Bissinger's study is essentially a study of neighborhoods. Major characters are examined within their varying neighborhood contexts. The Mayor's "Achilles' heels" are identified as "neighborhoods and crime." The author also repeatedly uses public housing as a major public policy problem for the city. In those respects, the perspectives and priorities of this book dovetail almost perfectly with Congressman Fattah's. See, for example, Bissinger, *Prayer for the City,* 188, 280, 321, and passim.

22. Mondics, "In GOP Congress."

23. The technique is described in Poole and Rosenthal, *Congress.*

24. Laura Winter, "Fattah Feels the Arm-Twisting," *Philadelphia Daily News,* May 23, 2000.

25. Ibid.

26. "House of Representatives to Vote Today to Grant China Permanent Normal Trade Status," National Public Radio, May 24, 2000.

27. William Bunch, "Fattah Expected to Back Talmadge, " *Philadelphia Daily News,* April 20, 2001.

28. See Mondics, "In GOP Congress."

29. "Helping More Students to Prepare for College through 'Gear Up,'" www.ed .gov.gearup, November 3, 1998.

30. Dan Page, "U.S. Rep. Chaka Fattah: Builder of Bridges," *Converge Magazine,* December 2000 (www.convergemag.com/Publications/CNVGDec00/in-close.shtm).

31. Ronald Roach, "New Political Leadership," *Black Issues in Higher Education,* October 2, 1997.

32. In Philadelphia, see: editorial, "High Hopes," *Philadelphia Inquirer,* February 9, 1998; Kevin Haney, "Clinton Educates Youth, Democrats," *Philadelphia Daily News,* May 20, 2000; Thera Martin Connelly, "President Clinton at Sulzberger," *SCOOP U.S.A.,* May 26, 2000. Nationally, see: "Plan Aims Poor Youth to College," *Richmond Times-Dispatch,* February 5, 1998; E. J. Dionne, "A Chance for College," *Washington Post,* October 13, 1998. His own best postmortem explanation will be found in "Forging New Partnerships," a forum held at the Brookings Institute, June 25, 1999. See www.brook .edu/comm/transcripts/19990625/fattah.htm.

33. Details taken from C-SPAN coverage, February 4, 1998.

34. For the Fattah–Souder relationship, see: Jake Tapper, "Capitol Hill's Odd Couple," www.salon.com, June 10, 1999; Stephen Burd, "House Committee Backs White House Plan for Colleges to Aid Needy School Children," *Chronicle of Higher Education,* March 19, 1998.

35. The partisan balance on the committee was 25 Republicans, 19 Democrats. The committee vote was 24-19, with one "present." All 19 Democrats and 5 Republicans voted "yes." All 19 "no" votes and the one "present" vote were Republicans.

36. See Linda Wright Moore, "Thanks to Fattah, Needy Students Now Have Hope," *Philadelphia Daily News,* October 4, 1998.

37. White House Briefing, "Remarks by President Clinton in Philadelphia," Federal News Service, May 19, 2000. Earlier, the President had mentioned it in his weekly radio address of August 9, 1999.

38. See Charles Dervarics and Ronald Roach, "Fortifying the Federal Presence in Retention," *Black Issues in Higher Education,* March 30, 2000, 21; Laura McClure, "Fattah Given Award for Service," *Daily Pennsylvanian,* April 27, 2000.

39. The preparatory work is described in Dale Mezzacappa, "Educators Discuss How to Help Less-Privileged Climb Ivory Tower," *Philadelphia Inquirer,* March 12, 1999.

40. An early progress report from the field is Tara H. Arden-Smith, "Studying Students Gear Up," *Boston Globe,* September 2, 2001.

41. Juliet Eilperin, "Morning Business," *Roll Call,* February 6, 1997.

42. See Peter Nicholas, "Fattah's Quest for House Clout," *Philadelphia Inquirer,* June 12, 2000.

43. "Democrats Hand Out Prime Panel Slots," *Roll Call,* December 14, 1999. See also Ethan Wallison, "Too Many Democrats, Too Few Spots," *Roll Call,* December 3, 1998.

44. Ethan Wallison, "Promises, Promises, Promises," *Roll Call,* December 2, 1999; Ethan Wallison, "Gephardt's Promises Prove Hard to Keep," *Roll Call,* September 25, 2000.

45. Nicholas, "Fattah's Quest for House Clout."

46. The saga is told in the following: Ethan Wallison and Ben Pershing, "Gephardt Faces Difficult Decision on Panel Slots," *Roll Call,* January 11, 2001; Ethan Wallison and Ben Pershing, "Democrats Won't Get Approps Seat," *Roll Call,* February 1, 2001; Ethan Wallison, "Hastert Changes Tune on Approps," *Roll Call,* February 5, 2001; Ethan Wallison and John Breshnehan, "Roemer Pushing Energy Panel Rule Change," *Roll Call,* February 8, 2001. See also Lauren Whittington, "Fattah, Moran Take Over Key Appropriations Subcommittees," *Roll Call,* March 12, 2001.

47. Bissinger, *Prayer for the City,* 283.

48. William Bunch, "Rep. Fattah Raises His Profile," *Philadelphia Daily News,* April 9, 2001.

49. Mondics, "In GOP Congress."

50. John Baer, "Fattah's A Major Player Now," *Philadelphia Daily News,* March 5, 2001.

51. Elmer Smith, "Chaka Fattah, The Back Room Brawler," *Philadelphia Daily News,* February 21, 2001.

52. Peter Nicholas, "For Phila. Politicians, A National Publicity Surge," *Philadelphia Inquirer,* March 14, 2001.

53. Baer, "Fattah's A Major Player Now."

54. William Raspberry, "Rich Schools, Poor Schools," *Washington Post,* April 6, 2000; "New York Crisis Emphasizes Funding Inequity in Schools," *Jacksonville Times-Union,* January 14, 2001; S. A. Reid, "$20 Million Goal Set for Inner-City Education Effort," *Atlanta Journal and Constitution,* May 24, 2001.

CHAPTER 5

1. Michael McIntyre, "Stokes Stuck with His Ideas, Supporter's Say," *Cleveland Plain Dealer (PD)*, January 18, 1998. For evidence of his "iconic" status, see James Sweeney, "Name Branding, Louis Stokes Is Tops in Local Landmark Labels," *PD*, November 6, 2001.

2. See the following in the *PD*, "Stokes' Clout for Cleveland," July 3, 1994; "Stokes in the Eleventh District," September 26, 1994; "Cleveland Gets Budget Goodies: Stokes Steers Millions from Helm of Appropriations Panel," September 27, 1994; "Waking Up to a New Reality: Debate Begins Over What GOP Sweep Means for Blacks," November 13, 1994. See also Francesca Contiguaglia, "Congress Losing Its Institutions," *Roll Call*, January 26, 1998, B-41.

3. Tom Brazaitis and Sabrina Eaton, "Rep. Stokes to Retire: Clevelander Rose from Poverty to Heights of Power," *PD*, January 17, 1998. See also Brazaitis, "Stokes Era Comes to an End."

4. Brazaitis, "Stokes Era Comes to an End."

5. Sabrina Eaton, "Stokes to Serve on Party's Leadership Panel," *PD*, December 14, 1994.

6. Roger Lowe, "Wylie, McEwan in Top 20 of Bad Check Writers," *Columbus Dispatch*, March 17, 1992.

7. Actually, he dropped to 69 percent in 1992 and rebounded to 77 percent in 1994. From 1978 to 1992, his average general election vote was 84 percent.

8. An excellent discussion of the effects of the scandal on the House elections of 1992 is Gary Jacobson and Michael Dimoock, "Checking Out: The Effects of Bank Overdrafts on the 1992 House Elections," *American Journal of Political Science* 38, no. 3 (August 1994): 601–24. On Stokes's 1992 result, see Paul Shepard, "It's No Contest, Stokes a Winner," *PD*, November 4, 1992.

9. One change he noted, however, was that publisher W. O. Walker, a Republican, had died. "At his death," said Stokes, "Carl and I were feuding with him. We had a falling out, and things were not the same."

10. Douglas Arnold, "Congress, the Press, and Political Accountability," unpublished book manuscript, September 2000 (with the kind permission of author.)

11. Winegardner, "The Congressman."

12. Hallett, "Congressman Says He Has No Preferred Successor."

13. From records at the Cuyahoga County Board of Elections.

14. For suggestions of change inside the subcommittee, see Jeffrey Katz, "Partnership Takes Toll on Lewis and Stokes," *Congressional Quarterly*, December 16, 1995, 3807–3809.

15. Rep. Julian Dixon, "Stokes Paved Way for Members," *Roll Call*, September 13, 1999, 13–20; Rep. William Gray, "Shades of Gray," *Roll Call*, May 11, 2000, 54.

16. Three years later, in the aftermath of the September 11 attack, he was asked "What are you most proud of from your tenure in Congress?" He remarked that, as chairman of the Intelligence Committee, "we set up the Undergraduate Training Program for

minorities to get college scholarships if they were willing to commit to working for the CIA after graduating." And he noted that the Defense Intelligence Agency and the FBI followed. It was a small example of his committee clout on behalf of African Americans (Paul Kane, "Serving with Intelligence," *Roll Call,* September 20, 2001).

17. Winegardner, "The Congressman," 60.

18. *Congressional Record,* 100th Congress, 1st sess., 133, no. 121, July 22, 1987, p. E2978.

CHAPTER 6

1. Brazaitis, "Stokes Era Comes to an End."

2. Fran Henry, "Tubbs Jones, All Pro Keeps Family, Career in Perspective," *PD,* February 12, 1995.

3. Rachel VanDongen and John Mercurio, "Voters Go for Moderates in Primaries," *Roll Call,* May 7, 1998.

4. Henry, "Tubbs Jones, All Pro."

5. Evelyn Theiss, "Embrace Diversity, Jones Urges," *PD,* January 25, 1993.

6. Paula Giddings, *In Search of Sisterhood: Delta Sigma Theta and the Challenges of the Black Sorority Movement* (New York: William Morrow, 1998), 304.

7. Audio interview with Deya Smith, "Politically Black Dot Com," November 11, 1999 (www.politicallyblack.com/audio111199.htm).

8. Steve Luttner, "Mayor White Blasts Ohio Senators; Says Blacks Should Have Been Consulted on Judgeships," *PD,* May 8, 1993; Mary Ann Sharkey, "Politically Correct Numbers," *PD,* May 9, 1993.

9. "Prosecutor Still Wants Judgeship," *PD,* May 11, 1993.

10. On the career pattern from law enforcement office to legislative office, see Joseph Schlesinger, *Ambition and Politics: Political Careers in the United States* (Chicago: Rand McNally, 1966), 91–98 and passim.

11. Sabrina Eaton, "Tubbs Jones Ready to Adjust to Congress," November 8, 1998; KET, "Mrs. Jones Goes to Washington," *Law Alumni News Bulletin,* Case Western University School of Law, Spring 1999.

12. Joe Hallett, "White Won't Seek Post, But Others Will Weigh Options," *PD,* January 17, 1998.

13. Brent Larkin, "Congressman's Decades at an End," *PD,* January 18, 1998.

14. Stephen Koff, "Tubbs Jones Might Run for Ohio Governor," *PD,* December 1, 2001; Mark Naymik, "Tubbs Jones for Governor Not a Very Likely Campaign," *PD,* December 6, 2001.

15. Sabrina Eaton, "Rep. Jones Maintains Low Profile While Learning Her Job," *PD,* July 4, 1999.

16. Steve Luttner and Ulysses Tomassa, "Jones Topples Old Guard," *PD,* January 13, 1991. A women-in-politics analyst later singled out Tubbs Jones's triumph as a "stunning defeat of the older order" (Eleanor Mallet, "Breaking Up the Old Order: Women Take Control of Public Institutions," *PD,* August 8, 1993).

17. Larkin, "Congressman's Decades at an End."

18. Ulysses Tomassa, "Jones Wins Easily in Prosecutor Race," *PD,* November 4, 1992.

19. James Ewinger and Robert Vickers, "Tubbs Jones Enters Race for U.S. House; Cuyahoga Prosecutor to Seek Stokes' Seat," February 11, 1998.

20. Rachel VanDongen, "Cleveland's 30-Year Itch," *Roll Call*, April 30, 1998. See also "More Shop Talk, *Roll Call*, April 27, 1998.

21. VanDongen, "Cleveland's 30-Year Itch."

22. Joe Hallett, "Tubbs Jones Wins Easily in 11th," *PD*, May 6, 1998.

23. VanDongen and Mercurio, "Voters Go for Moderates in Primaries."

24. Sabrina Eaton, "Tubbs Jones Takes House Seat Easily," *PD*, November 4, 1998.

25. An excellent analysis of George Forbes can be found in Nelson, "Cleveland: The Evolution of Black Political Power."

26. An earlier work grounded in that assumption is Fenno, *Senators on the Campaign Trail.*

27. Hallett, "Tubbs Jones Wins Easily in 11th"; editorial, "11th Congressional District," *PD*, October 7, 1998.

28. Jonathan Riskind, "Tubbs Jones Confident of Win," *Columbus Dispatch*, November 2, 1998; Robert Vickers, "Tubbs Jones Prepares to Win," *PD*, October 11, 1998.

29. Ewinger and Vickers, "Tubbs Jones Enters Race"; editorial, "Mrs. Jones Goes to Washington," *PD*, November 22, 1998.

30. Joe Hallett, "11th District Decision Waits on 11th Hour," *PD*, April 26, 1998.

31. James F. McCarty, "100 Percent Gore Vote Wasn't Enough," *PD*, December 11, 2000; See also Robert Vickers, "Feeling Taken for Granted by Gore; Some Blacks Object to Suburban Focus," *PD*, November 3, 2000.

32. Joe Hallett, "11th District Race Was Too Clean to See," *PD*, May 8, 1998.

33. McCarty, "100 Percent Gore Vote Wasn't Enough"; Vickers, "Feeling Taken for Granted by Gore."

34. Alan Achkar and Zach Schiller, "Comeback City?" *PD*, January 6, 2000.

35. Sarah Cohen and D'Vera Cohn, "Continental Shift," *Washington Post National Weekly Edition*, April 9–15, 2001.

36. Northern Ohio Data and Information Service," Profile Report, House District 11," Urban Center, Cleveland State University, Cleveland, 1999.

37. Sara Fritz, "Mayors Project High Hopes for a Revival under Clinton," *Los Angeles Times*, November 21, 1992.

38. Achkar and Schiller, "Comeback City?"

39. Sandra Livingston and Ron Rulti, "Building Brain Power; Region Stuck in Second Gear until Education Level Rises," *PD*, July 9, 2000. See also Livingston and Rulti, "Ohio Plays Catch Up," *PD*, July 11, 2000.

40. Clare Ansberry, "In Cleveland, A Center of the U.S. Slowdown, Good News Softens Bad," *Wall Street Journal*, May 9, 2001. See also Bob Paynter and Marcia Pledger, "Comeback City Fights Old Shoe Image," *PD*, October 14, 2001.

41. Jennifer Scott Cimperman, Peter Krause, and Sandra Livingston, "1000 LTV Jobs in Peril," *PD*, April 11, 2000"; PR Newswire Press Release, "Congresswoman Tubbs Jones and Steel Caucus Introduce Steel Revitalization Act," February 28, 2001; Elizabeth Marchak, Sandra Livingston, and Peter Krause, "Steel Bill Would Cost up to 32,000 Jobs, Opponents' Study Says; Trade Group Opposes Quotas, Tax," *PD*, May 1, 2001.

42. Vickers, "Tubbs Jones Prepares to Win."

43. "I love this pretty black face," she told them. Mark Russell and Richard Peery, "Race a Subtle Election Issue," *PD*, December 2, 1992.

44. Joe Hallett, "Tubbs Jones Likely to Seek Stokes' Job; Announcement from Prosecutor Expected Today," *PD*, February 10, 1998.

45. Vickers, "Tubbs Jones Prepares to Win."

46. Mark Russell and Richard Peery, "3 Leaders, 3 Styles; Stokes, Forbes, White Moved City Forward," *PD*, December 2, 1992.

47. Thomas Edsall, "Clinton Gains from Eased Race Tensions in Big Cities," *Washington Post*, October 8, 1992.

48. Russell and Peery, "Race a Subtle Election Issue."

49. Russell and Peery, "3 Leaders, 3 Styles."

50. See, for example, Theiss, "Embrace Diversity, Jones Urges"; Jesse Tinsley, "Tubbs Jones Targets Issue of Race; People Vote along Racial Lines, She Says," *PD*, February 26, 1998.

51. Tinsley, "Tubbs Jones Targets Issue of Race."

52. Larkin, "Congressman's Decades at an End."

53. Vickers, "Tubbs Jones Prepares to Win."

54. Riskind, "Tubbs Jones Confident of Win."

55. Russell and Peery, "Race a Subtle Election Issue."

56. Robert Vickers, "As the Torch Passes, Blacks Sense a Void," *PD*, December 19, 1999.

57. Ibid.

58. Ibid.

59. Editorial, "Cuyahoga County Prosecutor," *DP*, April 26, 1998.

60. Editorial, "On Balance, McMickle," *DP*, April 26, 1998.

61. Ibid.; Brent Larkin, "McMickle's Race Is Uphill All the Way," *PD*, February 22, 1998; Elizabeth Auster, "The Greater of Goods in Race for Congress," *PD*, March 26, 1998.

62. Auster, "Greater of Goods."

63. www.house.gov.

64. Editorial, "11th Congressional District," *PD*, October 7, 1998.

65. Dan George, "Tomorrow's Leaders Today," *PD*, May 10, 2000. See the section on George Whitfield.

66. See "Teens Come Together to Confront Violence," *PD*, April 19, 2000.

67. Angela Townsend, "Youths Corner Attention," *PD*, January 16, 2000.

68. Vickers, "As the Torch Passes."

69. James McCarty, "Tubbs Jones Faces Henley as She Makes Her Way in Congress," *PD*, February 11, 2000.

70. Ohio Credit Union Foundation News, www.ohiocul.org/foundation/OCUFnews .htm, p. 2 [cited July 6, 2000]. See also editorial, "Learn to Avoid Trouble from Predatory Lenders," *Brooklyn Sun Journal*, July 12, 2001.

71. Remarks delivered by Franklin D. Raines, Fannie Mae Black History Month Celebration, Washington, D.C., February 8, 2001. See also Fannie Mae Press Release,

"US Representative Stephanie Tubbs Jones and Fannie Mae Announce New $100 Million Affordable Housing Partnerships to Improve Cleveland Neighborhoods," February 23, 2001.

72. Nicholas Kulish and Jacob Schlessinger, "How Fannie Mae Gave the Slip to Adversaries Seeking to Rein It In," *Wall Street Journal,* July 5, 2001.

73. Statement of Norman D'Amours, presented at the Predatory Lending Forum, sponsored by Rep. Stephanie Tubbs Jones, Cleveland, Ohio, July 6, 2000, www.nuca.gov.

74. Elizabeth Auster, "Stephanie Tubbs Jones: Building a Better Bully Pulpit," *PD,* August 19, 2001.

75. At the same time, the experience confirmed my conviction that only black political scientists can do justice to the kinds of relationships I am trying to describe. As an example, see Frederick Harris's stunning account of another black politician participating in an event in a black church (*Something Within,* chap. 2).

76. Jennifer Gonzalez, "New Mayor Assumes Office in Warrensville Heights," *PD,* January 17, 2000.

77. Joe Hallett, "Democrats Back Tubbs Jones for Stokes' District," *PD,* March 7, 1998.

78. Grant Segall, "New Face, New Feeling at Democrats Annual Picnic," *PD,* September 7, 1999.

79. Ibid.

80. April McClellan-Copeland, "Political Caucus Gets Back to Roots," *PD,* September 4, 1999.

81. Joel Rutchick, "Black Democrat Group Picks Fisher in Governor's Race," *PD,* March 29, 1998.

82. Mark Naymik, "Schools CEO Seen as Asset for Bonds," *PD,* April 17, 2001; Angela Townsend and Janet Okoben, "Forbes Talked into Talking on Schools," *PD,* April 13, 2001; Angela Townsend, "NAACP Backing Schools' Tax Issue," *PD,* April 15, 2001.

83. Dave Davis, "Rep. Stokes Backs Levy," *PD,* October 16, 1994. To add to this similarity, the manager of the 1994 campaign was the same man who was managing the 2001 campaign. He was Arnold Pinkney, a longtime Stokes ally and a one-time president of the Cleveland School Board.

84. Scott Stephens, "School Levy Backers Still Courting Stokes," *PD,* October 12, 1994.

85. Davis, "Rep. Stokes Backs Levy."

86. Patrice Jones and Scott Stephens, "School Levy Heads for Second Defeat," *PD,* November 9, 1994.

87. Angela Townsend and Janet Okoben, "Voters OK Millions to Fix Unsafe Buildings," *PD,* May 9, 2001; Olivera Perkins and Michael O'Malley, "Support for School Issue Scarce on West Side," *PD,* May 9, 2001.

88. Robert Vickers, "Poll Shows Tubbs Jones Has Mayor White's Number," *PD,* May 28, 2000.

89. RVD, "Member vs. Member for Cleveland Mayor," *Roll Call,* May 18, 2001.

90. Mark Naymik, "Tubbs Jones Won't Run for Mayor," *PD,* July 2001.

91. Ibid. See also Rachel VanDongen, "Tubbs Jones Decides against Mayoral Run," *Roll Call,* July 5, 2001.

92. Scott Stephens, "Pinkney Legendary for Orchestrating Political Campaigns," *PD,* October 24, 2001.

93. Brent Larkin, "A Gift for Pierce—But the Price Is Racial Politics," *PD,* September 2, 2001.

94. Mark Naymik, "Mayoral Race Tight, Poll Reveals," *PD,* September 9, 2001.

95. Editorial, "Cleveland Mayor: Jane Campbell's Strength, Vision and Compassion Offer Cleveland Its Best Hope in These Critical Times," September 23, 2001. See also Kevin Hoffman, "Not Everyone Loves Raymond: Is the PD Giving Ray Pierce a Raw Deal?" *Cleveland Free Times,* October 10–16, 2001.

96. Christopher Quinn, "Field Narrows to Campbell and Pierce," *PD,* October 3, 2001.

97. Ibid.

98. Mark Naymik, "Pierce Scores Points by Adding Pinkney to the Team," *PD,* September 7, 2001.

99. Larkin, "A Gift for Pierce"; Mark Naymik, "Endorsements Offer More than Momentum to Candidates," *PD,* October 22, 2001.

100. Brent Larkin, "Campbell Win," *PD,* November 7, 2001; Mark Naymik and Scott Stephens, "An East Side–West Side Winner," *PD,* November 8, 2001.

101. Eaton, "Tubbs Jones Ready to Adjust."

102. Sabrina Eaton, "Freshman Tubbs Jones Named to Democrats' Steering Committee," *PD,* November 18, 1998.

103. Eaton, "Tubbs Jones Ready to Adjust."

104. Eaton, "Freshman Tubbs Jones Named."

105. Smith, "Politically Black Dot Com."

106. Naymik, "Tubbs Jones Won't Run for Mayor."

107. Smith, "Politically Black Dot Com."

108. Ibid.

109. News Release, "Congresswoman Stephanie Tubbs Jones and Deborah Pryce Protect Children through Passage of CAPE Act," October 4, 1999. See also Smith, "Politically Black Dot Com."

110. *Congressional Record,* daily ed., March 10, 2000, 49350–57. Public Law 106-177.

111. Smith, "Politically Black Dot Com."

112. Ibid.

113. Eaton, "Rep. Jones Maintains Low Profile."

114. Ibid.

115. McCarty, "Tubbs Jones Faces Henley."

116. Eaton, "Rep. Jones Maintains Low Profile."

117. McCarty, "Tubbs Jones Faces Henley."

118. Eaton, "Rep. Jones Maintains Low Profile."

119. Ethan Wallison, "Who's Part of the NEXT Generation of Hill Leaders?" *Roll Call,* January 24, 2000.

120. "Fifty for the Future," *Time,* December 5, 1994.

121. Auster, "Stephanie Tubbs Jones."

122. Robert Vickers, "Protest of Police Shooting Turns Violent," *PD*, April 11, 2001; Robert Vickers and T. C. Brown, "Violence Spreads in Cincinnati," *PD*, April 12, 2001; Robert Vickers and T. C. Brown, "NAACP Chief Urges Calm in Cincinnati," *PD*, April 13, 2001.

123. Auster, "Stephanie Tubbs Jones."

124. Ibid.

CHAPTER 7

1. In Jordan's case, insufficient exposure kept me from utilizing all categories. In Stokes's case, because he did not incorporate whites into his other connective strategies, a discussion of "minority connections" was added.

2. All four districts fall in the category designated by Swain as "historically black districts" and Canon as "old districts." This leaves a good deal of room—and plenty of incentive—for students to examine the activity of African American House members in other types of districts. It is worth noting, however, that when Swain turns to her "newly black districts" and when Canon turns to his "new districts," both find evidence of balancing activities undertaken in the home constituency. See Swain, chapter 4 in *Black Faces, Black Interests,* and Canon, chapter 5 in *Race, Redistricting, and Representation.*

3. Canon, *Race, Redistricting, and Representation,* chap. 5.

4. Fenno, *Congress at the Grassroots.*

5. For example, Lublin, *Paradox of Representation;* Carol Swain rejects the idea early on, but returns to it as one of several relevant factors in her final accounting (*Black Faces, Black Interests,* 217, 237 n. 4).

6. Dawson, *Behind the Mule.*

7. Tate, "Political Representation of Blacks in Congress," 623–38.

INDEX